WINDOWS

WINDOWS

The official guide to

Microsoft's operating

environment

Nancy Andrews

MICROSOFT.
P R E S S

PUBLISHED BY

Microsoft Press
A Division of Microsoft Corporation
16011 N.E. 36th, Box 97017, Redmond, Washington 98073-9717

Library of Congress Cataloging in Publication Data
Andrews, Nancy
  Windows.
  Includes index.
  1. IBM Personal Computer XT—Programming. 2. IBM Personal
  Computer AT—Programming. 3. Microsoft Windows (Computer programs).
I. Title.
QA 76.8.I2594A54   1986   005.265   86-2512

ISBN 0-914845-70-5

Printed and bound in the United States of America.

1 2 3 4 5 6 7 8 9 RRDRRD 8 9 0 9 8 7 6

Distributed to the book trade in the
United States by Harper and Row.

Distributed to the book trade in
Canada by General Publishing Company, Ltd.

Distributed to the book trade outside the
United States and Canada by Penguin Books Ltd.

Penguin Books Ltd., Harmondsworth, Middlesex, England
Penguin Books Australia Ltd., Ringwood, Victoria, Australia
Penguin Books N.Z. Ltd., 182-190 Wairau Road, Auckland 10, New Zealand

British Cataloging in Publication Data available

Trademark information located at the back of the book

TABLE OF CONTENTS

ACKNOWLEDGMENTS

Putting together a book requires the efforts of many more people than just the author. To all who had a part in this book, I'd like to say thank you— specifically to Claudette Moore for working with me on the details of the outline, to Ron Lamb for his professional editing and his gentle prodding and encouragement, to Chris Kinata for his technical expertise and wry comments, and to Mike Halvorson for his good work and strict attention to detail. Also thanks to the Windows development team for answering questions and offering suggestions.

INTRODUCTION

When Microsoft Press asked if I would be interested in doing a book on Windows, Microsoft's operating environment for IBM machines, I was initially skeptical about this new product. But after looking briefly at a pre-release copy of Windows, I fell in love. It had the best of all worlds: a graphic user interface (a screen resembling a desktop, and drop-down menus, icons and dialog boxes), plus the ability to run MS-DOS applications such as Microsoft Word and Lotus 1-2-3. In other words, I could have the advantages of a graphic environment without giving up my old favorites. I could write with Microsoft Word, leave Word for an instant to check my electronic mail, and then return to exactly where I'd left off in Word with a few quick keystrokes. I could combine text in a wide variety of fonts with graphics (a Lotus 1-2-3 graph or an illustration drawn with Microsoft Paint) in the Windows word-processing application, Microsoft Write, and produce an elegant report quickly and easily.

This book introduces you to the advantages of Windows. It shows you how to increase productivity using Windows tools, the new Windows applications Write and Paint, and your favorite applications. It takes a hands-on approach. Most of the chapters include a sample task that you can follow along with on your computer. You'll do something useful and at the same time learn how to use Windows quickly and painlessly.

Section 1 describes the basics of using a Windows application, including choosing commands from menus, shrinking applications to icons so they are readily available for future use, and having several applications share the screen. It shows how to use the desktop applications: programs such as Calculator, Cardfile, and Calendar that come with

Windows and that can replace your traditional calculator, cardfile, and calendar. You'll learn to use these tools separately and together to perform useful tasks, such as writing a proposal or putting together information for an annual report.

Section 2 explains what is meant by the new category of applications called Windows applications. It explains what they are, how they work, and the advantages of using them. Then it gives hands-on experience using Microsoft Write and Paint and Micrografx's In·a·Vision. It concludes with previews of a short sampling of additional Windows applications.

Section 3 discusses running standard applications with Windows. *Standard applications* is the term used to describe the DOS applications you were able to use before Windows, such as WordStar and R:base 5000. This section shows you how to set up Windows to work with standard applications, how to develop efficient strategies for using Windows and standard applications, and how to combine information from several standard applications into a Windows application such as Microsoft Write to produce a sample company proposal. Using these tools with Windows, you can complete the proposal in less time than it would have taken before Windows.

Section 4, the last section, shows how additional equipment can give you Windows in color and with memory beyond your machine's normal limit. By adding IBM's Enhanced Graphics Adapter (EGA) to your system, you can display Windows in eight colors or in very high resolution black and white. By adding Intel's AboveBoard, you can give your PC up to two megabytes of RAM. The final two chapters detail how to use this extra equipment with Windows and the advantages and disadvantages of adding this equipment.

HOW TO USE THIS BOOK

You perform just about any action in Windows by using either the keyboard or a mouse, a popular add-on pointing device. If you don't have a mouse, you can still do anything with Windows that you could do with a mouse. Even if you do have a mouse, you may find it easier to use the keyboard for a particular task, particularly if your hands are already on the keyboard. Which one you use is a matter of circumstance and personal preference. So, rather than tell you which one to use, when I give instructions in this book, I describe both methods or a general method that can be done either way. Instructions look something like this:

Do this with either the mouse or the keyboard.

M *Here's how to do something with the mouse.*

K *Here's how to do the same thing with the keyboard.*

There are several ways to choose commands from menus using the keyboard, most of which involve pressing the Alt key. A keyboard step might read like this:

K *Use Alt-Edit-Copy.*

This means "Use the keyboard to choose the Copy command from the Edit menu any way you like." In the first few chapters of the book, keyboard and mouse steps are delineated in detail. In later chapters, after you know how to choose commands from menus and start applications, there is less detail and you will notice that most of the steps are general, rather than being separated into mouse and keyboard instructions.

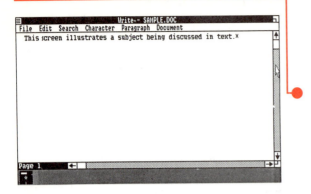

This book is designed for ease of reading, with graphics appearing mainly on the left side of each page and text on the right. Where a picture of the screen or a printout illustrates the subject being discussed in the text, you'll see a dot to the left of the text and a line leading to the proper graphic, as shown here.

From time to time, you'll notice a box containing the title ABOUT... and a small block of text. These ABOUT... boxes contain information about using Windows that you may not find in the documentation, information I've learned from the people at Microsoft and on my own. (The title comes from Windows' About... command, which gives you information about an application.)

EQUIPMENT YOU'LL NEED

Windows requires DOS version 2.0 or later, a graphics adapter card, and a monochrome graphics monitor or color monitor. Windows also requires 256K of memory and two disk drives. However, with only 256K of memory, it is difficult to run several applications at once or really take full advantage of Windows' capabilities. The system I used in developing the models for this book is a standard IBM PC with 512K of memory and a 10MB hard disk. All the models used in this book will run as described on a system like this. If you do not have a hard disk, you can most likely still use the models in the book, but you will have to do a fair amount of disk swapping. I strongly recommend a hard disk.

Chapters 3 and 6 include the use of the desktop application Terminal. To use Terminal, you will need a modem.

If you have an IBM PC AT or a COMPAQ Deskpro 286, Windows will run considerably faster than on an IBM PC or IBM PC XT. As long as you have at least 512K of memory, however, the models in this book will work on these machines as well.

Now that you know all you need to know about using this book, you're ready to turn to Chapter 1 and start learning about Windows.

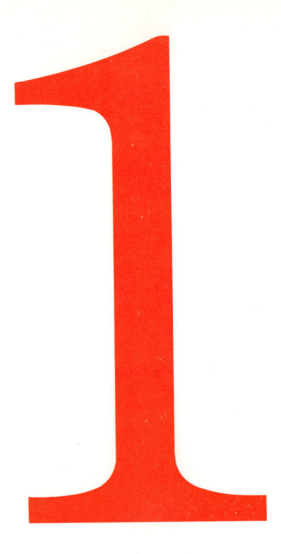

Chapter 1
Introducing Windows

1

INTRODUCING WINDOWS

When we turned on our PCs before Windows, we were greeted by a cryptic A> prompt. We were on our own to determine what to do next. Now we have Windows. When we turn on our machines, we are still greeted by the A> prompt, but all we have to do is start Windows and we can then do all our work from the Windows desktop—working intuitively with the program's equivalents of familiar tools and objects you might keep on your desk. After you've worked with Windows a short while, you'll probably take for granted the way you use Windows' desktop and familiar tools. But just because you may find Windows easy to use doesn't mean it was easy to create. Let's take a brief look at how it was done.

CREATING WINDOWS

Windows is not the first product to use a desktop metaphor. Research done at XEROX's Palo Alto Research Center indicated that when computers resemble familiar objects, people can transfer familiar skills to the computer more easily and work much as they used to work by hand. In early 1983, Apple Computer introduced the first microcomputer for the Apple world that used a desktop metaphor, the Lisa, and in early 1984, Apple released a scaled-down version of the Lisa, the Macintosh.

In early 1983, Microsoft started work on Windows, an operating environment with a desktop metaphor for the IBM world. Microsoft showed a test version of Windows to a select group of OEMs (original equipment manufacturers) in the spring of 1983. The majority of OEMs at the Windows demonstration said they supported the concept of Windows and said that Microsoft (rather than any other company then designing an operating environment) would get their support. It made sense to them to align themselves with an operating environment from Microsoft because Microsoft already had marketed the predominant microcomputer operating system, MS-DOS.

So Microsoft made a commitment to produce Windows and announced it at a lavish press conference on November 10, 1983, promising shipment in May of 1984. Then they started serious work.

In February 1984 the first Windows software developers' seminar was held, introducing software developers to Windows technology so the developers could build Windows applications. Feedback from the seminar and continued work on their own led the Windows development team to realize that Windows could be even better than the original plan. They polished the user interface and added two major tasks—memory management with virtual storage and dynamic linking and loading, two parts that make Windows and Windows applications usable on a limited-memory PC. At the same time they were developing Windows, they were also rewriting the C Compiler, the programming tool they were using to construct Windows, to support these additions.

Because of additions to Windows' design, in May of 1984, rather than shipping Windows, Microsoft sent out only a rough software vendor's toolkit to use in building applications, and announced a new retail date of November 1984. But when November 1984 arrived, Windows was still not ready to ship and a new date, June of 1985, was announced. The press, which up to this point had been reasonably loyal, now called Windows "vaporware," and speculated that perhaps Microsoft had found the task of producing Windows, with a graphic user interface, memory management, and device independence, just too difficult. But the software developers, who had been getting regular updates of the toolkit and Windows, remained loyal, recognizing that it would be a significant product, and that the delays were justified by the complexity of the task.

In June 1984, Microsoft shipped a final version of Windows to software developers and OEMs. But this was virtually unnoticed because Windows was not yet in the stores. Microsoft used the time between June and November 18, the date Windows finally appeared in the stores, to create their own Windows applications: Write, Paint, and the desktop applications. Including actual Windows applications in the retail version was necessary because when the average users look at Windows, they don't see its sophisticated memory management or graphic-device independence. They can see only the effect these behind-the-scenes features have on graphics and multiple applications sharing the screen.

Now that you know the story behind it, let's look at Windows, the operating environment that will change the way people work with computers. To understand a bit about how Windows does this, we'll first see what Windows looks like, and then we'll move on to some of its behind-the-scenes features.

WHAT WINDOWS LOOKS LIKE

The main work area of the initial Windows screen is similar to the center of a large desk and is designed to work the way you would work on a real desk. The computer task you are currently working on occupies the main area of the screen, just as a current task would occupy the center of your desk.

Windows

Because many people frequently work on more than one task at once, Windows lets you divide the screen into separate areas, called windows, each of which can display a separate task. If you start a new task, Windows will automatically resize the existing windows for you, to make room for a new window to display the new task. You can easily switch from task to task and transfer information between tasks and their windows.

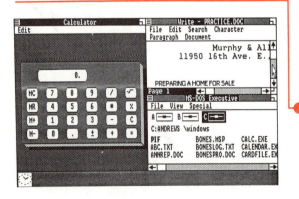

how to type the exact syntax and parameters of every command (which usually requires keeping the manual close at hand). Instead, you choose commands from Windows' menus, which are always located just beneath the title bar and which expand in drop-down fashion when you select them.

Dialog boxes

If a command needs additional information, Windows presents a dialog box that asks for the information in an easy-to-understand format.

Filling in dialog boxes is easier to remember than typing the parameters of a command, and is much less prone to error. For instance, perhaps you have had the experience of incorrectly typing the DOS command for file-copying as *COPY∗.∗ B:* instead of *COPY∗.∗ B:* and receiving the somewhat obtuse message "Bad command or file name." Interpreted, this message means you forgot the space between the *Y* and first asterisk. Using the Copy command in the same way with Windows is much easier: You choose the Copy... command from the File menu and complete the resulting dialog box as shown here.

The visible parts of Windows—the windows, icons, scroll bars, the title bar, drop-down menus, and dialog boxes—make up Windows' graphic user interface, which all Windows applications use. Windows' graphic user interface defines a standard for the way applications work; once you've learned to use one Windows application, the next one will be even easier because you will already know the basics—how to start it, how to choose commands, how to complete dialog boxes, and how to transfer information. This makes Windows applications easier to learn and use than DOS applications (also called standard applications—that is, applications not specifically designed for Windows), because before Windows there were no agreed-upon conventions for design of the user interface; designing the user interface was up to the programmers who designed the applications.

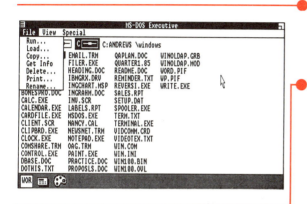

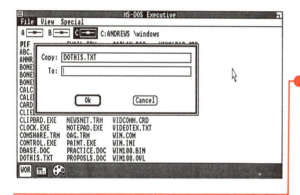

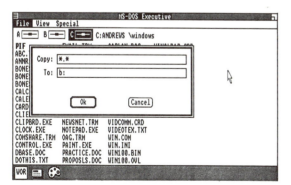

The Windows environment also encourages a "hands-on" approach to learning. You can readily see each component and command of a Windows application because of the graphic user interface. You feel free to look at the commands in each of the menus, you quickly learn how to use Windows, and you carry these skills over into every Windows application you use. Standard applications, on the other hand, often force you to fumble through the pages of a thick manual, looking for the name or syntax of a command, which tends to discourage carefree investigation.

BEHIND-THE-SCENES FEATURES

In addition to the desktop metaphor and the graphic user interface, Windows has some remarkable features that you can't see.

Windows expands the 640K limit of the PC

Even though Windows lets you run several applications at once, when you run more than one large application at a time, you eventually run into the inevitable PC memory limit of 640K, making the benefit of switching between several applications of marginal value. Fortunately, Windows allows you to overcome the memory barrier. If you have a hard disk or expanded memory, Windows uses the hard disk or additional memory to swap out one application and bring in another. You can return to exactly where you were in the first application with a couple of keystrokes. This allows you to switch between more applications than would fit in conventional memory at once.

Windows takes care of peripheral details

Before Windows, if you used a standard application without a mouse and later added a mouse, you would have had to upgrade the software to a version that supported the mouse. With Windows, if you add a mouse or other pointing device, a new printer, graphics card, or a new monitor, Windows will take care of the details of seeing that your current Windows applications will work with your new hardware. This is called device independence.

WINDOWS BENEFITS

It's easy to see why Windows would be beneficial for a person new to computers: It standardizes the way applications look and makes them easy to learn and use. But what does Windows have to offer seasoned PC users, people who are comfortable with DOS and the cryptic A> prompt, those who know and love standard applications such as Lotus 1-2-3 and Microsoft Word?

You can run standard applications

Not all applications are Windows applications. In fact, though the number of Windows applications is growing, there are far more standard applications. And chances are, if you're a seasoned PC user, you're loyal to a standard application, such as Multimate or VisiCalc, that was written before Windows. But using Windows does not mean abandoning the software you used before Windows. The same programs you used before Windows will work with Windows in just about the same way they work without Windows. And you'll get the additional benefits that using Windows adds, such as running more than one application and switching between them, and transferring information from one application to another.

Before Windows, if you wanted to transfer information from one program to another (from a database to a word-processing program, for example) you had very little choice: You couldn't transfer information between independent programs because of their different file formats, so you bought an integrated package, containing perhaps a database, a word processor, and probably a few other applications, all designed to work together. Theoretically, this sounds good; but it usually means giving up one

ABOUT...

Pop-up windows

Perhaps the most consistent feature of the Windows operating environment is the application window. Having menus, scroll bars, title bars, and other window components that are the same for each application you use allows you to be more comfortable and productive. But the application window is not the only type of window. There are also pop-up windows, which are overlaid (rather than being tiled) in response to commands you have chosen. Pop-up windows either display information or prompt you for information. A good example of a pop-up window is the one that appears when you choose the Get Info command from the File menu of the MS-DOS Executive. Like an application window, the Get Info window has a System menu and a title bar. But like other pop-up windows, it has only two commands on the System menu: Move and Close. You can't turn a pop-up window into an icon, as you can an application window.

of the high-power single-application tools you may be used to using for one of lesser capability that is part of the package, so that you can transfer information from one to the other. Windows, on the other hand, lets you run the programs with the features you like best, switch easily between them, and integrate and consolidate information from several different programs into a Windows application. You can, for example, put together a report in Microsoft Write that includes a report from R:base, some financial data from Multiplan, and a chart from Lotus 1-2-3. Windows takes care of the translation between programs, even programs that use different file formats.

Windows increases productivity

The ability to switch easily from one application to another (without saving your work first and quitting one application, then loading and opening your work in another) saves time and increases productivity. If, for example, you're writing an article using Microsoft Word and want to pause a minute and check your electronic mail, with one keystroke you can leave Word and go to Terminal, Windows' telecommunications application. You can check your mail and then almost instantly return to Word right where you left off. This is a wonderful timesaving feature for most of us who work on several tasks at the same time.

This ability to do more than one task at a time is called non-preemptive multitasking. In a nutshell, this means that the active application has Windows' attention until the application wants to or has to give it up. When an application loses Windows' attention, a process called context switching helps the application remember where it left off, so that when it eventually gets Windows' attention again, it will restart in the same place it stopped. For example, if Write is the active desktop application and Cardfile and Calendar are the inactive applications, Windows will give its attention to Write until you switch over to Cardfile or Calendar. Some exceptions to this are Clock, which continues to run, and Terminal, which can continue to receive data. Future versions of

Windows may support preemptive multitasking, in which several applications will seem to be running at the same time, with each getting a slice of the processor's time.

Mouse, light pen, or keyboard?

Windows gives you a choice of choosing and carrying out a command either with a mouse, a light pen, or a keyboard. If you have a mouse or a light pen, you may find some tasks quicker and easier to do by just pointing to them. But if your hands are already on the keyboard, it may be easier to execute a command from the keyboard. Almost anything you can do with a pointing device you can also do with the keyboard, including using Microsoft Paint. The choice is yours.

Windows in color!

The Apple Macintosh, which, as mentioned earlier, also uses a graphic user interface, has very high-resolution graphics, but no color. Windows with standard equipment (a PC, color-graphics adapter and monitor) also has no color; it runs in high-resolution black and white. But if you add an enhanced graphics adapter, such as the IBM EGA, you can have Windows in color. And with the addition of an enhanced graphics monitor, Windows is truly impressive with both color and very high resolution.

WINDOWS TRADEOFFS

Any new hardware or software has some tradeoffs, limitations that come with the benefits it offers. And this is true of Windows under current conditions. The two major tradeoffs for Windows features are speed and memory.

Because Windows is a graphic application, it runs slightly slower than text applications. Graphic applications write to the screen one pixel at a time, whereas text applications write one character at a time. A screen can display 2,000 characters, but is made up of 128,000 pixels. If you're running Windows with a standard display, it's acceptably fast.

But if you're running Windows on a PC with an enhanced graphics adapter and monitor in very high-resolution color, you may find it running slower than you'd like.

Another tradeoff is the amount of memory Windows requires. Memory on the PC is limited to 640K. Even with Windows' sophisticated memory management, you probably won't be able to run as many applications as you'd like at once. Ideally, you'd most likely want to run two or three favorite standard applications and some of the desktop applications, such as Clock, Calendar, and Terminal, as icons. Right now, there just isn't enough memory for all these at once. Because Windows allows you to run more than one application at a time, it has outgrown traditional memory needs. But a future version of Windows will most likely take advantage of expanded memory (memory above 640K, as RAM) and memory will no longer be a problem.

Right now, even with these limitations, the benefits of using Windows—the increase in productivity, the ability to run both standard applications and Windows applications, the ability to transfer information from these applications to Windows applications, and the ability to switch quickly between applications—are definitely worth the tradeoffs. As future versions of Windows are released—versions that include options such as the ability to use more than 640K of memory as RAM—Windows will be mandatory for the PC user who places a high value on productivity.

Chapter 2
Getting Started with Windows

Chapter 3
Using Calendar, Cardfile, and Terminal

2

GETTING STARTED WITH WINDOWS

In this chapter, you'll finally get your hands on the keyboard (and the mouse, if you have one) and start Windows.

First, we'll tour Windows and the MS-DOS Executive, the window that opens when you start Windows. (As its name suggests, this window is in charge of MS-DOS, the disk operating system for the IBM PC, XT, AT, and compatibles.) We'll look at the features of Windows that are generic to all applications; that way, you'll know what they do in whatever Windows application you use. Then we'll look at the specific commands that are part of the MS-DOS Executive. You'll see how to use the MS-DOS Executive for the tasks you may be used to doing from DOS.

The MS-DOS Executive window is the place where you start an application like Lotus 1-2-3 or Microsoft Write. It also takes care of most of the DOS commands, commands you may be used to typing in after the A>, B>, or C> prompt. For example, the MS-DOS Executive has commands to copy, delete, and print files, just as DOS does. Once you become familiar with the MS-DOS Executive, you'll find that having it do your DOS work for you is easier than the old way—typing DOS commands after the A> prompt—and there's less possibility of error. You'll never again type *CPOY* when you meant to type *COPY*.

Once you know about the MS-DOS Executive and how to put it to work, you'll learn to use three of the desktop applications: Clock, Notepad, and Calculator. Windows comes with seven desktop applications. Chapter 3 shows you how to use three more: Cardfile, Calendar, and Terminal. (The seventh application is Reversi, a game much like Othello. I won't spoil the fun you'll have figuring out Reversi on your own.)

Clock, Notepad, and Calculator are handy tools that come with Windows and you use them much as you would a real clock, calculator, or paper notepad lying on your desk. Clock is an analog clock, the kind most of us are used to looking at. You can shrink this clock to an icon so that it takes up no work space but continues to display the current time. Calculator has most of the functions of a hand-held model: It can add, subtract, multiply, and divide, and has memory functions and some special keys. You'll use Notepad much as you would a paper pad—to jot down notes and reminders. It won't replace your word processor for letters and reports, but it is instantly available for a quick note or memo. Having the desktop applications as part of Windows makes them instantly accessible: No one can sneak in, borrow them, and forget to return them; they will always be exactly where you need them, at the bottom of your Windows screen. Another advantage to using the Windows desktop applications rather than the ones lying on your desk is that Windows can transfer information from one desktop application to another. You can, for example, use Calculator to compute the total for a column of figures, then copy this total out of Calculator and paste it into Notepad.

In this chapter, we'll start Clock and shrink it to an icon displaying the current time in the corner of the screen. (Shrinking an application to an icon removes it from the work area, leaves it running in memory, and puts a small graphic that represents the application, called an icon, in the icon area at the bottom of the screen.) Then we'll start Notepad, write a short expense memo, start Calculator, add up our expenses, and then copy the calculated total to the memo. In addition to learning to use these accessories, you'll learn how to work with Windows: how to open one or more windows, how to start applications, how to choose commands from menus, how to shrink windows to icons for future use or close them if they're no longer needed, and how to transfer information between applications.

ABOUT...

Reversi moving options

While you're playing Reversi, if you want to see all of the legal moves you can make next, displayed one by one, hold down the Tab key.

Once you know these basics, you'll be comfortable with all Windows applications because they all work similarly, though the specific commands for each application will, of course, be different.

The chapter ends with a short explanation of how to run DOS commands not included on the MS-DOS Executive menus, such as DISKCOPY, which copies an entire disk's information to another disk. A short discussion of moving between directories when you're running Windows from a hard disk is also included. This information will complete your Windows orientation.

RUNNING WINDOWS

If you haven't already done so, you need to install Windows. Installing Windows is a one-time process that sets up the Windows program to work with your particular computer, printer, and other equipment. You install Windows by using a program called Setup that comes on your Windows disks. Setup provides step-by-step instructions which it displays on the screen. If you've already run the Setup program to install Windows, you can skip this section of the chapter and move on to the section titled "Starting Windows."

Installing Windows

To install Windows for your computer:

If you have a hard disk, start your computer in the usual way. If you're working on a floppy-disk system, start your computer with your DOS disk in drive A. Enter the time and date after the prompts.

Insert the setup disk in drive A, close the drive door and, if drive A is not the current drive, type:

```
A:
```

■ *Press the Enter key.*

> On the IBM keyboard, the Enter key
> is the one with the arrow that looks
> like this: ↵ It's also known as the
> Return key and looks different on
> non-IBM keyboards.

■ *Now type:*

SETUP

■ *Press the Enter key.*

> Instructions you type are shown in
> uppercase in this book, but you can
> type them in either upper- or lower-
> case. DOS ignores capitalization.

The Setup program will begin. Just follow the
instructions on the screen. Installing Windows takes
some time and disk-swapping, but you only need to
do it once and then Windows will be set up for your
computer and peripherals. Later, if you add another
printer, you can tell Windows what you've done
using the Control Panel; you don't have to run the
Setup program again. If you change the kind of
graphics card or adapter you are using or if you add
a pointing device, you will need to run Setup again
and specify your new equipment.

Starting Windows

The way you start Windows varies, depending on
whether you have a hard-disk or floppy-disk system.
As I mentioned in the introduction, Windows works
best with a hard disk, so instructions in this book
are for hard-disk users. The steps for starting
Windows on a floppy-disk system are similar and
instructions in the documentation and Setup program are straightforward.

If you have a hard disk, here's how to start Windows:

■ *To move to the Windows directory, type:*

CD \WINDOWS

If you accept the default settings, the Windows Setup program creates the \WINDOWS directory when it sets up the program on your system. The CD, or Change Directory, command moves you to the directory you specify. If you don't accept the default settings and specify a different directory name for the Windows files, you can specify that directory with the CD command.

■ *Now type:*

WIN

■ *Press the Enter key.*

In a few seconds, you'll see the Microsoft logo moving across the screen and then the initial Windows screen.

Later, when you're using Windows regularly, you can put these steps into an AUTOEXEC.BAT file. AUTOEXEC.BAT is a file that is run automatically each time you start your computer. So, if you put these startup steps in AUTOEXEC.BAT, each time you turn on your computer, Windows will automatically be loaded. The AUTOEXEC.BAT file I use looks as shown here.

If you have an AUTOEXEC.BAT file, yours may have different commands.

```
C:\)type autoexec.bat
astclock
prompt $p$g
set files=20
set buffers=15
set path=c:\;c:\mouse1;c:\windows;
verify on
break on
cd \windows
win

c:\)
```

If you don't already have an AUTOEXEC.BAT file to which you can add these lines, here's how to make one:

■ *After you start your computer and see the C> prompt, but before starting Windows, type:*

COPY CON AUTOEXEC.BAT

■ *Press Enter.*

■ *Next, type:*

TIME

■ *Press Enter.*

■ *Type:*

DATE

■ *Press Enter.*

■ *Then type:*

CD \WINDOWS

■ *Press Enter.*

■ *Finally, type:*

WIN

■ *Press Enter.*

■ *Now press the F6 key and press Enter.*

```
C:\>COPY CON AUTOEXEC.BAT
TIME
DATE
CD \WINDOWS
WIN
^Z
         1 File(s) copied

C:\>
```

Pressing F6 adds a ^Z just below the last line you typed on the screen. When DOS runs the AUTOEXEC.BAT file, this is the mark it looks for to tell it that it's reached the end of the file. The lines that say TIME and DATE will prompt you to set the current time and date; without them, DOS would bypass the usual time and date prompts. If you set them when you start your computer, the Windows clock and calendar will be set accordingly.

Your AUTOEXEC.BAT file is written on your disk, and each time you start your computer, it will run.

THE WINDOWS SCREEN

Let's look at the initial Windows screen. First, I'll identify the parts of the screen that are common to all Windows applications and then we'll look specifically at the MS-DOS Executive, which opens automatically when you start Windows. The screen shown here reflects the system I am using: a PC with two floppy disk drives (A and B) and a hard disk drive (C).

The title bar
The title bar at the top of the screen contains the title of the current window (MS-DOS Executive). Each window you open will have a title bar.

The System menu
In the upper left corner of the screen is a small box called the System menu box. You'll find one of these on every application that can run in a window.

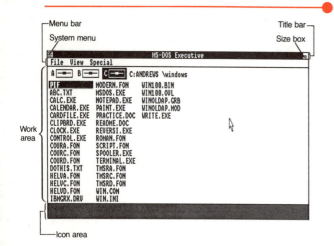

SECTION 2
Chapter 2: Getting Started with Windows

Commands in the System menu move, shrink, expand, close, describe, and change the size of the windows they're displayed in. To display the System menu, if you have a mouse, position the pointer over the System menu box and hold down the mouse button or press the Alt-Spacebar key combination. The System menu will continue to be displayed until you release the mouse button or press the Esc key.

Notice that some of the command names are dimmed. This is Windows' way of telling you that these commands aren't currently available for you to use.

We'll use commands from the System menu later in this chapter when we use the desktop applications.

The size box

In the upper right corner of the screen is the size box. In some windows, the size box appears in the lower right corner or in both the upper and lower right corners. If you have a mouse, you can drag the size box to change the size of a window. If you don't have a mouse, you'll use the Size command from the System menu and the direction keys with this box to size windows. The size box must cross a window border in order for the sizing feature to be activated. (This means you'll sometimes need to move the size box in the opposite direction of the way you want to size a window to cross a window border and then pull it back to the size you want the window to be.)

The menu bar

Just below the title bar is the menu bar. The menu bar contains the names of the command menus. Rather than typing the names of commands, you select commands from these menus in Windows applications. Each application has its own menus and commands.

The work area

Just below the menu bar is the work area. It's the working area for the application you're running. Right now the MS-DOS Executive window is open and the work area displays the directory of the current drive.

The icon area

The gray area at the bottom of the screen is the icon area. There is nothing in the icon area now because the only Windows application running is MS-DOS Executive and it's displayed in the work area. But if you were in the middle of a busy Windows session, your icon area might look as shown here.

The icon area is the place to leave an application you're not currently using but plan to use later. It's like pushing something aside on your desk rather than putting it away in a drawer. When we use the desktop applications, we'll keep Calculator in the icon area so it's easily accessible.

THE MS-DOS EXECUTIVE WINDOW

Now let's take a closer look at the MS-DOS Executive window's work area. I'll identify the parts of the work area, and then we'll look at the commands on each of the menus so you'll have a clearer idea of what the MS-DOS Executive does and how to use it.

At the top of the work area are the drive icons. These represent the computer's disk drives. The current drive (in our example, drive C) is highlighted. To highlight a different drive and see a directory of its files:

M *Point to the drive A icon (or the drive B icon, if you're using a floppy-disk system) and click the mouse button to see a directory of drive A.*

K *Press Ctrl and the letter of the drive whose directory you wish to see. For example, for a directory of drive A, press Ctrl-A.*

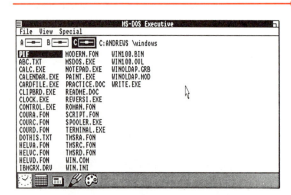

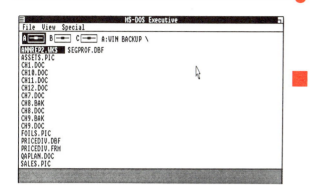

The drive A icon is highlighted and you can see a directory listing for drive A in the work area. (The files shown here are the ones that were on the disk I had in drive A when I created this image.)

Now return to drive C.

If you have a hard disk, you may wish to see other directories on that disk in the MS-DOS Executive window. Most hard-disk users divide their disks into various directories to better organize the information stored there. These directories are hierarchical and are called tree-structured directories because they can branch into multiple subdirectories. A typical directory tree might look as shown here.

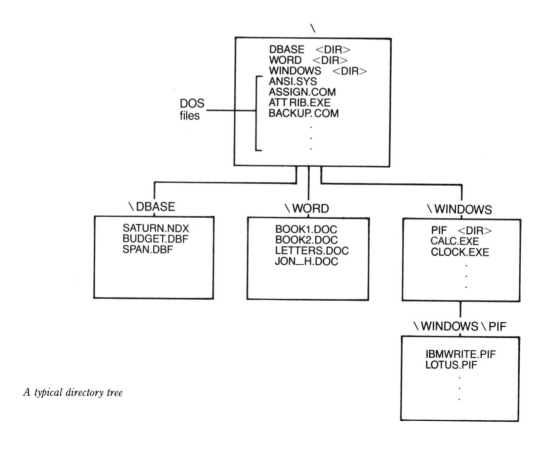

A typical directory tree

SECTION 2
Chapter 2: Getting Started with Windows

There is a section at the end of this chapter that explains how to move between directories.

Looking back at the MS-DOS Executive window displayed when drive C is the current drive, next to the drive icons you see the pathname. It shows what part of the directory tree you're in. The pathname consists of the drive name (for example, C:) followed by the volume name, if there is one. The volume name in this example is ANDREWS because the dealer who installed my hard disk assigned it the volume name of its owner. Following the volume name is the current directory pathname, \WINDOWS. Most people give directories names that clearly identify their contents. The \WINDOWS directory name indicates that this is the place my Windows files are stored.

Below the drive icons and the pathname is a directory listing showing the files contained in the current directory.

Files

The files displayed in the directory on your screen right now most likely are ones that came with Windows. Files beginning with WIN (for example, WIN100.BIN and WINOLDAP.MOD) are ones the Windows program uses. The files CALC.EXE, CALENDAR.EXE, CARDFILE.EXE, CLOCK.EXE, NOTEPAD.EXE, REVERSI.EXE, and TERMINAL.EXE are the desktop application files. DOTHIS.TXT is a sample file you can use to try out Notepad. The files named WRITE.EXE and PAINT.EXE contain Microsoft Write and Microsoft Paint, two applications that were bundled with the first release of Windows. Write and Paint are discussed in detail in Chapter 5. All the files ending with .FON are fonts. We'll discuss using different fonts with Write and Paint in Chapter 5. Also included is a print spooler, SPOOLER.EXE, which allows printing to take place while the computer is doing other tasks. When we use Notepad and, at the same time, print a memo later in this chapter, you'll see how the Spooler works. You should also have a file something like EPSON.DRV for your specific printer. The file named CONTROL.EXE contains Control Panel. You use Control Panel to set the time or date and also when you add new printers to your system. The file name MSDOS.EXE lets you run two MS-DOS Executive windows so that, for example, you can have one displaying the files in drive A and the other window displaying the files in drive B, allowing you to view both at the same time.

Notice that the very first directory entry, PIF, is displayed in bold type. Windows puts any entries that are themselves directories at the beginning of the directory listing (ahead of files) and displays them in bold type. (I have moved the highlight to a different entry in this illustration, so that you can see the difference in type style more easily.)

PIF is the directory that contains program information files for many of the standard applications you'll use with Windows. The PIF directory also contains PIFEDIT.EXE, a program information file editor that resides in the PIF directory. You use it to create or modify program information files for standard applications like Lotus 1-2-3 or Microsoft Word, so that they will run with Windows. PIFs contain information such as the amount of memory required for an application.

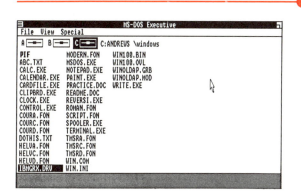

Menus and commands

The MS-DOS Executive has three menus: the File menu for tasks such as copying, deleting, renaming and printing files; the View menu for displaying directories; and the Special menu for tasks such as creating directories to organize files into convenient groups, changing directories, and formatting disks.

Displaying menus   If you have a mouse, you can see the commands on any menu by pointing to the menu and pressing the mouse button. To display the System menu with the keyboard, press Alt-Spacebar. From this display, you can display other menus using the left or right direction keys. You can also directly display the menu of your choice by pressing Alt and the first letter of the menu you wish to see (for example, Alt-F displays the File menu). Menus remain displayed until you release the mouse button or press Esc or Enter.

Choosing commands   If you're using a mouse, there is only one way to choose a command. Drag over the menu selections until the command you want to use is highlighted. Then release the mouse button.

There are several ways to choose commands from the keyboard. Once the appropriate menu is displayed (by pressing Alt and the first letter of the menu name), use the direction keys to highlight the command of your choice or press the first letter of the command (for example, C for Copy). Then press Enter to carry out the command. A shortcut for choosing commands is to hold down the Alt key, press the first letter of the menu, and then press the first letter of the command. If you do both of these steps with the Alt key depressed, the command will automatically be executed when you release the Alt key; you won't need to press Enter to carry out the command.

I won't try to tell you which method to use when choosing commands with the keyboard; it's up to you to choose which method to use. As I said in the introduction, instructions in this book for choosing commands with the keyboard look like this:

Use Alt-*Menu name-Command name*

For example, I might say "Use Alt-Edit-Copy" and it means you can choose the Copy command from the Edit menu whichever way you prefer.

The File menu

The File menu has seven commands.

Run...   The Run... command runs an application or program you've written. (Commands followed by ... indicate that the program needs more information from you to carry out the command. Windows will present a dialog box requesting the information it needs.) You'll use the Run... command rather than selecting the program name from the MS-DOS Executive window when you need to provide additional information, such as a pathname or volume name, in order to run a program. For example, I use the Run... command to start Edlin, the line editor, and specify the name of the file I want to edit in the Run dialog box.

Load... The Load... command opens the application you specify as an icon instead of automatically opening it in a window.

Copy... The Copy... command copies a file to a different directory or disk, or makes a copy with a different name in the same directory. The advantage of using the Copy... command from Windows rather than DOS is that you can select more than one file to be copied, and Windows will perform the copying of all the selected files in one step. (You select more than one file with a mouse by clicking on the first file you want to copy to select it, then holding down the Shift key and clicking on each additional file you want to select. You can select more than one file to copy with the keyboard by moving the underline to the first file you wish to copy and then pressing Shift-Spacebar to select it. Then hold down the Ctrl key, use the direction keys to move the underline to the next file to copy, and press Shift-Spacebar to select it. Continue like this until all the files you wish to copy are selected.)

Get Info The Get Info command displays the selected file's name and extension, its size (in bytes), and the date and time it was created or the date of its most recent change.

Delete... The Delete... command deletes the selected file or group of files.

Print... The Print... command prints the selected file or directory.

Rename... The Rename... command is the one to use to change the name of the selected file.

The View menu

The View menu lets you display the directory listings in the MS-DOS Executive window in a variety of ways. The default display is the one you see in the MS-DOS Executive window when you start Windows: Directory names and file names are displayed in the short format, the entire directory is displayed, and files are organized alphabetically by name. The selection of these options is indicated by check marks beside the names of the corresponding commands in the View menu. The commands are divided into three groups (as indicated by the horizontal lines across the menu) and you can select one option from each group.

Short   When Short is checked, only file names are displayed in the MS-DOS Executive window.

Long   If you select Long, the contents of the current directory will be displayed in an expanded format, which includes the name, extension, size, and the date and time of creation or last revision of files. Directories are denoted simply by *<DIR>*.

The portion of the information displayed in bold-face represents the selected command in the last group on the View menu (By Name, By Date, By Size, or By Kind). For example, if you've chosen By Date, the dates for all the displayed files will be displayed in bold type.

All   All files in the directory are listed when All is checked.

Partial...   You use the Partial... command to view only certain files. The Partial... command displays a dialog box that looks as shown here.

Specify the type of files you wish to see. For example, specifying *.BAT* would list only the batch files. (The ∗ is a wildcard that tells Windows to list all files ending with .BAT.)

Programs   If you select the Programs command, the MS-DOS Executive window displays only program files (those with .COM, .EXE, and .BAT file-name extensions).

Commands in the last group on the View menu select the order in which the files will be displayed on the screen.

By Name   By Name arranges the files alphabetically by name.

By Date   By Date arranges files chronologically by the date and time each file was created and lists the most recently created files first.

By Size   By Size orders the files according to size, from largest to smallest.

By Kind   By Kind orders files alphabetically by file-name extension. For example, a file ending with .BAT would precede those ending with .COM and .EXE. Files with the same extension are sorted alphabetically by name.

The Special menu

The Special menu has a command to end the current Windows session and return to DOS and commands that replace the DOS utilities MD (Make Directory), CD (Change Directory), FORMAT, FORMAT/S, and VOL (Volume).

```
Special
End Session
Create Directory...
Change Directory...
Format Data Disk...
Make System Disk...
Set Volume Name...
```

End Session   You use the End Session command to leave Windows and return to DOS. You don't need to shrink windows that are expanded or to close desktop applications that are running before using the End Session command. Windows will take care of that for you, and prompt you to save any information that's unsaved. (But you do need to close any standard applications, such as Multiplan and Lotus 1-2-3, before ending your Windows session.)

Create Directory...   The Create Directory... command replaces the DOS MD utility and lets you create a new directory. You can use this command to organize your files into convenient groups.

Change Directory...   Change Directory... replaces the DOS CD utility and is used to change from one directory to another, usually on a hard disk. If you have a mouse, you can also change directories by clicking on the part of the pathname you want to go to. A keyboard shortcut is the Backspace key, which moves you one directory closer to the root.

Format Data Disk...   This command lets you format a disk from the MS-DOS Executive window. It is the same as the DOS Format utility with no parameters.

Make System Disk...   The Make System Disk... utility lets you format a bootable disk (one that contains DOS Startup files) from the MS-DOS Executive window. It replaces the FORMAT/S utility.

Set Volume Name...   You use the Set Volume Name... command to give a disk a descriptive title to help you identify its contents. The volume name is displayed in the MS-DOS Executive window as part of the pathname, so if all your disks have volume names, it's easy to check to be sure you're using the right disk.

Those are all of the MS-DOS Executive menu commands. We'll use some of these commands as we work with the desktop applications.

Now that you've toured the MS-DOS Executive window, it's time to use Windows, start some of the desktop applications, and do some useful work. This is the fun part—the desktop applications are as useful and no more difficult to use than the accessories lying on your desk, and they'll never get buried under last week's mail. In the process of learning to use the desktop applications, you'll learn how Windows applications work. You'll learn how to start programs, choose commands from menus, transfer information from one window to another using the Clipboard, shrink applications to icons so they'll always be available at the bottom of your Windows screen, and save and print files.

USING CLOCK

First, we'll start Clock and see how to start an application from the MS-DOS Executive window. Then we'll shrink Clock to an icon in the icon area. You can shrink any Windows application to an icon. This leaves it accessible in memory without having to start it or load it from disk again. The Clock icon is called a dynamic icon because even when it is a very small icon on the bottom of the screen, it continues to run and display the correct time. We'll also learn how to use Control Panel to set the time displayed by Clock in case it's displaying the wrong time, and how to start Clock as an icon.

Starting an application
Let's start Clock now, so you can see what it looks like.

M *In the MS-DOS Executive window, point to the file named CLOCK.EXE and double-click the mouse button. If you're using a mouse with two buttons, all Windows functions can be performed using only the left button.*

K *Use the direction keys until CLOCK.EXE is highlighted. Press the Enter key.*

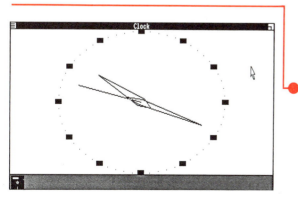

This starts Clock. Notice how the Clock window replaces the MS-DOS Executive window in the work area and MS-DOS Executive shrinks to an icon that resembles a floppy disk in the icon area.

Shrinking an application to an icon

Even though this is a rather nice clock, you probably won't want it taking up the entire work area. But it would be nice to be able to glance at it and note the time. What you can do is shrink it to an icon where it won't take up any of the work area and will still display the correct time.

To shrink an application to an icon:

M   *Double-click on the title bar.*

K   *Use Alt-Spacebar-Icon to display the System menu and choose the Icon command.*

Notice that the work area is cleared and Clock joins the MS-DOS Executive icon in the icon area at the bottom of the screen.

Starting an application as an icon   You may wish to start Clock or another application as an icon. If you just want Clock to display the correct time, but not take up space in the work area, it is simpler to start it out that way; this will eliminate having the Clock window replace the MS-DOS Executive window and then having to shrink it to an icon. Be sure the MS-DOS Executive window is open and the \WINDOWS directory with the CLOCK.EXE file is displayed.

Then hold down the Shift key and double-click on CLOCK.EXE, or use the direction keys to select the file named CLOCK.EXE, then hold down the Shift key and press Enter.

Clock will start as an icon in the icon area and the MS-DOS Executive window will continue to be open in the work area. You can open any application as an icon, just as you did with Clock. Applications can also be started as icons using the File menu and the Load... command, as noted earlier in this chapter. You might want to use the Load... command if the application you're starting as an icon needs parameters specified.

Using Control Panel

Having a clock that displays the wrong time could be a bit disconcerting, so Windows provides Control Panel for setting the correct time for Clock.

We need to start Control Panel from the MS-DOS Executive window, so we must first move the icon for the MS-DOS Executive into the work area.

To move an application from the icon area back into the work area:

M *Position the mouse pointer on the icon of the application you want—in this case, the MS-DOS Executive icon. (Notice that when the mouse pointer is positioned in the icon area, the pointer shape changes from an arrow to a small rectangle.) Hold down the mouse button and drag the MS-DOS Executive icon into the work area. Release the mouse button.*

K *Press Alt-Tab until the MS-DOS Executive icon is selected. (When the icon is selected, it is framed by a white border.) Use Alt-Spacebar-Move to display the System menu and choose the Move command. Press Enter.*

You'll see the MS-DOS Executive window in the work area displaying the Windows directory or the current directory (the directory you're currently in).

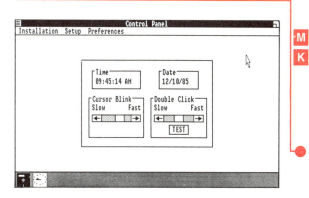

M *Double-click on the file named CONTROL.EXE.*

K *Use the direction keys to highlight the file named CONTROL.EXE. Press Enter.*

The Control Panel window replaces the MS-DOS Executive window in the work area and MS-DOS Executive is displayed as an icon in the icon area.

Changing the time   First, we'll use Control Panel to change the time.

M   *Click on the part of the time you wish to change—the hours, minutes, or seconds. This selects that part of the time. (For example, to change the time from 9:45:14 to 9:52:14, you'd click on 45, the minutes.)*

K   *Use the right and left arrows to select the part of the time you wish to change.*

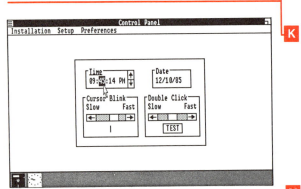

When you select part of the time either by clicking or using the direction keys, a box containing a pair of vertical arrows appears at the edge of the Time box. You use these arrows to change the time.

M   *Click the top arrow to set the clock ahead. Click the bottom arrow to set the clock back.*

K   *Press the up direction key to set the clock ahead. Press the down direction key to set the clock back.*

Other settings you can change in the Control Panel window are the date, the cursor-blink rate, and the mouse double-click speed, although you won't be able to set the double-click speed if you don't have a mouse. The Tab key is used to move from one control panel section to another.

You set the date the same way you set the time. To change the cursor-blink rate, simply drag the box to the left or right or use the direction keys. Mouse users may wish to change the mouse double-click speed. If you need to double-click more than once to get Windows to carry out a command, you may wish to experiment with setting different double-click speeds until you find the one that best matches your clicking speed.

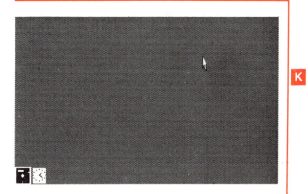

Windows saves the Control Panel settings in a file called WIN.INI, which contains important information needed by Windows. With standard equipment, the time and date changes you made will be in effect only until you shut off your computer.

When your clock is properly set, choose the Close command from the System menu to close Control Panel. We'll close this application rather than shrink it to an icon because we're not likely to need it again, and applications running as icons take up memory.

M *Position the mouse pointer on the System menu box in the upper left corner of the screen. Hold down the mouse button to display the menu. Drag the mouse pointer over the menu selections. When the command you want is highlighted (in this case, the Close command), release the mouse button. A shortcut is to double-click the System menu box, which will close any application.*

K *Use Alt-Spacebar-Close to display the System menu and choose the Close command.*

The Control Panel window disappears. If you need it again, you can run it from the MS-DOS Executive. The work area is now empty, and the Clock and MS-DOS Executive icons are in the icon area.

WORKING WITH CALCULATOR

Now we'll look at Calculator and see how it works. Calculator is easy to use because it works much like a hand-held model. Later, after we've used Notepad for an expense memo, we'll use Calculator to total up expenses.

We need to start Calculator, like all applications, from the MS-DOS Executive, the same way we started Clock and Control Panel. So first we'll need to open the MS-DOS Executive, which is now an icon.

Starting Calculator

To move the MS-DOS Executive icon into the work area to start it:

M *Position the mouse pointer on the MS-DOS Executive icon. Hold down the mouse button and drag the icon into the work area. Release the mouse button.*

K· *Press Alt-Tab until the MS-DOS Executive icon is selected. Use Alt-Spacebar-Move, and then press Enter.*

The MS-DOS Executive should now be running.

To start Calculator in the work area:

M *Double-click on the file named CALC.EXE.*

K *Use the direction keys to select the file named CALC.EXE. Press Enter.*

Calculator will replace the MS-DOS Executive in the work area and the MS-DOS Executive again becomes an icon.

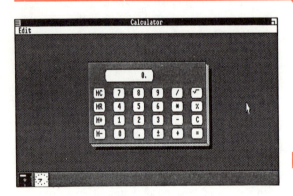

The calculator in the window performs the basic arithmetic functions—addition, subtraction, multiplication, division, and calculation of square roots and percentages. It also has its own memory.

Using Calculator

To use Calculator:

M *Click on the figures you wish to compute. For example, to add 1.83 and 7.9, click the 1, the decimal point, the 8, and the 3. Then click the plus (+) sign. Click the 7, the decimal point, and the 9, and click the equal (=) sign.*

K *Enter the figures you wish to compute. You can use either the numbers in the top row of the keyboard or you can depress the Num Lock key and use the numeric keypad.*

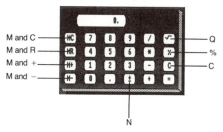

M and C ——— +MC ———

M and R ——— +MR ———

M and + ——— +M+ ———

M and − ——— +M− ———

——— Q

——— %

——— C

N

Keyboard equivalents for Calculator buttons

The total appears in the display at the top of the calculator.

Some Calculator buttons have typing key equivalents, as shown here.

Notice that Calculator has only one menu in the menu bar: the Edit menu. The Edit menu has two commands: Copy and Paste. If you pull down the Edit menu, you'll notice key names to the right of the commands: F2 beside Copy and Ins next to Paste. A key name on a menu tells you that you can carry out that command with that key. Carrying out a command with the key (or keys) shown on a menu usually is a faster method of choosing a command from the keyboard than any other keyboard method because it eliminates displaying the menu. Even if you have a mouse, you may find it easier to use the keyboard shortcuts (when you remember them) rather than reach for the mouse, if your hands are already on the keyboard.

You use the Copy command to copy a total from Calculator to use in another application. We'll do this later when we transfer a calculated total to Notepad. You can use the Paste command to bring a figure in from another application. For example, if you have the figure $9,264,771.69 in a Windows spreadsheet, you could simply select the figure, copy it to the Clipboard for temporary storage, open the Calculator window, and choose the Paste command. Windows automatically copies that figure (without the dollar sign or commas) into the Calculator display. Using the Clipboard eliminates entering the same figure twice, which reduces the chance of typing errors. If the Clipboard contains a formula, Windows will paste in the result of the formula.

USING NOTEPAD

Before you can start Notepad, you need to move the MS-DOS Executive back into the work area again, since the MS-DOS Executive window is the place from which all applications that are not already icons must start. We'll put the MS-DOS Executive in the Calculator work area, which will shrink Calculator to an icon and put it in the icon area at the bottom of the screen, ready for us to use later.

To move the MS-DOS Executive from the icon area back into the work area:

M   *Position the mouse pointer on the MS-DOS Executive icon. Hold down the mouse button and drag the icon into the work area. Release the mouse button.*

K   *Press Alt-Tab until the MS-DOS Executive icon is selected. Use Alt-Spacebar-Move to display the System menu and choose the Move command. This moves the icon into the work area. Then press Enter to start the MS-DOS Executive.*

> You'll see the MS-DOS Executive window in the work area, with the Windows directory displayed, and Calculator is now an icon.

M   *Double-click on NOTEPAD.EXE to load it.*

K   *Use the direction keys to highlight NOTEPAD.EXE. Press Enter.*

> You'll see the Notepad window appear in the work area.

Right now the work area is empty, much like a blank sheet of paper in a notepad on your desk. Before we type a memo, let's look at the Notepad menus to get an overview of what Notepad can do.

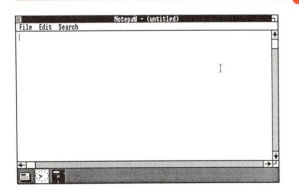

The File menu

The File menu has five commands.

```
File
New
Open...
Save
Save As...
Print
```

New   Use the New command when you are
working on a note and need to start a new one.
Choosing the New command gives you a blank
Notepad window that's like a clean sheet of paper.

Open...   Use the Open... command to open an
existing Notepad file, perhaps something that you
created earlier and now need to change, add information to, and print.

Save and Save As...   The Save and Save As...
commands are for saving your notes. Use Save
As... the first time you save a note. Notepad will
display a dialog box asking you to name the note.
Names can be at most eight characters long. Notepad adds the .TXT extension to the name you specify. After naming your Notepad file, if later you want
to save changes or additions, use the Save command. Save simply saves your changes in the file
you specified earlier with the Save As... command.

Print   Use the Print command when you want
to print a note. Notepad will set up the Spooler and
your note will begin to print. While your note is
printing, you can continue to use the computer for
other tasks; you don't need to wait until printing
is completed.

The Edit menu

```
Edit
Undo        Sh/Esc

Cut         Del
Copy        F2
Paste       Ins
Clear

Select All
Time/Date   F5

Word Wrap
```

The Edit menu has eight commands. Notice how
some of the commands are followed by key names.
You can use commands that are followed by key
names either by choosing them from the menu or
by pressing the keys indicated. Once you learn the
commands, you may find the keyboard alternative
faster than the menu.

Undo   The Undo command undoes your last
Notepad action. For example, if you delete a paragraph and then suddenly realize it was the wrong
paragraph, rather than typing the deleted paragraph
again, you can use the Undo command.

Cut, Copy, and Paste   Cut, Copy, and Paste are
three commands that use the Clipboard as a temporary storage place. For example, if you want to
transfer information from Notepad to the Clipboard,
you would use either Cut or Copy. Cut deletes the
selected text from Notepad and puts it on the
Clipboard; Copy puts a copy of the selected text on
the Clipboard. You use the Paste command to put
information from the Clipboard into Notepad.

Clear   Use the Clear command to delete selected
text from Notepad.

Select All   Select All selects all the information
in the Notepad file that's currently open. This is
handy if you wish to copy the entire note to the
Clipboard. First you'd use the Select All command
and then the Copy command.

Time/Date   Choosing the Time/Date command
inserts the time and date currently recorded by the
computer's clock and calendar into your note at
the cursor position.

Word Wrap   If you choose Word Wrap, Notepad
will automatically start a new line for you when you
reach the right margin. You won't need to press
Enter at the end of each line.

The Search menu
    The last menu in the Notepad menu bar is the
Search menu. It has two commands: Find... and
Find Next.

Find   You use the Find... command to search for text in your Notepad file. You specify the text to search for and whether Notepad should match upper- and lowercase characters when searching for the text you specified.

The search text you specify stays in the Find box until you clear it, change it, or close Notepad.

Find Next   Use the Find Next command to find additional occurrences of the text specified in the Find... command.

Those are all of the commands on Notepad's menus. As you can see, it is a very simple word processor—more sophisticated than your paper pad, but it will never replace your word-processing software for heavy-duty writing. What it's good for is what its name indicates—simple notes you jot down quickly. Notepad does not add formatting information; it produces straight text files. So you can also use it for tasks like editing an AUTOEXEC.BAT file, tasks that you perhaps used to do in DOS with Edlin.

Now it's time for the useful work promised earlier: writing a short expense-reimbursement memo using Notepad. This exercise will show you how to use this new desktop application. Then, we'll use Calculator to total expenses, and have Windows copy the total from Calculator to Notepad.

Before beginning to type the memo, let's choose the Word Wrap command from the Edit menu. That way, Notepad will take care of the right margin and will start new lines for us.

Choose the Word Wrap command from the Edit menu.

Notepad puts a check mark in front of Word Wrap to indicate that it is turned on, and all we need to do now is begin to type.

■   *Type the expense-reimbursement memo shown here.*
Press the Enter key where you see [Enter] and the
Tab key where you see [Tab]. (Instead of typing the
date, you can choose Time/Date from the Edit menu,
and Notepad will insert the current time and date
for you.)

TO: Mary Slakker[Enter]
FROM: Nancy Andrews[Enter]
DATE: 9:59AM 12/4/1985[Enter]
RE: COMDEX Expense Reimbursement[Enter]
[Enter]
Mary, here is a list of my expenses for Fall
COMDEX, November 21-24, 1985.
I'd appreciate it if you could get me a check
before the weekend. Thanks.
[Enter]
[Enter]
[Tab]Hotel:[Tab][Tab]$313.12[Enter]
[Tab]Meals:[Tab][Tab]$214.65[Enter]
[Tab]Taxis:[Tab][Tab]$ 52.80[Enter]
[Tab]Airfare:[Tab][Tab]$352.00[Enter]
[Tab][Tab][Tab]———————[Enter]

If you make an error while typing, use the
Backspace key to erase the character to the left of
the cursor. If you discover an error that is not in the
current line (for example, if you've typed *November*
as *Novmeber,*) you can still correct it. You simply
move the insertion point to the right of the characters you wish to delete or change, press the
Backspace key to delete the incorrect characters,
then type the characters you want.

Notepad inserts the characters you type, and
moves the rest of the text right to make room for
the new characters.

Scrolling in Notepad

Notice the bars on the right and bottom edges of the work area. These are scroll bars. You'll see them on all Windows applications that are larger than one screen. There were no scroll bars on the MS-DOS Executive window because the entire directory could be displayed in the window. But if the entire directory hadn't fit, the MS-DOS Executive window would have had scroll bars, too. You scroll information on the screen by positioning the mouse pointer on the box in the scroll bar and dragging the box in the direction you want to scroll. When you release the mouse button, the screen will scroll in the direction you've moved the box. You can also scroll by clicking the scroll bar or arrow, as described in Chapter 1.

To scroll the expense memo down the screen:

M *Position the mouse pointer on the scroll box on the right and drag it about halfway down the scroll bar; then release the mouse button.*

K *Press the PgDn key. (The up and down direction keys scroll one line at a time. PgUp and PgDn scroll one screen at a time.)*

Move the insertion point to the end of the memo and press Enter two or three times to create two or three blank lines at the end of the memo.

Type the last line:

Receipts are attached.

Your screen should look as shown here.

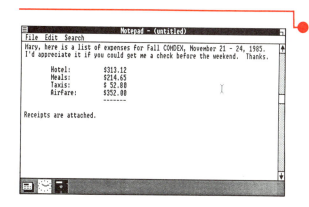

Adding expenses with Calculator

Now we'll use Calculator to total our expenses. We'll also see how to have two windows open at the same time: Calculator and Notepad. This is handy because we can see both the column of expenses in the memo and Calculator at the same time, and we don't have to flip from one to the next to see the figures and use Calculator. We'll also learn how to use the Clipboard to copy information from one window to another (in this case, the calculated total from Calculator into the memo).

Since Calculator is an icon on the bottom of the screen, all we need to do is drag it into the work area and it will be ready to use.

The position of the window that Windows opens in the work area for Calculator depends on where we place the icon. If we place it on the left or right border of the work area, Windows splits the work area vertically and places the new application (in this case, Calculator) in the right or left half of the work area. If we place the Calculator window icon on the top or bottom of the screen, Windows splits the work area horizontally, and places the Calculator window in the top or bottom half of the work area.

We'll place the icon on the right border of the Notepad window.

M *Move the mouse pointer to the Calculator icon. Hold down the mouse button and drag it to the right border of the Notepad window. Release the mouse button.*

K *Press Alt-Tab until the Calculator icon is selected. Use Alt-Spacebar-Move to display the System menu and choose the Move command. Now use the direction keys to position the Calculator icon on the right border of the Notepad window, and press Enter.*

Magically, the Calculator window opens and is positioned on the right half of the screen. The figure *9.73* in the Calculator display is the result of the calculation we did earlier.

Now we can see both Calculator and the column of expenses we need to total. So, we'll use Calculator to do the work.

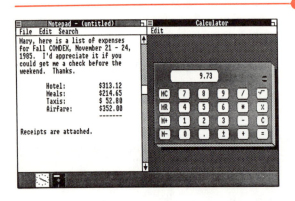

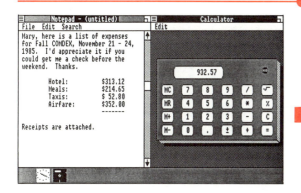

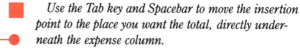

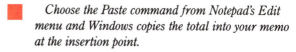

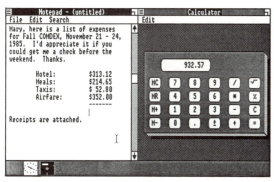

M *Click the C button to clear your previous calculation. Enter the first figure (313.12) by clicking Calculator's buttons. Now click the plus sign (+) button and enter the next figure, 214.65. Continue until you've entered all four figures and clicked on the equal sign (=) for your total.*

K *Press C to clear the previous calculation. Use the numbers in the top row of the keyboard and type in the figures. Press the equal sign (=) key when you're finished.*

Windows automatically performs the calculations and displays the total on the Calculator display.

Using the Clipboard

The next step is to copy the total from Calculator to Notepad using the Clipboard.

Choose the Copy command from the Edit menu.

Windows automatically copies the Calculator total into the Clipboard.

To get this total into the Notepad memo:

Use the Tab key and Spacebar to move the insertion point to the place you want the total, directly underneath the expense column.

Choose the Paste command from Notepad's Edit menu and Windows copies the total into your memo at the insertion point.

Now click in front of the total amount for an insertion point and type a dollar sign.

Now all that's left is to save the memo, and then print it. To save the memo:

■ *Choose the Save As... command from the File menu.*

Save As... displays a dialog box asking for a name for your memo.

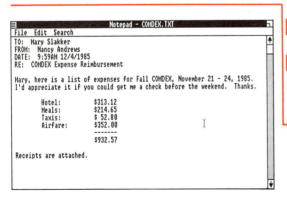

Save file as: C:\windows

[   ] [Save]
                      [Cancel]

■ *Type a name for the memo. Give the file a name that will remind you of its contents, perhaps something like COMDEX.*

M *Click the Save button.*

K *Press the Enter key.*

Your memo is saved on disk. Windows gives Notepad files the .TXT extension. Notice that the title of the memo (COMDEX.TXT) now appears in the title bar of the window.

Zooming a window

Before you print, you may wish to proofread your memo to check one last time for typos. To do this more easily, you can zoom the Notepad window so that it takes up the entire screen and overlaps the icon area. When you zoom a window, other applications in the work area are covered by the zoomed window, but they'll reappear when you return the window to its previous size.

To zoom the Notepad window:

M *Double-click in the size box in the upper right corner of the Notepad window.*

K *Use Alt-Spacebar-Zoom to display the System menu and choose the Zoom command.*

Watch the Notepad window expand and fill the entire screen.

Notepad - COMDEX.TXT

File Edit Search
TO: Mary Slakker
FROM: Nancy Andrews
DATE: 9:59AM 12/4/1985
RE: COMDEX Expense Reimbursement

Mary, here is a list of expenses for Fall COMDEX, November 21 - 24, 1985.
I'd appreciate it if you could get me a check before the weekend. Thanks.

     Hotel: $313.12
     Meals: $214.65
     Taxis: $ 52.80
     Airfare: $352.00

                 $932.57

Receipts are attached.

After proofing your memo and correcting any errors, return the window to its previous size.

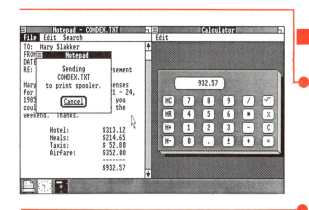

M *Double-click on the size box a second time.*

K *Use Alt-Spacebar-Zoom to choose the Zoom command from the System menu a second time.*

The screen returns to the way it was before you used the Zoom command.

If you printed the memo now, it would have the narrow margins shown on the screen because Word Wrap from the Edit menu is selected. If you want wider margins for your printed memo, choose Zoom again to expand the Notepad window, or close Calculator before you print.

Printing a memo

Printing your Notepad memo is really easy.

Choose the Print command from the File menu.

Windows displays the message shown here.

The Spooler is a place Windows reserves in memory for documents that will be printed. Copying to memory is faster than sending information to the printer at the rate the printer can accept. Once the memo is in the Spooler, you'll see the Spooler icon in the icon area, and your memo will begin to print. If you have sent more than one file to the Spooler, your files will be printed on a first-come, first-served basis.

Even though the printer is running, Notepad and Windows are free for you to use for other tasks. You can close Notepad or start a new memo. The printer shares the CPU (central processing unit) with Windows.

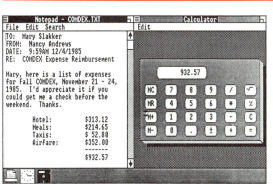

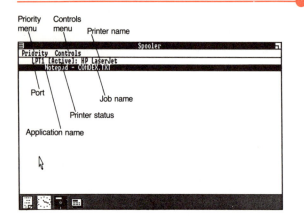

Priority menu
Controls menu
Printer name
Port
Job name
Printer status
Application name

Once your memo has begun to print, it is possible to modify what the printer is doing by moving the Spooler icon into the work area. The Spooler's Controls menu has a Terminate command that will cancel the current printing task. The Controls menu also has Pause and Resume commands that temporarily stop and start the printing process. The Spooler also has a Priority menu that lets you specify how fast you want to print your work.

Closing a window

Memory is a limited resource, so it's a good idea to close applications you won't be using again for, say, the rest of the day. For example, you might want to close Notepad now because you're finished writing memos for today, but leave Calculator in the icon area because you'll need it a little later for some budget calculations. Icons take up memory, but closed applications take up no memory.

It's a good idea to shrink applications that you use regularly to icons. If you shrink them to icons rather than close them, they're accessible anytime from the icon area; you don't need to open the MS-DOS Executive window and start them first.

To close Notepad:

M   *Double-click on the System menu.*

K   *Use Alt-Spacebar-Close.*

> The window closes, the application disappears from the work area, and it isn't even represented by an icon. If you do need to use Notepad again, you can use the MS-DOS Executive window to start it.

Those are the basics of the three desktop applications Clock, Calculator, and Notepad. Each time you start Windows you may wish to open these three applications as icons so they'll be readily available when you need them.

BUT THERE'S NO A>

Now you know how to use Windows applications, how to start them, how to choose commands from menus, and how to transfer information between applications. But you still need to know two things to complete your Windows orientation: If you're used to using DOS commands, you'll need to know how to run the DOS commands that are not included on the MS-DOS Executive menus, and if you have a hard disk, you'll want to know how to move around your hard disk's directories.

Running DOS commands

You may have noticed that a few of your favorite DOS commands (such as DISKCOPY, the command that copies an entire disk of information from one disk to another; and TYPE, the command that displays a text file on the screen) are not shown on the MS-DOS Executive menus. Don't worry; they are available, and you can run them from the MS-DOS Executive window. Here's what to do.

First, open the MS-DOS Executive window. We'll move the icon into the work area (not on the border); then it will replace the Calculator window and Calculator will become an icon. This eliminates the extra step of first shrinking Calculator to an icon.

M *Position the mouse pointer on the MS-DOS Executive icon and drag it into the work area. Release the mouse button.*

K *Press Alt-Tab until the MS-DOS Executive icon is selected. Use Alt-Spacebar-Move. Then press Enter.*

Now here's how to run a DOS command (in the following example, DISKCOPY):

Move to the directory containing the DOS utility you want to use.

We'll move to the \DOS directory with the file named DISKCOPY.COM on it. You'll see a directory something like the one shown here.

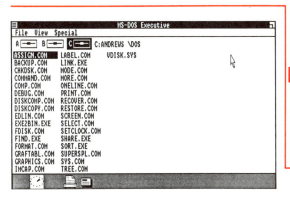

If you're using a DOS command that doesn't require parameters, you can simply select the command from the directory.

M   *Double-click on the name of the DOS command you want. For example, double-click on DISKCOPY.COM to run DISKCOPY.*

K   *Use the direction keys to select the command you want (in this case, DISKCOPY.COM). Press Enter.*

If you need to specify parameters for the command (as in DISKCOPY A: B:), use the Run command.

■   *Choose Run from the File menu.*

You'll see a dialog box.

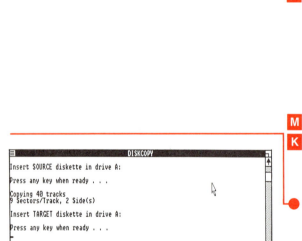

■   *Press the End key.*

This moves the blinking insertion point to just after the last M in DISKCOPY.COM.

■   *Type the parameters you need. If you're using DISKCOPY, for example, specify the source, target, and any other extra parameters (for instance, type \1 to copy only the first side of the disk). Consult your DOS manual for more in-depth coverage of DISKCOPY and any other DOS commands you wish to use.*

M   *Click the OK button.*

K   *Press Enter.*

DISKCOPY replaces the MS-DOS Executive window, runs, and displays its information on the screen.

The DISKCOPY information will remain in the work area until you close it by using the Close command on the System menu or until you move another icon, such as the MS-DOS Executive icon, back into the work area.

To return to the MS-DOS Executive without closing DISKCOPY, drag its icon back into the work area.

The DISKCOPY icon will then be in the icon area, ready for later use.

If you're finished copying disks for today, you can close DISKCOPY by using the Close command on the System menu. Then drag the MS-DOS Executive icon back into the work area.

Moving around hard-disk directories

If you're running Windows on a system with a hard-disk drive, you'll notice that so far the MS-DOS Executive window has only displayed the \WINDOWS directory for drive C. Because hard disks are so large, most hard-disk users group information on their disks into various subdirectories to better organize information stored there and make finding stored information easier. (It's easier to find a file in one of several small, logically grouped and named subdirectories than in one large directory.) You, no doubt, have several directories on your hard disk, and it would be a good idea to be able to see files in these directories as well as files in the \WINDOWS directory so that you can load programs and copy and delete files no matter which directory they're stored in.

Before Windows, when you typed a DIR command, directories that were themselves entries in the current directory would be listed followed by <DIR>. As we've mentioned before, Windows lists directory names that are entries in the current directory in bold type, drops the <DIR>, and lists them at the beginning of the directory listing. We have seen that the only directory entry in the \WINDOWS directory is one called PIF (for Program Information Files). You can move to a directory that is part of the current directory listing either by double-clicking on the name of the directory or by selecting the name and pressing Enter.

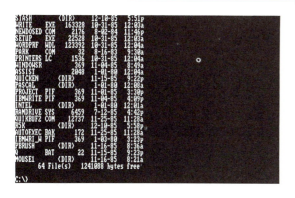

To see what's in the PIF directory (Recall that this is the place Windows stores information about standard applications, such as Lotus 1-2-3 and Microsoft Word, so it can run them.):

M *Double-click on PIF.*

K *Select PIF (if it is not already selected) and press Enter.*

The MS-DOS Executive window now displays the files in the PIF directory. (Your PIF directory may look different from the one shown here.)

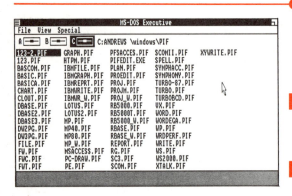

To move back to the Windows directory:

M *Notice the name of the directory and path next to the drive icons. To move to a directory above the current directory, simply double-click on the part of the path to which you wish to go.*

K *Press the Backspace key. Each time you press the Backspace key, you'll move up one directory level.*

For example, if the full pathname were ANDREWS\WINDOWS\PIF and I wanted to go back up to the WINDOWS directory, I would point to WINDOWS and double-click the mouse button or press Backspace. The WINDOWS directory would be displayed once again.

You can also move up or down directories with either the mouse or the keyboard by using the Change Directory command.

■ *Choose the Change Directory command from the Special menu.*

You'll see a dialog box that looks like the one shown here.

■ *Type the name of the directory you want to go to. Include a pathname, if necessary. Press Enter.*

If you have a hard disk, you can simply change to the directory where your favorite DOS utilities are located and run your favorites simply by double-clicking on the file name or by selecting the name and pressing Enter. If the DOS utility needs parameters as DISKCOPY did, simply use the Run command from the File menu and specify them as we did before.

You've completed your Windows orientation and have some practical experience using Windows. You know how to start an application, open a second window for another application, and use the Clipboard to transfer information from one application to another. You know how to zoom a window so it fills the entire screen and how to shrink an application to an icon. You've chosen commands from menus, displayed directories and moved from one to another. You've also used commands on the MS-DOS Executive menu for DOS functions and learned how to execute DOS commands not available on the MS-DOS Executive menus. In addition, you know how to use Notepad, Clock, and Calculator. Not bad for one chapter.

The next chapter shows you how to use three more desktop applications: Terminal, Calendar, and Cardfile. Now that you know how Windows applications work, these should be easy to learn and you'll find them useful tools.

3

USING CALENDAR, CARDFILE, AND TERMINAL

In Chapter 2, we discussed three of the seven desktop applications Windows comes with: Clock, Calculator, and Notepad. This chapter shows you how to use three more: Calendar, Cardfile, and Terminal.

Calendar is much like a desktop calendar and appointment book. The advantage of an electronic calendar is that it doesn't take up any space on your desk, it won't get buried under stacks of paper and books, and you can set alarms to remind you of appointments you've scheduled. When it's time for an appointment (or at a designated number of minutes before an appointment), an alarm will ring and a box will flash on the screen with an appropriate reminder.

Cardfile works much like a manual 3x5-card filing system. You put information on each card, and Windows files the cards in alphabetical order. Then, when you need the card again, you can ask Windows to find it and you'll have the information on it at your fingertips.

The Terminal is a simple communications program you can use to connect your computer to other computers or to online information services, such as Dow Jones News/Retrieval or NewsNet. Terminal isn't a substitute for a sophisticated communications package any more than Notepad will replace your word processor. Terminal does not have features such as automatic redial, automatic logging on, and keyboard macros. Instead, you'll use Terminal for simple communications tasks, such as checking your electronic mailbox or dialing NewsNet to see if information you requested has arrived.

Chapter 2 showed you how to choose commands from menus, run more than one application at once, and transfer information between applications using Clock, Calculator, and Notepad. Calendar, Cardfile, and Terminal (and all other Windows applications) work the same way as Clock, Calculator, and Notepad. So in this chapter, rather than say "This is Calendar (or Cardfile, or Terminal) and here's how it works," I'll present a scenario, similar to one you may have faced at some point in your career, and show how Calendar, Cardfile, and Terminal can work with you to get this job done.

For the scenario we'll follow in this chapter, imagine that you are the director of documentation for a mid-sized software company, and you've just been given the task of chairing a committee studying videotex. It's your job to determine the feasibility of videotex, putting all documentation and technical specifications on line for in-house and customer use. The company is interested in this possibility because they have a lot of time-sensitive information that is frequently updated and distributed to a scattered audience. With this information on a computer in a videotex format, the company could shorten delivery time and provide instant updates. Your committee's task is to do preliminary videotex research: to analyze company needs, to survey similar companies that have converted documentation and technical specifications to videotex, and to track current developments in the videotex field. You are to give a preliminary report to management in one month.

You've just received Windows. You don't have the time or the staff to do all this work by hand, so you determine to put the desktop applications to work to help with this project.

In the process of organizing your committee to do this research, you'll learn to use Cardfile, Terminal, and Calendar. First, we'll set up Cardfile with information about each committee member. Then we'll set up Terminal to work with an information service, and set up the information service to search for current videotex articles. Then we'll use Calendar to schedule committee meetings and deadlines. Finally, we'll go through a typical day (the day of a committee meeting) to show you how to use these desktop applications (and Notepad) once we've set them up.

USING CARDFILE

We'll use Cardfile to store information about committee members: their areas of expertise in the company, the tasks assigned them on the committee, the due dates for these tasks, and members' phone numbers. One of the added benefits of Cardfile is that, if you have a Hayes or Hayes-compatible modem attached to your computer, Cardfile will automatically dial any phone number on a card, and after the connection is made, prompt you to pick up the phone and talk.

Cardfile, like all applications, must be started from the MS-DOS Executive window.

Start Windows or, if you're currently working in Windows, shrink the applications you're working with to icons, and open the MS-DOS Executive window by moving its icon into the work area.

If you need help starting Windows, see Chapter 2.

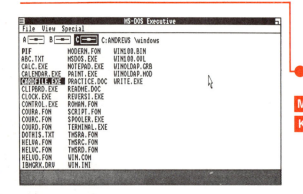

The MS-DOS Executive window is now open in the work area.

M *Double-click on the file named CARDFILE.EXE.*

K *Select the file named CARDFILE.EXE using the direction keys. Press Enter.*

The Cardfile window opens in the work area, and MS-DOS Executive becomes an icon.

The top line of each card is the index line. Cardfile uses the information you type here to sort the cards alphabetically. We'll use the index line for the names of the committee members.

Let's look at Cardfile's menus to get an overview of what Cardfile does.

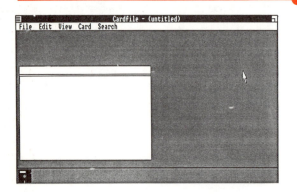

```
File
New
Open...
Save
Save As...
Print
Print All
Merge...
```

```
Edit
Undo      Sh/Esc
Index...  F6
Cut       Del
Copy      F2
Paste     Ins
Restore
✓Text
 Picture
```

The File menu

The File menu has seven commands.

The commands New, Open..., Save, and Save As... on the File menu are the same commands found in most Windows applications. The New command is for opening a new Cardfile file, and the Open... command is for opening an existing file. The Save command is for saving changes or additions to a file; if the file hasn't been named, you will be prompted for a file name. The Save As... command allows you to save the current file under a new name while retaining the original copy of the file on disk under the old file name.

There are two print commands. The Print command prints the card at the front of the file. The Print All command prints all the cards contained in an entire file.

The Merge... command is unique to Cardfile. It is used to combine another Cardfile with the current file and sort it again alphabetically.

The Edit menu

The Edit menu has eight commands.

The Undo, Cut, Copy, and Paste commands perform the same functions in Cardfile as they do in Notepad. Undo reverses your latest revision. Cut deletes selected text and copies it to the Clipboard. Copy works much the same as Cut, but instead of deleting the selected text, it makes a copy of it for the Clipboard and leaves the selected text intact on your card. Paste takes the information in the Clipboard and pastes it onto the card at the front of the file at the insertion point. You can paste information onto a different card, in a different location on the same card, or into a separate application, just as we did in Chapter 2 when we copied some information from Calculator into the Clipboard and then pasted it into Notepad.

The Index... command is used to change the text in the index line. You cannot simply move the cursor to the index line with the keyboard and make changes; instead, you need to use this command. If, for example, you enter names in first-name, last-name order, and later decide that you want them arranged alphabetically by last name, you would need to use Index... and change the order to last-name, first-name.

The Restore command allows you to change your mind. It will restore the card at the front of the file to its original state as long as it's the front card. This is similar to Notepad's Undo command, except that Restore will take out all of the changes in the body of the top card while Undo only undoes your most recent change. Once you've scrolled to another card, you can't restore information on the previous card.

A card can contain text, pictures, or a combination of text and pictures, which can be overlaid, if desired. When you open Cardfile, the Text command has a check mark in front of it on the Edit menu. If you decide to paste in a picture (for example, from Paint through the Clipboard), or edit one, choose Picture. That way, Cardfile will paste in the information properly. When you're finished, choose Text to reset the Edit menu to handle text.

The View menu

The View menu changes the way information is displayed on the screen. It has only two commands, Cards and List.

The Cards command is the default display. It displays information as if it were on 3x5 cards. Check the List command if you wish to see only a list of index lines for the cards in your file.

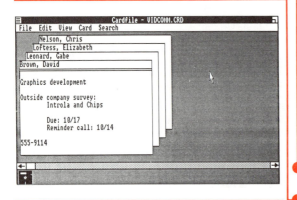

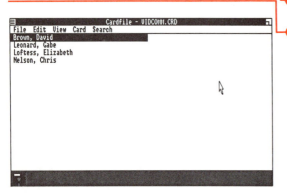

The Card menu

You use commands on the Card menu when you want to add, delete, or duplicate cards, or have Terminal automatically dial a phone number.

The Add... command adds a new card to the front of the file. Delete removes the card that's at the front of the file. Duplicate makes an exact copy of the card at the front of the file. If you have several similar categories of information you want to put on several different cards, it might be quicker to make one card, then duplicate it and make minimal changes, rather than add a new card and re-enter the information for each category.

The Autodial... command instructs Windows to dial phone numbers listed on the card on the front of the file. If you have a Hayes or Hayes-compatible modem, Cardfile will search for the first number on the front card that is six digits or longer and dial it. Make sure you have the entire phone number, complete with related area and access codes. Cardfile will pass over hyphens, so you may include them if you wish in the phone number (but avoid hyphens in the text, as Cardfile will attempt to "dial" groups of six or more hyphens). If you have more than one phone number on the card and want to dial a number other than the first one, select the number you wish to dial before choosing the Autodial... command or type the number you want in the Dial section of the Autodial... command dialog box. When a connection is made, you are prompted to pick up the phone.

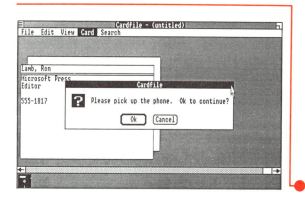

The Search menu

The last menu is the Search menu. It has commands for locating cards and information on cards in the file.

Use the Go To... command to have Cardfile locate a specific card for you. The Go To... command displays a dialog box where you type all or part of the index line of the card you want to bring to the front. You needn't type the entire line, just enough to identify the card.

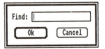

The Find... command will search for text in the body of one or more cards in your file. It displays a dialog box where you type the text you wish to find. If you wish to find additional occurrences of the text specified in the Find... command, use the Find Next command. It doesn't display a dialog box, but immediately begins searching for the specified text.

Now that you have an overview of the commands on Cardfile's menus, it's time to enter information on the cards and use Cardfile to organize the committee and tasks.

You have a committee of five: four committee members and you, the chair. One of the tasks you have to accomplish is to survey your company to determine its needs: How important are graphics, and if graphics are important, what level of graphic support is needed? You decide to have two of your committee members do this survey. Elizabeth Loftess, Publication Coordinator, will survey documentation needs and Chris Nelson, a programmer, will survey technical-specification needs. The second task is to survey outside companies that currently use videotex systems. You've uncovered four companies you'd like information from: Paragon, Chips, Introla, and Macrosoft. You decide to assign the other two committee members, David Brown and Gabe Leonard, to do this outside survey; each will contact two companies. That leaves you with the last task: tracking current videotex news. You're comfortable with that because you have a modem and the Windows Terminal program and you've used information services before for research projects.

Now that you've assigned tasks, it's time to put this information on cards in Cardfile. Start with committee member Elizabeth Loftess.

M *Double-click on the index line of the card (the top section of the card).*

K *Use Alt-Edit-Index to choose the Index command from the Edit menu.*

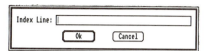

You will see a dialog box with a blink-ing insertion point in the Index Line text box.

■ *Type the name of the first committee member:*

Loftess, Elizabeth

Type the names in last-name, first-name order so Cardfile will alpha-betize by last name.

■ *Click the Ok button or press Enter.*

The dialog box disappears and the name you typed appears on the index line of the first card.

Notice the blinking insertion point just below the index line. This is where Cardfile will put the text you type.

■ *Start by pressing Enter for a blank line at the top of the card. This will add white space, which will make the information you enter easier to read.*

■ *Next, type her title:*

Publication Coordinator

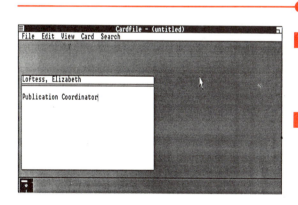

■ *Press Enter twice for another blank line and type the next line, her committee responsibility:*

In-house survey / documentation

■ *Press Enter. Press Tab and then type the due date for her task:*

Due: 10/3

She'll be the first committee member to report to the group at the 10/3 meeting. Add a reminder to phone her the Monday before her report is due.

Press Enter, then press Tab and type:

Reminder call: 9/30

> If you make errors while typing, use the Backspace key or the Undo command to correct them just as you did in Notepad.

Press Enter twice and then type her phone number:

555-6641

> You can use Cardfile to dial for you when you make the reminder calls. Use the Autodial... command and Cardfile will dial this number.

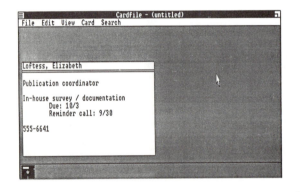

Your completed card will look as shown here. That's all there is to entering information on a card. Cardfile only lets you add as much information as there is room for on the card—no scribbling on the back and in the margins. If you try to add more, Cardfile will just beep and ignore what you're typing. If you have more information than will fit on one card, you can always add another card with the same index line and number the second card. For example, to add another card for Elizabeth Loftess, I would type #2 on the index line after her name. Notice that as this second card is added, scroll bars appear. These can be used to move from card to card in files of two or more cards. Then when Cardfile alphabetizes the cards, it will put the first card ahead of the second one (with #2 in its index line).

To add the rest of the members to Cardfile:

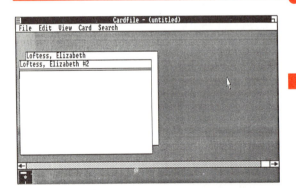

Choose Add... from the Card menu.

> Cardfile prompts you for index information for the next card and then puts a blank card in front of the file and moves Elizabeth Loftess's card behind the new card.

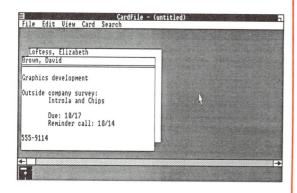

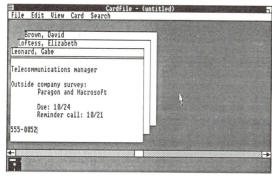

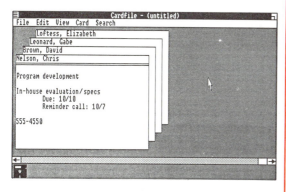

■ *Follow the same steps to add information to cards for the remaining three committee members, as shown here.*

Notice how when you add a new card, Cardfile takes the card in front, files it in alphabetical order, and then gives you a blank card at the front of the file at the correct position for the index name you have specified.

You can only make changes to the card at the front of the file. To bring a card to the front of the file, hold down the Ctrl key and press a letter key. Cardfile will scroll to the first card beginning with that letter. (In our sample Cardfile, to see the card for Chris Nelson, hold down the Ctrl key and press N. Chris Nelson's card will scroll to the front of the file.) You can also move through the cards using the Scroll bars at the bottom of the window or by clicking on the desired index line.

If you have a large file, you may wish to use the Go To... command on the Search menu, which displays a dialog box. You simply type the first few characters of the index line of the card you want to find, click Ok or press the Enter key, and Cardfile brings that card to the front. We'll use these commands when we get to the "typical day" part of the scenario.

Before switching to Terminal, save the information in your cardfile.

■ *Choose the Save As... command from the File menu. Name your file something like VIDCOMM.*

Windows adds the .CRD extension in order to identify this file as belonging to Cardfile.

USING TERMINAL

Now that your cardfile is set up, we'll set up Terminal to use the information service you need to do your research. We'll use NewsNet's NewsFlash service to research current publications. You give NewsFlash a keyword or words to search for (in this case, videotex). NewsFlash will search new information as it's added to the system, and the next time you dial, NewsFlash will tell you if it found anything since the last time you signed on. Then you can scan the material and, if anything looks good, you can save it on disk to read thoroughly later, and perhaps copy parts of it for the committee. NewsNet is likely to have several articles for you each day, so you should dial up daily so you don't get inundated with more information than you can handle.

Let's look at Terminal and its menus so you can see how it works and get on with the task of setting up the information services to find the information you want.

Move the MS-DOS Executive into the work area.

Cardfile automatically becomes an icon in the icon area.

M *Double-click on the file named TERMINAL.EXE in the MS-DOS Executive window to start Terminal.*

K *Select the file named TERMINAL.EXE in the MS-DOS Executive window and press Enter to start Terminal.*

The Terminal window has the standard menu bar (as all Windows applications do) and the work area is blank.

Because you've used Windows applications before, you'll find information on the File and Edit menus familiar. If you've used other communications programs before, you'll find information on the Control and Settings menus familiar. If not, read on and I'll explain it.

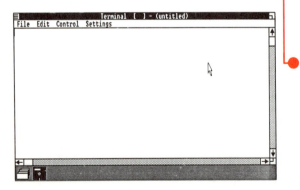

The instructions that follow are for a Hayes or Hayes-compatible modem. If you have a different type of modem, you may have to consult the manual that came with it and a good telecommunications primer. You might find Steve Lambert's *Online: A Guide to America's Leading Information Services* (Microsoft Press, 1985) useful. It has an excellent chapter on setting up your system for telecommunications and chapters on each of the major information services.

The File menu

The File menu contains four commands.

You use the New command to open a new Terminal file, and the Open... command to open an existing terminal file. When you work with Terminal, you set up and save a file with the settings you need for the service or computer you're calling. Then each time you call the service, you can open the file with the settings you need. That way, you won't have to enter the settings each time you call.

To save Terminal settings, use the Save or Save As... command. You can use the Save As... command to save a new file. It prompts you for a name for the file. Use the Save command to save an existing file after you've made changes. Terminal won't prompt you for a name, but will save it under the existing filename.

The Edit menu

The Edit menu has two commands. You use these two commands to transfer information to and from the Clipboard just as in Notepad and Cardfile.

Use the Copy command to copy selected text from Terminal into the Clipboard. Then you can paste it into another application, such as Notepad, to use, for example, as part of a memo. Commands currently unavailable for use appear on menus in light gray print. Copy appears in light gray because no text is selected. After selecting text, when you pull down the Edit menu, Copy will be dark and available to use.

File
New
Open...
Save
Save As...

Edit
Copy   ^F2
Paste

Use the Paste command to paste text from the Clipboard into Terminal. Terminal will paste the contents of the Clipboard at the blinking insertion point. Paste is in light gray on the menu because the Clipboard is empty. It will darken when there is something in the Clipboard to paste.

I've found the Paste command especially useful. I compose messages in Notepad when I'm not paying for time (because I'm "online"), then copy them to the Clipboard, and use Terminal's Paste command to paste them into the message I'm sending.

The Control menu

The Control menu has five commands.

The first command on the Control menu is the Connect command. You use this command to actually make the connection, after you've used the commands on the Settings menu to set up the communication parameters. Choosing Connect instructs Terminal to have your modem dial the number (in this case, the number of our information service), and make the connection. When you connect Terminal, a check mark appears in front of the Connect command on the Control menu.

Then a dialog box appears. The number following "Waiting for answer:" is the number of seconds Terminal will let the phone ring before hanging up. When the connection is made, the dialog box disappears.

To disconnect, you choose Connect again. This removes the check from in front of the Connect command and disconnects you.

To send incoming information to the printer at the same time as it appears on the screen, use the Print command. Terminal puts a check mark in front of Print on the Control menu, a P in the title bar, and the Spooler icon in the icon area.

Sending information to the printer uses the Windows print spooler, which allows you to keep using Terminal (or any other Windows application) at the same time your information is printing.

To stop printing, choose Print again. Both the check mark and the P in the title bar disappear.

Control	
Connect	^F3
Print	^F4
Capture	^F5
Pause	^F6
Break	^F7

Control	
✓Connect	^F3
Print	^F4
Capture	^F5
Pause	^F6
Break	^F7

Waiting for answer: 59

[Cancel]

Terminal [P] - (untitled)
File Edit Control Settings

Use the next command (Capture) to save the incoming information on disk. Terminal can do this almost as fast as it scrolls on the screen. Then, if you wish, you can edit it and print it later when you're disconnected from the service.

The Capture command saves incoming information in a file at the same time that it's displayed on the screen. After choosing the Capture command, you'll see a dialog box. Type the name of the file you want Terminal to put incoming text in and click the Save button or press Enter. When you look at the Control menu, you'll see a check mark in front of Capture on the menu and a C in the title bar.

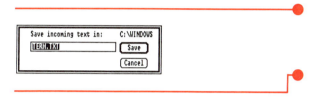

Terminal saves the captured information in a text file. You can use this information in applications such as Notepad or Write, to scroll through, read, delete parts that aren't useful, and save the useful parts to use later.

Sometimes information scrolls off the screen faster than you can read it. The Pause command temporarily stops the scrolling (by sending a Ctrl-S, or XOff, signal) and allows you to view information that has been sent to a buffer. The buffer can hold up to 999 lines of information. To start receiving data again, choose Pause a second time.

The last command on the Control menu is the Break command. Use the Break command to send a signal to get the attention of the host computer or to interrupt program execution.

The Settings menu

You need to use the commands on the Settings menu before you connect to specify the type of hardware you're using and the system or computer you're connecting to.

We'll set up Terminal to work with the communication parameters of NewsNet. If you connect to systems other than this, you'll need to consult the user's guide for the system you're connecting to.

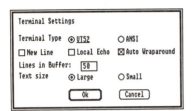

Terminal... The first command on the Settings menu is the Terminal... command. The dialog box that appears when you choose Terminal... is where you tell the system or computer you're connecting to what kind of terminal to emulate. NewsNet expects a VT52 type of terminal, which is Terminal's default setting. For other services, consult the user's guide.

Terminal also has New Line and Local Echo turned off (no X in those two check boxes) and Auto Wraparound turned on (an X in that box) as defaults. These are the settings we need for the service we're connecting to in our example. If the service you're connecting to moves the insertion point down one line at the end of each line but does not move it to the start of the new line, check the New Line box. If the system you're connecting to does not display, or echo, your keystrokes on the screen, check the Local Echo box. The service we're connecting to does not provide automatic wraparound, so we're keeping Terminal's default of Auto Wraparound turned on. This returns the insertion point to column 1 of the screen after it reaches column 80.

Terminal's default number of lines in the buffer is 50. The buffer is the place where incoming information is temporarily saved. You can specify any number of lines from 25 to 999 by simply typing that number in the Lines in Buffer text box. As the buffer is filled, the earlier information in it is replaced by newer information. An interesting use for the Pause command is to look at information that has scrolled too fast for you to read. When you choose Pause, Terminal puts scroll bars on the screen, so you can scroll back up to see what you missed. This gives you the option of selecting a section of the text and copying it to the Clipboard for pasting into another document, such as a Notepad file. This is, of course, more effective if you specify a larger buffer in the Lines in Buffer text box. (You can specify up to 999 lines.) The difference between using Pause this way and using Capture is that with Capture, you need to know in

ABOUT...

Terminal's Pause

If you've used other communications pro-grams, you may be used to using Ctrl-S to stop incoming information and Ctrl-Q to re-start. Terminal's Pause command (F6 on the keyboard) is better than Ctrl-S/Ctrl-Q be-cause, in addition to sending an XOff signal to stop incoming information, it puts scroll bars on the screen so you can scroll back, look at information that has come in, and perhaps cut and paste to another application. Crtl-S stops incoming information but does not activate the scroll bars, which give you the option of going back and looking at what's scrolled off the screen.

advance what you want to save. Pause, however, is better for "backing up" to see something that has scrolled off the screen and copying a small section of it to paste somewhere else.

Another interesting use of the Clipboard in Ter-minal is to send information out that you have pre-pared earlier. You can write a message in Notepad, for instance, copy it to the Clipboard, and when the remote system is waiting for your input, you can choose Paste from the Edit menu. The text in the Clipboard will be read into Terminal and will be transmitted to the remote system. The obvious ad-vantage of this is that you don't have to spend con-nect time being tongue-tied (or finger-tied!) while trying to think what to say, and you'll save a signifi-cant amount of time. You can even run Notepad (or another application) at the same time as Terminal, and prepare your message offline and send it when you are connected.

Terminal's default Text Size setting (the size that text normally appears in a window) is Large. If you need to fit more text on the screen, change Text size to Small.

Communication... Once you've used the Terminal... command to set up your computer to match the system you're connecting to, you're ready for the Communication... command. When you choose the Communication... command, you'll see a dialog box. Set the Baud Rate (the speed at which information is transferred, specifically the number of signal changes per second) to 1200 if you have a 1200-baud modem. Set it to 300 if you have a 300-baud modem or 2400 if you have a 2400-baud modem. We'll set word length, parity, and stop bits for the requirements of the service we're connec-ting to. (Word length is the number of bits used to send each character. Parity is a code used to detect errors when information is sent from one computer to another, and stop bits are sent to indicate the end of a character.) Most services use a word length of 8, no parity, and 1 stop bit, but if you're not getting clear transmission, check the user's guide. (I once couldn't connect to a service I wanted to use until

```
Communications Settings
Baud Rate:    [1200]
Word Length  ○4  ○5   ○6  ⊙7   ○8
Parity       ⊙Even     ○Odd      ○None
Stop Bits    ⊙1        ○1.5      ○2
Handshake    ⊙XOn/XOff ○Hardware ○None
Connection   ⊙Modem    ○Computer
Port         ⊙COM1:    ○COM2:
             [  Ok  ]  [ Cancel ]
```

I changed the word length to 7 and parity to Even. Once I did that, it worked perfectly.) User's guides for the services contain specific information on their word-length, parity, and stop-bit requirements.

Handshake refers to how Terminal tells the other system or computer to start or stop transmission of information. XOn/XOff is the best of all possible worlds, and both NewsNet and Dow Jones support XOn/XOff. With XOn/XOff selected, if you pause the display and the buffer fills up, Terminal will send an XOff character to temporarily stop transmission. That way, you won't lose any information, regardless of the size of your buffer. When you stop pausing, Terminal sends an XOn character, and then transmission begins again. Both the Terminal program and the service you're connecting to need to use XOn/XOff for this method to work. If you're connecting directly to another computer without a modem, you might need to select Hardware. If you're connecting to a service that does not support XOn/XOff, select None.

Connection choices are Modem or Computer. Leave the Connection setting on Modem (the default) if you're connecting to a service or computer using phone lines and a modem. If you're directly wired to another computer, choose Computer.

Terminal's default Port setting is COM1. (The COM1 or COM2 port is the place you connect a modem, serial printer, or mouse.) If you have a device other than a modem connected to the COM1 port of your computer and your modem connected to the COM2 port, select COM2.

Phone...   With a Hayes or Hayes-compatible modem, you can set up the Phone... command in the Settings menu so that Terminal automatically dials the number you specify.

When you choose the Phone... command, the Phone Settings dialog box appears. In the Connect To text box, you type the phone number of the service or computer you're connecting to. The phone number should be specified exactly the way you'd dial it (for example, include a 1 and an area code if you're calling a long-distance number outside your area code).

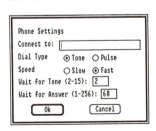

ABOUT...

Tiling

If you have two horizontal windows on your screen and place an icon on a vertical border of the top window, you might expect Windows to split one of the windows vertically. But Windows instead puts the new window on half of the screen vertically.

You can also insert commas in parts of the phone number to instruct the modem to pause before dialing the next part of the number. For example, if you dial a 9 for an outside line, put a comma after the 9. This allows time to wait for a dial tone before dialing the rest of the number.

The Dial Type options are Tone (the default) and Pulse. If you have a push-button phone and hear a tone after each number you dial, you have a tone phone. If you have a rotary-dial telephone or hear a clicking sound when you dial, you have a pulse telephone.

The Speed options control how fast Terminal dials the phone. Fast is Terminal's default. If Terminal has trouble connecting, change the speed to Slow and try again.

Wait For Tone represents the number of seconds Terminal waits for a connect tone after the phone it's trying to reach answers (2 is the default).

Wait For Answer represents the length of time (in seconds) Terminal will let the phone ring before hanging up. You can set this option from 1 to 256 seconds (60 is the default). Most services answer after one or two rings, so you may wish to change this setting to 30 seconds.

Those are all the commands on Terminal's menus. The Settings menu has quite a bit of information, especially if you're new to telecommunicating. But I'll show you exactly which settings to use with the service we're connecting to, so you can get started and gain confidence to carry on and perhaps try new services on your own.

Connecting to NewsNet

Let's assume that you're already a NewsNet subscriber, and have an account number, password, and the NewsNet Pocket Guide they send to new subscribers. (The guide has a summary of their commands and services.)

Now you want to set up a NewsFlash profile. What this does is instruct NewsNet to search incoming material in your subject area for the key word or words you specify. At midnight of the day you complete the NewsFlash profile, NewsNet will begin checking for information. The next time you log on, if anything has been added to the NewsNet database that contains a "hit" (match) for your profile, you'll get a message. Then you can read the articles of interest to you or save them to disk to read later.

First, we'll set up Terminal to work with NewsNet. Then we'll set up the NewsFlash profile.

We'll use the Settings menu to set up our NewsNet session. We don't need to use the Terminal... command because NewsNet expects the system you're using to have the same settings as Terminal... command defaults. But you may need to change some of Terminal's defaults in the Communications Settings dialog box.

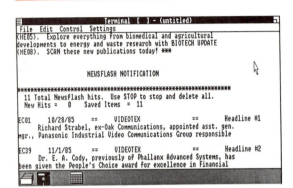

■ *Choose the Communication... command from the Settings menu.*

■ *When the Communications Settings dialog box appears, if your baud rate is not 1200 (File's default), type a new baud rate (300 if you have a 300-baud modem or 2400 if you have a 2400-baud modem).*

■ *Keep Terminal's defaults (Word Length of 7, Even Parity, and 1 for Stop Bits).*

■ *You can keep Terminal's default Handshake option (XOn/XOff) because NewsNet supports this. Now you won't have to worry about losing information if you pause too long.*

■ *Click in front of the appropriate Port (COM1 or COM2), depending on which port your modem is connected to, and click Ok or press Enter.*

Your Terminal and Communications settings now match NewsNet's. All that's left before you connect is completing the Phone Settings dialog box.

■ *Choose Phone... from the Settings menu.*

■ *Type the phone number you'll be using to call NewsNet in the Connect To text box.*

I use Telenet to reach NewsNet, so I type in the Telenet number for my area.

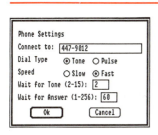

■ *Specify the dial type of your phone: Choose Tone if you have a tone telephone; otherwise, choose Pulse.*

■ *For now, accept Terminal's defaults for Speed, Wait For Tone, and Wait For Answer.*

If you have difficulty connecting, you may need to change the Speed setting to Slow or increase the Wait For Tone number. Some phone systems require slower dialing. You may wish to change Wait For Tone and Wait For Answer later, based on your experience and preferences. But the defaults should be fine for the first few times you connect.

Before connecting, save the settings so you won't have to reset them each time you dial NewsNet.

■ *Choose Save As... from the File menu.*

You'll see a dialog box.

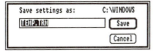

■ *Type a name up to eight characters long for your file (for example, NEWSNET).*

Terminal will add the extension .TRM so you can easily identify it as the name of a Terminal file.

■ *Click Save or press Enter.*

Now, to connect to NewsNet:

■ *Choose Connect from the Control menu.*

If you have a Hayes-compatible modem, you'll hear the phone number being dialed. Terminal will connect you to the phone number of the network or directly to NewsNet, depending on which phone number you specified in the Connect To text box with the Phone... command in the Settings menu. Notice that the scroll bars have disappeared.

Once connected to NewsNet, you'll be asked to "Please sign on."

■ *Type:*

ID

■ *Type a space, your identification number, another space, and your password (for example, ID 0000 PASSWORD). Then press Enter.*

You're now logged on to NewsNet and ready to set up NewsFlash to search for videotex articles. In a few seconds, you'll get introductory News-Net messages and then see the NewsNet prompt.

■ *After the -- > prompt, type:*

FLASH

■ *Press Enter.*

■ *To create a NewsFlash profile, type:*

ADD

You'll see the message, "Enter service code, ALL, STOP, or HELP."

ABOUT...

Buffer size

What is the best buffer size in Terminal? Should it be as large as possible (999 lines) so you can pause and scroll back through lots of information, or should you accept the default, a reasonably small buffer of 50 lines? The answer depends on the kind of work you do with Terminal. If you sometimes receive large documents, it is probably a good idea to have a very large buffer so you'll be able to scroll back through a large amount of text. On the other hand, a large buffer can become a problem if you like to run memory-hungry applications (such as Microsoft Word) at the same time you're using Terminal. So, if you like to use Terminal with large applications, you should probably opt for a small buffer.

Service codes are the categories NewsNet uses to group information. For a list of service codes, see the NewsNet Pocket Guide, page 2.

We'll conduct our search in the service codes EC (Electronics and Computers) and TE (Telecommunications).

■ *Type:*

EC,TE

■ *Press Enter.*

You'll see the message, "Enter exception to service code, DONE, or HELP."

■ *Type:*

DONE

■ *Press Enter.*

You'll see the message, "Enter keyword(s), keyword phrase(s), or <RETURN> for help."

■ *Type:*

VIDEOTEX∗

■ *Press Enter.*

This will find all occurrences of the word *videotex* and also articles with information on videotext, an alternate spelling. The asterisk is a wildcard character that tells NewsNet to match the eight characters (videotex), no matter what other characters may follow.

You'll see the message, "Enter CONTINUE to continue, STOP, or HELP."

■ *Type:*

STOP

■ *Press Enter.*

That's all there is to creating a NewsFlash profile.

■ *Now type:*

QUIT

■ *Press Enter.*

■ *To leave NewsNet, at the NewsFlash prompt, type:*

OFF

■ *Choose Connect from the Control menu.*

Terminal displays a dialog box asking you to confirm that you want to disconnect.

```
Are you sure that you
want to disconnect?
  [ Yes ]      [ No ]
```

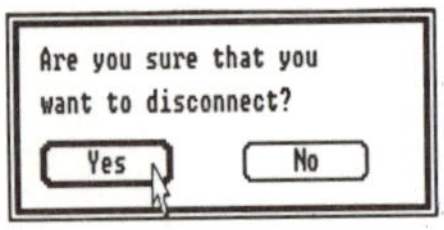

■ *Click Yes or press Enter.*

Terminal removes the check mark from in front of Connect and disconnects you from the network.

Starting at midnight tonight, NewsFlash will begin doing your research. At first, check in with News-Net daily to see how many "hits" you're getting. If you're getting two or three a day, it's a good idea to dial up daily and read these articles or save them on disk. That way, you won't accumulate a huge backlog. If you're not getting "hits" daily, you may only need to check every three or four days.

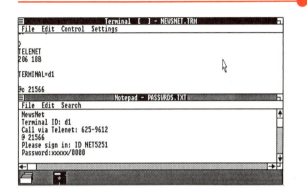

```
≡              Terminal  [  ] - NEWSNET.TRM           ⌐
 File  Edit  Control  Settings
⟩
TELENET
206 18B
                                              ⌐
TERMINAL=d1

⟩c 21566
≡              Notepad - PASSWRDS.TXT              ⌐
 File  Edit  Search
 NewsNet                                          ▲
 Terminal ID: d1
 Call via Telenet: 625-9612
 @ 21566
 Please sign in: ID NET5251
 Password:xxxxx/0000                              ▼
←|                                              |→
```

I keep my passwords and sign-on information in a small Notepad file. Then when I'm about to dial, I open a Notepad window on the bottom of the screen so I can refer to the sign-on information I need. Once I'm connected, I close the Notepad window so Terminal can have the entire workspace.

In the description of a "typical day" later in the chapter, you'll get more practice with NewsNet. You'll dial NewsNet, check for "hits," and record those of interest. Then you'll open the TERM.TXT file you saved information in and edit it so you can distribute selected information to the committee members.

Now you know how to use Terminal and connect to a reasonably difficult-to-use information service. You'll find that the advantage of using an information service, once you're comfortable with the protocol of each service, is that it will do your research for you. All you need to do is dial, then read and save the information you want to use later. And Terminal is a handy program to have in the icon area of your "desktop"; just drag its icon into the work area, and you're ready to go.

USING CALENDAR

Now let's look at Calendar, an application that's easy to learn and easy to use. It works with menus and commands just like the other desktop applications and you use it much like you would a paper calendar—to schedule appointments and remind yourself of upcoming deadlines.

Move the MS-DOS Executive into the work area in the middle of Terminal. Terminal becomes an icon.

M   *Double-click on the file named CALENDAR.EXE to start Calendar.*

K   *Select CALENDAR.EXE and press Enter.*

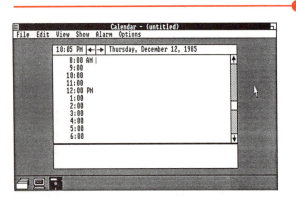

Calendar starts. The work area looks much like an appointment calendar. When Calendar starts, it displays the current day's page of appointments. It also displays the current date and time on the top line. If you have a mouse, you can click the arrows between the time and date to move to the next or previous date. If you don't have a mouse, you can use the Next and Previous commands on the Show menu to accomplish the same thing. The main part of the Calendar work area is for appointments, and the small rectangular space at the bottom is a scratch pad. You can use the scratch pad to jot down notes or reminders about your appointments by selecting the scratch pad with the mouse or Tab key.

We'll use Calendar to schedule the five videotex committee meetings and your tasks as chair of the committee. But before we start to schedule, let's look at the commands on the Calendar menus to get an overview of what Calendar can do and how it works.

The File menu

The File menu has six commands.

The New and Open... commands are used the same way as in other desktop applications. New opens a new Calendar file, perhaps for an additional user. Open opens an existing Calendar file.

Save and Save As... are used to save Calendar files. Use Save As... the first time you enter appointments and save a Calendar file. After that, each time you make changes to Calendar, use the Save command before you exit to save the changes.

The Print... command prints your appointments. By printing out your appointments, you can put them in your pocket and take them with you, just as you would a pocket calendar. Choosing the Print... command displays a dialog box. Specify the first date you want Calendar to print in the From text box and the last date you want printed in the To text box. To print only one day's appointments, leave the second box blank.

The Remove... command is unique to Calendar. You can use it to specify a range of dates to make room on your disk for other days. Every several months, it's a good idea to use the Remove command and delete old information.

The Edit menu

The Edit menu has three commands the other desktop applications have.

If an appointment is changed, you can select the original appointment, choose Cut from the Edit menu, then Paste the appointment text back in on the day it's rescheduled—no more crossing out or attempting to erase rescheduled appointments and then rewriting them again. Calendar uses the Clipboard to transfer information the same way as the other desktop applications.

The View menu

The View menu has two commands.

The Day command is Calendar's default view. Day displays information much like an appointment book. To see an entire month, much like a desktop calendar, choose the Month command. The Month view is useful when you're scheduling committee meetings on the five Thursdays in October. You can use the Month view to determine which dates the Thursdays fall on and then use the Day view to schedule the meetings.

Notice the keyboard commands listed after the command names on the menu (F9 for Day and F10 for Month). You'll find that pressing F9 and F10 to change between views is faster than choosing from the menu.

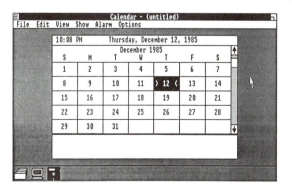

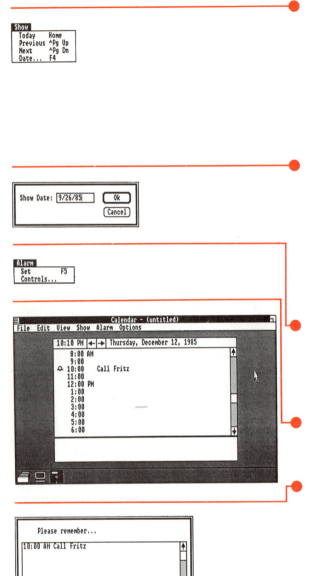

The Show menu

The Show menu has four commands.

Choosing the Today command takes you back to the current day if you're in the day view, or the current month if you're in the month view, from a day or month in the future or past.

The Previous command takes you to the previous day or month, depending on the view. The Next command takes you to the following day or month.

The Date... command is like the Go To... command in Cardfile. It takes you to the date you specify in the dialog box. You can also use the scroll bar to move quickly between months or years.

You can choose any of the commands on the Show menu (and, as mentioned in Chapter 2, many other commands on other menus in Windows) with a key or key combination: the Home key to choose Today, Ctrl-PgUp to choose Previous, Ctrl-PgDn for Next, and F4 for the Date command.

The Alarm menu

The Alarm menu has just two commands.

To use the alarm, you must be viewing Calendar with the Day command. Move the insertion point to the time you want the alarm to ring and choose the Set command. This will set the alarm and put a small bell icon to the left of the appointment time to indicate the alarm is set. You can set alarms for as many appointments on your calendar as you like.

When the alarm goes off, if Calendar is active, the alarm sounds and Calendar displays a dialog box reminding you of the appointment. If Calendar is an icon or a non-active window, the alarm will sound and the icon or title bar will flash. To see the reminder message and stop the alarm, just click the flashing icon or calendar title bar.

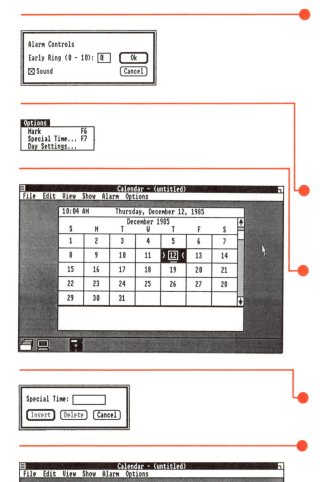

The alarm will sound unless you set it to be silent with the Controls... command. The Controls... command displays a dialog box. When Calendar starts, any alarm you set will sound. If you'd rather have a silent alarm (only the message box displayed or the icon flashing), you can turn the sound off by clicking in the Sound box. The Alarm Controls dialog box is also the place you set the alarm for an early ring. If you'd like the alarm to go off five minutes early to remind you of your scheduled appointment, simply type *5* in the Early Ring text box.

The Options menu

The last menu is the Options menu. You can use it to customize your electronic calendar so it resembles the appointment calendar you're used to using.

You can use the Mark command to mark special days in the month view. Calendar puts a small box around the number you mark. This is a good command to use to mark the date your committee report is due.

The Special Time... command is used to indicate an appointment at a time not listed on the calendar or to delete a special time that was set previously. For example, a special time might be a lunch date scheduled for 12:20 PM. After choosing this command, you'll see a dialog box. Type a time in the Special Time text box, click the Insert button, and the special time will be inserted at the appropriate place on your calendar.

To delete a previously set special time, choose the Special Time command, type the time you want to delete, and click the Delete button.

Chapter 3: Using Calendar, Cardfile, and Terminal

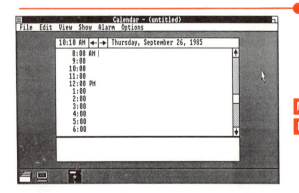

The Day Settings... command can be used to change the appearance of the Calendar window. Day Settings... displays a dialog box. The Interval option controls the intervals between times listed in the Calendar. Calendar's initial display has 60-minute intervals. You can change this to 15- or 30-minute intervals. You can make it have the same intervals as the paper calendar you're used to using. Calendar displays times in a 12-hour clock format, but you can change this option to a 24-hour clock format by clicking the button in front of 24. Starting Time is the earliest time Calendar lists on the Day view. The default starting time is 8 AM. You can change this to whatever time you wish.

That's all there is to Calendar. It's a fairly simple and useful desktop application, and now that you're a seasoned user of the desktop applications, you'll find Calendar easy to use. Let's use it now to schedule committee meetings and tasks.

Move to the date of the first meeting, 9/26/85.

M *Choose the Month command from the View menu. Click in the vertical scroll bar to change the date to September 1985. Double-click on the date of the first meeting—Thursday, September 26.*

K *Use Alt-View-Month to change to the Month view. Use Control-PgUp and Control-PgDn to move to September 1985. Use the direction keys to select the date of the first meeting—Thursday, September 26. Press Enter.*

Calendar displays the Day view for the date you selected.

Now enter information for the day of the first meeting. If the insertion point isn't already at 8:00 AM, move it there now.

M *Click anywhere on the line containing 8:00 AM.*

K *Use the up and down direction keys to move the insertion point to the line to the right of 8:00 AM.*

This gives you a place to type information for an 8:00 AM task.

You want to call the information services first thing the day of the meeting to get the latest news to report to your committee.

■   *Type your 8:00 AM task:*

   Call NewsNet

M *Click in the* 9:00 AM *line.*

K *Press the down direction key to move the insertion point to the right of* 9:00 AM.

■   *Type your 9:00 AM task:*

   Prepare agenda

You can use the scratch-pad area at the bottom of each day's calendar.

M *Click in the scratch-pad area to put an insertion point there.*

K *Press the Tab key to move the insertion point from the appointment area to the scratch pad.*

Notice that the blinking insertion point moves to the scratch-pad area.

The scratch-pad area is a handy spot to jot down items you may wish to include in your agenda. You can type whatever you wish in this area, perhaps some reminders for your agenda.

To return to the appointment area of Calendar:

M *Click in the appointment area.*

K *Press the Tab key again.*

You're compulsive—you don't want anyone to forget the meeting. And since Cardfile will dial for you, this task won't be difficult.

M *Click in the line that reads* 10:00 AM.

K *Use the direction keys to move to the line that reads* 10:00 AM.

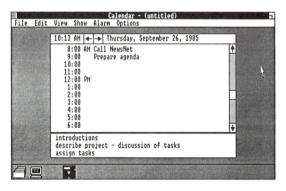

■ *Type this task:*

Reminder calls to committee

You decide you'd like to set an alarm for the committee meeting to go off 10 minutes before the meeting. That way, you'll be sure to have time to get organized.

■ *Now, move down to the* 1:00 PM *line and type:*

Videotex Committee, E106, 1-3pm

■ *Choose Controls... from the Alarm menu.*

You will see a dialog box. Notice the cursor blinking in the Early Ring box.

■ *Type:*

10

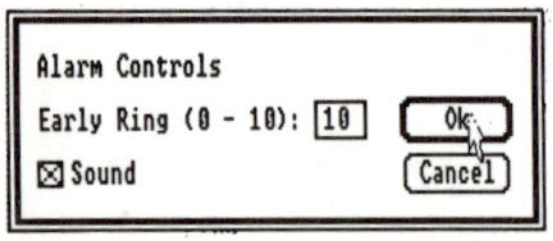

```
Alarm Controls
Early Ring (0 - 10): [10]   ( Ok )
⊠ Sound                    (Cancel)
```

■ *Click Ok or press Enter.*

■ *Choose Set from the Alarm menu.*

The small bell icon appears to the left of *1 PM*, indicating the alarm is set. It will ring at 12:50, giving you the time you need to get ready.

That's all there is to entering information on Calendar, using the scratch pad at the bottom, and setting the alarm.

You could enter similar information on the dates of future committee meetings. Each of these meetings has one member presenting information. You could

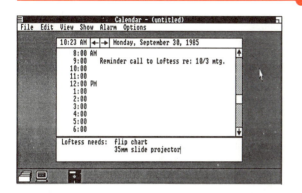

include reminder calls to the person giving a presentation on the Monday before the Thursday meeting and notes in the scratch pad about equipment you have agreed to procure for the presentation.

You could use the Mark command on the Options menu to mark the date the final committee report is due. This may keep you from procrastinating longer than you should.

Enter as much information as you'd like in Calendar. If you wish, use commands on the Options menu to make the display resemble your appointment book. For instance, you can change the interval time between appointments and set the starting time so it suits your schedule.

When you're finished making changes—adding information or changing the format—save this information using the Save As... command on the File menu. Name your calendar something like YOURNAME or MYCAL; you can use as many as eight characters for the name. Calendar adds the .CAL extension.

Next time you wish to start Calendar, double-click on your Calendar file (for example, NANCY.CAL or MYCAL.CAL) rather than on CALENDAR.EXE. This will both start Calendar and load your Calendar file. You'll see the information you've just entered here and can continue to use it just like your desktop calendar. When you're finished with Calendar, it's a good idea to shrink it to an icon and leave it available in the icon area. That way, it's already loaded, and if you've set any alarms, they'll ring.

A TYPICAL DAY WITH CARDFILE, CALENDAR, AND TERMINAL

You've set up Cardfile, Calendar, and Terminal to help you with the videotex committee. Now let's see how this setup works on a typical day, the day of your first meeting.

You arrive at your office a few minutes before 8 AM, turn on your computer, and start Windows. After checking your electronic mail (with Terminal) and returning a phone call (using Cardfile), you want to look at your calendar, so you open Calendar.

■ *After starting your computer and Windows, open your Calendar file.*

Your Calendar file starts with the page for today's date displayed.

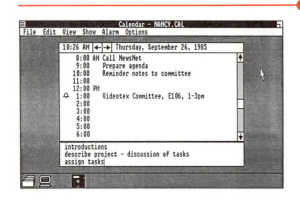

Your first task is to dial NewsNet to see whether there's any interesting news to report to the committee. What you'd really like is a short article or quote to start the discussion. So you'll use this service and hope to get lucky.

If Terminal is not an icon, you'll need to start Terminal from the MS-DOS Executive window to dial NewsNet. Rather than shrinking Calendar to an icon and then opening the MS-DOS Executive window, it's quicker to drag the MS-DOS Executive icon into the work area.

M *Drag the MS-DOS Executive from the icon area into the work area and release the mouse button.*

K *Press Alt-Tab until the MS-DOS Executive icon is selected. Use Alt-Spacebar-Move and press Enter.*

MS-DOS Executive is now running in the work area.

Checking the news

Now we'll check NewsNet for any "hits" to see whether we can get any information to use at today's meeting.

■ *Start Terminal by selecting your NewsNet file, the one named NEWSNET.TRM, and either double-clicking with the mouse or pressing Enter.*

■ *Dial NewsNet as you did before (either directly or through a network), and sign on to NewsNet.*

After the introductory messages, if you have any NewsFlash "hits," you'll see a message. NewsFlash tells you the total number of "hits" and displays their headlines. In this example, you have several.

You scan the headlines until you find one that reads "PRIVATE IN-HOUSE VIDEOTEX SYSTEMS SLOWLY MAKING CORPORATE INROADS & EXTENDING TODAY'S TELEWORK OPTIONS..."

NewsNet's messages are easy to follow, so just read the message (usually a menu line) and enter one of the choices.

The message you'll see after the NewsFlash notification reads, "Enter Headline Numbers or ALL to read, MORE, AGAIN, SAVE, STOP, or HELP."

You want to read the NewsFlash "hit" on the second headline, so type:

2

The article begins to scroll across the screen. Scan it as it scrolls by to see if there is any information of interest. If it's scrolling a bit fast and you'd like to freeze the display, press Ctrl-F6 or use the Pause command from the Control menu. If you can remember Ctrl-F6, you'll find it faster than the menu. You'll then be able to stop the scrolling and read the information that has disappeared off the top of the screen. Pressing Ctrl-F6 a second time restarts the scrolling.

The article begins as shown here.

You decide to save the article. You think you may be able to use it to motivate the committee and perhaps begin a discussion to clarify some terminology.

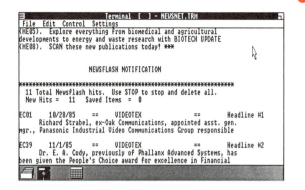

To capture part of this article to use later, you'll have to start it again, but this time turn on Capture before you start. As the article scrolls on the screen, Terminal saves it in a disk file. You might also want to turn on Print and get a paper copy at the same time.

Turn on Capture before telling NewsNet you want to read the article. That way, Terminal will capture the beginning of the article, including the headline and source.

To turn on Capture:

M   *Choose Capture from the Control menu.*

K   *Use Alt-Control-Capture.*

> You'll see a dialog box asking for a name for the file you want to save the text in.

   Type:

VIDEOTEX

   Press Enter.

> Terminal will save this information in a file called VIDEOTEX.TXT.

   Choose Print from the Control menu.

   To re-read and this time capture the article, type:

2

> Three new things have now happened on the screen: a C (signifying Capture) and a P (signifying Print) have appeared in the title bar and the Spooler has appeared as an icon.

When you come to the end of the article, again choose the Capture command from the Control menu to turn off Capture, and choose the Print command to turn off printing.

> The C and P will disappear, but the Spooler remains as an icon until you close it or quit Windows.

Now you have the article you want in a file called VIDEOTEX.TXT and can use it later with Notepad.

NewsNet finishes displaying the article a second time and you see the message, "Enter Headline Numbers or ALL to read, MORE, AGAIN, SAVE, STOP, or HELP." Now type:

STOP

Press Enter.

> You'll see the message, "Current NewsFlash notification completed. Total saved items = 0."

Once you read a NewsFlash "hit," unless you save it, it's gone. You saved this article that you wanted on disk, so there's no need to have NewsFlash save it as well. But sometime you may find an article of interest and not have time to read it fully or capture it. That's the time to use NewsFlash's Save command. Then NewsNet will save the "hit" and it will be part of your NewsFlash Notification next time you log on.

Now you're back at NewsNet. Type:

OFF

Press Enter to leave NewsNet. Choose the Connect command from the Control menu to disconnect from the network. You may also want to close the Spooler, which is an icon.

That's all there is to using NewsNet's NewsFlash. Don't you think it's better than checking a library's entire periodical section yourself?

Now we're finished with Terminal for today, so we can close it.

To close Terminal:

M   *Double-click the System menu box.*

K   *Use Alt-Spacebar-Close.*

Making the agenda

Now that you've checked the information service, you're ready for your second task. Let's use Notepad and the file named VIDEOTEX.TXT, the one we just made from NewsNet, so we can use the article in the agenda.

■   *Start Notepad.*

> First, you'll need to drag the MS-DOS Executive icon back into the work area and start Notepad from the MS-DOS Executive window.

■   *Use the Open command from the File menu and open the file named VIDEOTEX.TXT.*

> This file will have a lot of extraneous information in addition to the information you want. So, delete the NewsNet prompt and the second headline. Also delete any NewsNet prompts you may have received after the end of the article.

M   *Select the text you want to delete by dragging over it. Choose Cut from the Edit menu.*

K   *Use the direction keys to move the insertion point to the beginning of the text you want to delete. Hold down the Shift key and use the direction keys to move the insertion point to the end of the text you want to delete. Press the Del key to cut the selected section.*

The part of the article you want to use in the
agenda is the section beginning, "Why videotex?".
But you think the first sentence might be useful to
include in reminder notices you'll send to the committee later, so you decide to save the first sentence to use later in a second Notepad file.

■ *Move the MS-DOS Executive icon into the work
area and position it on the left border of the work
area. Start Notepad.*

Now you'll have two Notepads on the
screen; the one on the left is blank
and the one on the right has your
NewsNet article.

■ *Select the first sentence of the NewsNet article.
Choose Cut from the Edit menu.*

This puts the sentence into the
Clipboard.

■ *Make the left Notepad active by clicking in it or by
pressing Alt-Tab.*

■ *Choose Paste from the Edit menu and the sentence
will be pasted into this Notepad.*

■ *Choose the Save As . . . command from the File
menu and name this file REMINDER. Then shrink
it to an icon for use later.*

■ *Now delete the second sentence and paragraph
so that the article begins with the "Why videotex?"
paragraph.*

■ *Now type the text of the agenda. Type it at the top of
the page; the NewsNet article will follow the agenda.*

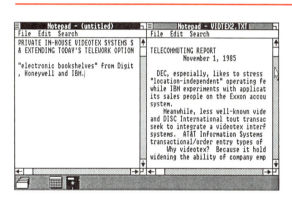

You may wish to open a window for Calendar and check your list in the scratch pad. That's where you made notes about agenda items. To do this:

■ *Position the Calendar icon on the right border of the Notepad window.*

Calendar will open in a window on the right half of the screen.

■ *Double-check to be sure your agenda includes the items in the scratch pad of the Calendar file, and then shrink Calendar back to an icon.*

■ *Now use the Print command from the File menu to print a copy of the agenda.*

Your printed agenda will look like the agenda shown here.

■ *Save the agenda with the Save As... command from the File menu and close Notepad.*

Printing Cardfile

Now you've finished your second task, making the agenda. The only task left on your calendar is notifying committee members. You used Cardfile yesterday and phoned the committee to remind them about the meeting, but you'd like to use Cardfile one more time to make a printed copy of the cards to use to jog your memory in the meeting when you assign committee members their tasks.

■ *Move the Cardfile icon into the work area.*

This opens the Cardfile file containing your videotex committee members.

■ *Choose Print All... from the File menu.*

```
═══ Notepad - VIDTEX2.TXT ═══   ═══ Calendar - NANCY.CAL ═══
File  Edit  Search              File  Edit  View  Show  Alarm
                                Options
   " Why videotex? Because it hol   11:03 AM ←→ Thursday, September 26
widening the ability of company emp
with the ever-increasing base of di   8:00 AM Call NewsNet
information...from home, from custo   9:00    Prepare agenda
locations or from literally anyplac  10:00    Reminder notes to commit
office". The main selling point is   11:00
with respect to the rapid delivery   12:00 PM
manuals, policy directives, vacatio ⌐ 1:00    Videotex Committee, E10
etc. -- to many employees, regardle   2:00
needn't be specially schooled in ho   3:00
computer because of the more famili   4:00
screen. Extending this ease-of-use   5:00
also been prototyped  (as at Buick   6:00
) to link key players within produc
   Videotex, in fact, can be used     introductions
                                      describe project - discussion of task
                                      assign tasks
```

```
Agenda - Videotex Committee Meeting - 9/26/85

1:00    Opening remarks
        Introduce members
        Explain videotex concepts and popularity - use NewsNet quote
        Discuss availability of equipment and services

1:30    Description of tasks
        Overview
        Clarification of terminology
        Discussion

2:00    Assign individual tasks
        (see Cardfile printout)

2:30    General discussion

3:00    Adjourn


    " Why videotex? Because it holds promise for significantly
widening the ability of company employees to access and interact
with the ever-increasing base of digitized corporate
information...from home, from customer sites, from branch
locations or from literally anyplace within the extended "virtual
office". The main selling point is ease of use, particularly
with respect to the rapid delivery of corporate information:
manuals, policy directives, vacation policies, holiday schedules,
etc. -- to many employees, regardless of their locations. Users
needn't be specially schooled in how to operate a personal
computer because of the more familiar page-oriented videotex
screen. Extending this ease-of-use feature further, systems have
also been prototyped  (as at Buick, Ralston-Purina and elsewhere
) to link key players within product delivery networks.
    Videotex, in fact, can be used as a kind of neutral "front
end" on existing data bases of all kinds for information delivery
in a friendly and familiar fashion to all types of non-technical
users -- including customers.  Thus, at Illinois Bell, large
corporate accounts may access the phone directory electronically
via a videotex system.  With 9,000 updates to the directory each
day, electronic access affords accuracy and convenience where
print publishing simply cannot. "

-- from The Telecommuting Report, November, 1985
```

A dialog box appears, saying: "Sending VIDCOMM.CRD file to print spooler."

In a short while, your Cardfile cards begin printing. Cardfile, like all Windows applications, uses the Spooler, so you don't have to wait until printing is finished to start another task.

Notifying the committee

Even though you phoned committee members yesterday to remind them about the meeting, you are compulsive and think an additional reminder on the day of the meeting wouldn't be too much. You decide to use the NewsFlash quote you saved as part of a message to your committee. You'll use your PC, Terminal, and your company's in-house electronic mail system to send the message.

You'll use Notepad to write a brief message to send with the quote; then copy the message to the Clipboard, open Terminal, connect to your company's electronic mail, and send the message to each person's mailbox. If electronic mail isn't available, you may wish to create this message in Notepad, print four copies, and send it through the regular company mail system.

■ *Move the MS-DOS Executive icon into the work area and open the file named REMINDER.TXT. This is the file you saved the NewsFlash reminder information in.*

■ *Delete the second sentence so all that's left is the quote you want.*

■ *Add this text at the beginning:*

Found this in NewsFlash this morning. It's from Telecommuting Report dated 11/1.

■ *After the quote, type:*

See you at our meeting at 1 PM today in Room E106. — Nancy

Your message will look like the one shown here.

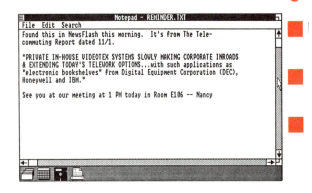

Choose the Select All command on the Edit menu to select the entire message.

Choose the Copy command (also on the Edit menu) to copy the selected message to the Clipboard.

Before starting Terminal and copying this message to committee members' electronic mailboxes, save the message by choosing the Save command on the File menu. That way, you'll have an extra copy on disk just in case you need to refer to it.

Different companies have different types of electronic mail systems. We'll assume yours works like mine. The one I use allows me to connect over the phone, using a PC and modem. I keep the settings and phone number in a file called EMAIL.TRM. Then, when I use the electronic mail system, I simply load this file and dial, just as you did with NewsNet.

Now close Notepad and open Terminal from the MS-DOS Executive.

Choose the Connect command from the Control menu and sign on in your usual way.

Use your electronic mail system's commands to create the message. You'll see the blinking insertion point indicating the start of the message, like the one shown here.

Choose Paste from the Edit menu and the Notepad message will be pasted in.

Tell your system to send the message.

Follow this procedure for each person on the committee or, if your electronic mail has a forwarding capability, simply forward this message to the other committee members.

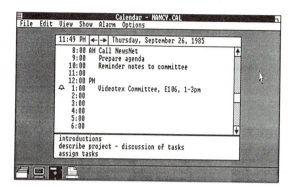

Now drag the Calendar icon back into the work area and check your tasks.

You've completed all of them: You checked NewsNet for current news, and got several quotes to use. You constructed the agenda for this afternoon's meeting, printed the cards in your cardfile as a reminder when you assign tasks, and you sent a reminder message to committee members. In addition, you set up an information service to do your research and learned to use three new desktop applications in the process. After accomplishing all this, you can take a break—perhaps by using the seventh desktop application, Reversi, for a quick game or two until 12:50, when your alarm will sound, giving you ten minutes to get ready for your 1 PM meeting.

SECTION 2
Chapter 3: Using Calendar, Cardfile, and Terminal

4

Windows divides applications—programs such as WordStar, dBASE III, Lotus 1-2-3, Microsoft Write, and Microsoft Paint—into two categories: standard applications and Windows applications.

Standard applications is a label Windows gives to the current generation of applications—ones that weren't designed specifically for Windows but were designed to run under DOS. Popular standard applications are WordStar, dBASE III, Lotus 1-2-3, and Microsoft Word. Even though these applications were not specifically designed for Windows, they will run with Windows. Chapters 8, 9, and 10 have specific information on using Windows with standard applications.

Windows applications are a new generation of programs. Microsoft Write and Microsoft Paint are two Windows applications you may have received when you purchased Windows, and the desktop applications, such as Notepad and Calendar, that come with Windows are mini-Windows applications. Windows applications differ from standard applications in three ways: All have the same graphic user interface; they take advantage of Windows' sophisticated way of managing memory; and Windows applications have device independence. I'll explain each of these individually.

CONSISTENT GRAPHIC USER INTERFACE

The Windows graphic user interface is important because it adds consistency between Windows applications, making them easy to learn and use. All Windows applications look generally the same: They have a title bar at the top of the window, a menu bar next, and then the work area. The work area has scroll bars on the bottom and right if information in the work area is larger than one screen. (Calculator, for example, does not need scroll bars; Notepad does.) At the bottom of every Windows application screen is the icon area.

Menu bar · Title bar · Work area · Icon area · Scroll bars

```
File
New
Open...
Save...
Print...
Change Printer...
Repaginate...
```

```
Copies: 1        Ok
☐ Draft Quality  Cancel
Page Range:
⦿ All
○ From:     To:
```

Standard applications, on the other hand, do not have a standardized appearance. Some applications, such as Microsoft Multiplan, display a menu at the bottom of the screen; others, such as Lotus 1-2-3, display a menu at the top; still others have no menu at all. Some require the menu to be displayed at all times; others let you decide whether or not to display the menu.

All commands for Windows applications are chosen the same way. You select commands from menus in the menu bar just above the work area. You choose a command from a menu in any Windows application by "pulling down" the menu (either with the mouse or with a few keystrokes) to display the choices and then choosing the command you want to execute. If the command requires more information, the application displays a dialog box requesting additional information.

Generally, you use the same keyboard or mouse techniques—displaying the menu and choosing the command you want from the displayed menu—for choosing a command from any menu of any Windows application.

Each standard application, on the other hand, has its own approach for choosing commands. Some require typing the entire command; others require typing only the first letter; still others require combinations of control keys and letters. This makes learning to use a standard application more difficult than learning to use a Windows application.

In addition to all Windows applications providing a similar appearance and similar ways to choose commands, some of the commands on Windows applications menus have similar names. For example, most Windows applications have a File menu that includes at least the following four commands: New (for opening a new file), Open (for opening an existing file), Save (for saving changes or additions to a file), Print (for printing information in the current file).

This feature makes it easy to know how to perform similar functions on many different Windows applications. Standard applications don't always use the same name for the same function this way. One application might use a command called Start, another a command called Load, and another a command called Open to open a file.

Using standard applications, it is difficult to transfer information from one application to another. This is because standard applications have their own user interface and probably their own unique file formats. Windows provides standard methods for data exchange between Windows applications. What this means is that you can transfer information—either text or graphics—from one Windows application to another Windows application. Typical Windows applications have an Edit menu with the Cut, Copy, and Paste commands, which use the Clipboard to transfer information between applications. What you do is cut and copy text or graphics from one Windows application into the Clipboard and paste it exactly where you want it in another Windows application.

Because of this consistency between Windows applications, learning to use a Windows application is similar to learning to drive a car: If you can drive a Honda, most likely you can also drive a Fiat or a Volvo. If you can use the Windows application Microsoft Write, most likely you can also use the Windows application Micrografx In·a·Vision. And the ability to transfer both text and graphics from one application to another without having to worry about file formats—to copy a chart or other graphic in the exact place you want it in your report—is a real plus.

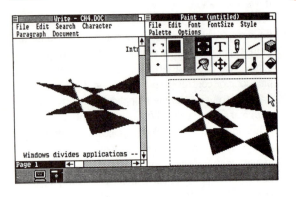

MEMORY MANAGEMENT

When Windows runs standard applications, it allots them the amount of memory they require and does not in any way interfere with this space. Windows does this so that standard applications "feel" just as they did running under DOS. If it needs to remove one standard application to make room for another, it removes the entire old application and then puts in the entire new one, as shown here.

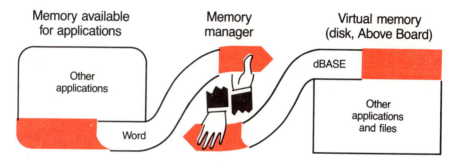

How Windows loads standard applications into memory

With Windows applications, Windows uses its own sophisticated memory-management system. If you try to run more than one Windows application at a time on a hard disk or expanded memory system and there is not enough memory available for all of the applications you're trying to load, Windows just puts in the parts of the application that it currently needs. It assigns part of the hard disk or extended memory to be swap space or "virtual memory" and keeps track of the rest of the program there. Windows decides which parts are needed and how to swap parts in and out, using the virtual memory (your hard disk or extended memory) for swap space. What this does is let you have more Windows applications running at one time than you could if you were using standard applications, as shown here.

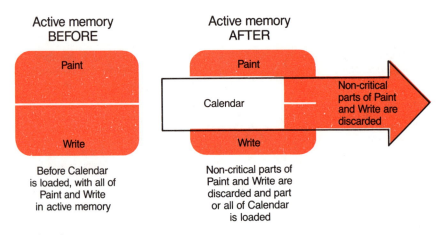

How Windows uses virtual memory

DEVICE INDEPENDENCE

Windows applications function independently of input devices such as mice and light pens, and output devices such as printers and plotters. Before Windows, if you used a standard application that didn't support a mouse, then added a mouse, you'd also have to upgrade your software to a version that supported the mouse. This won't happen with Windows applications; software will not become obsolete as new peripherals become available.

Right now Windows supports the peripherals listed here. (Windows will also run on cards fully compatible with those listed.)

Pointing Devices
Microsoft Mouse (bus or serial)
Mouse Systems PC Mouse
Manager Mouse (uses the Mouse Systems option)
VisiOn Mouse
Logitech Logimouse (serial version)
Kraft Joystick
The LightPen Company Lightpen
FTG Data Systems LightPen

Graphics Cards and Monitors
IBM Color Graphics Adapter and monitor
Compaq Personal Computer
Hercules Graphics Card
FTG Data Systems Single Pixel Board
EGA (Enhanced Graphics Adapter)
Enhanced Color Display

Printers and Plotters
Epson FX-80
Epson FX-85 (may not support all printer features)
Epson FX-100 (may not support all printer features)
Citizen MSP-25
NEC 3550
NEC P2/P3
HP LaserJet
HP LaserJet PLUS (may not support all printer features)
HP 7470A
HP 7475A
IBM Graphics
Epson MX-80 Graftrax+
IBM Proprinter
Okidata (IBM model) 92, 93, 192, 193
Okidata (Standard model) 92, 93, 192, 193
C-Itoh 8510
TI 850
TI 855
Epson LQ-1500
Toshiba P1351
Star Micronics SG-10

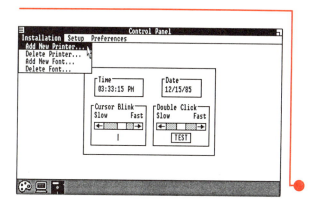

If you get a new printer, one that's on this list, you'd simply open Control Panel, and use the Add New Printer... command on the Installation menu.

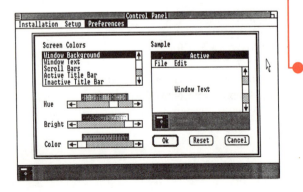

```
In order to operate correctly, Microsoft Windows needs to know
what kind of pointing device you have.

Follow these          - Find your pointing device on this list.
steps:                - Type the number for your pointing device.
                        (Or enter Q to quit Setup)
                      - Press the ⏎ key.

1: No pointing device
2: Microsoft Mouse (Bus/Serial)
3: Mouse Systems or VisiOn Mouse (COM1)
4: Mouse Systems or VisiOn Mouse (COM2)
5: Logitech Serial Mouse
6: Kraft Joystick Mouse
7: the Lite-Pen Company - Lightpen
8: FTG Data Systems Lightpen and Single Pixel Board

       pointing device: 1
```

```
In order to operate correctly, Microsoft Windows needs to know
what kind of graphics adapter you have.

Follow these          - Find your graphics adapter on this list.
steps:                - Type the number for your graphics adapter.
                        (Or enter Q to quit Setup)
                      - Press the ⏎ key.

1: IBM (or compatible) Color/Graphics Adapter or COMPAQ Personal Computer
2: Hercules Graphics Card (or compatible) with Monochrome Display
3: Enhanced Graphics Adapter (EGA) with Monochrome Personal Computer Display
4: EGA with Enhanced Color Display (Black and White only)
5: EGA with Enhanced Color Display or Personal Computer Color Display
6: EGA (more than 64K) with Enhanced Color Display

       graphics adapter: 1
```

To install a pointing device, EGA card, and monitor, you'd only need to run the Setup program one more time and, when prompted, specify your new equipment. (Setup will run faster the second time because it won't copy some of the files over again.)

What if you purchase equipment that is not on this list, perhaps something that was not available when Windows was released? You'd only need a device driver (software that connects the equipment to Windows) to be able to use this equipment with Windows. You'd most likely get the driver from the manufacturer of the hardware, but it could possibly come from Microsoft or from someone inside your company who can write a device-driver program. The benefit of this arrangement is that a larger number of peripherals can be supported, and the actual support can be made available by the hardware manufacturer at any time. The benefit to you is that your applications software won't need an upgrade because you've added new equipment. Windows and the device driver are all that are needed for an application such as Write to recognize the addition of a new graphics card.

If, for example, you're using a computer-aided design (CAD) Windows application with a standard 640- by 200-pixel monitor, and, a year from now when prices drop, you purchase a 1000- by 1000-pixel, 16-color monitor, you'd be able to run your same CAD program with no modifications (assuming that your CAD program took advantage of Windows' device independence) and take advantage of your new high-resolution color monitor.

Windows also has its own display options. If you're running Windows applications with a standard color-graphics adapter and monitor now, when you use the Preferences command in the Control Panel to set colors, Windows changes only the brightness of the various screen elements including text, background, scroll bars, and title bars.

If you add an Enhanced Graphics Adapter and monitor, however, you'll use the same part of the Control Panel, only you'll be able to set actual colors, not just shades of gray.

THE BEST OF ALL POSSIBLE WORLDS?

A reasonable question to ask at this point is: If this standardized graphic interface is so easy to learn and use, if transfer of information from any one application to any other application is so simple, and if sophisticated memory management and device independence are indisputably wonderful features, then why aren't there more Windows applications? That question is not easy to answer.

Most current programs were written for the plain-vanilla MS-DOS environment. DOS doesn't permit running several programs at once or cutting and pasting between programs. And even though programs written for DOS run as standard applications with Windows, they don't fully utilize the power of Windows. For standard applications to become Windows applications, applications programmers will have to modify them to take advantage of Windows' graphics tools, memory management, and device drivers. Windows is a new product; chances are that many will make the change to Windows.

Converting existing MS-DOS applications from a non-Windows environment to a Windows environment requires programmers to rethink their approach. Windows provides a new way of presenting an application to the user, and developers must consider how to take advantage of Windows' graphic capabilities. In some cases, this may mean totally new products. It could be compared to making a flying machine: Designers could start with their current vehicle, add wings and a more powerful engine, and end up with a flying automobile, or they could rethink the concept and design an airplane.

One advantage of Windows is that you don't have to wait for new applications. You can run your favorite existing applications with Windows right now and take advantage of some of Windows' features, and as new applications become available, you can switch to those that take advantage of all Windows' features.

5

USING WRITE AND PAINT

Microsoft Write and Microsoft Paint are two Windows applications bundled with the first release of Windows. Write is a simple word processor you'll find easy to use for your day-to-day writing tasks. Paint is a drawing program that you can use to create art for your memos and reports, to enhance graphics copied in from another program (such as a chart from Lotus 1-2-3), and to save and print artwork. Paint, too, works in the same way as other Windows applications, so it's easy to learn and use.

Write and Paint are useful on their own. But they can also be used to combine information from other applications, either Windows applications or standard applications. You can paste text from other text applications into Write, and use Write's tools to work with the text until it's exactly what you want. Likewise, you can paste graphics from other applications into Paint, and use Paint's tools to edit or enhance what you've pasted in. And you can combine a Paint graphic and Write document by copying the completed graphic from Paint into the Write document and paste it exactly where you want to illustrate a point. You can also paste part of a spreadsheet from Lotus 1-2-3 beneath the report text to show the numbers you need to reinforce a statement. With Write and Paint, you'll no longer need to have your figures on separate pages or need to send your report to your company's graphics department five days early so a graphic artist can cut and paste text and graphics into the right places by hand.

Let's look at Write and Paint to see how they work, first separately and then together. We'll look at Write's features and menus, and then construct a short business letter. Then we'll look at Paint's features and drawing tools and construct a graphic to accompany the letter. Then we'll copy the graphic into the letter, position it exactly where we want it, and print the final copy.

WRITE

Write has the features of most simple word processors—it can wordwrap, it allows you to set margins and tabs, it can move blocks of text, and it searches for one text string and replaces it with another. Because Windows is a graphic environment, Write can display different font sizes and types on the screen. Your document is displayed on the screen just as it will look when it is printed on your printer, showing only the options your printer allows. This feature is called WYSIWYG—What You See Is What You Get. If you know what your documents will look like before you print, you won't have to waste time and paper printing things you can't use because they weren't what you expected.

Write also has drop-down menus and dialog boxes just like the desktop applications and it is easy to use.

When you start Write, the screen looks as shown here.

The Write screen shows a title bar, menu bar, scroll bars, and a work area. The small mark that resembles a bug in the upper left corner of the work area marks the end of your document. Write displays the page number in the lower left corner.

Write has six menus: File, Edit, Search, Character, Paragraph, and Document. We'll take a look at each one.

The File menu

The File menu has six commands.

The first four commands on the File menu, New, Open..., Save..., and Print..., are similar to the commands on the File menus in the desktop applications. New opens a new, untitled document. Open... opens an existing Write document so you can edit and make changes. You use the Save... command to save a document after creating it or making changes. You can also give a document a title with the Save... command and indicate whether you want the saving action to be text-only or backup. You use the Print... command to print the current document.

The Print... command works by running the Spooler, so once you've sent a document off to be printed, you can use Write or any other part of Windows for another task. When Write sends a document to the Spooler, the Spooler icon appears in the icon area. In addition, Write displays a dialog box on the screen with a message telling you it is sending the document to the printer. This dialog box has a Cancel button. If you do not use the Cancel button, the box will eventually disappear, and the printer will begin to print your document.

The last two commands on the File menu are the Change Printer... and Repaginate... commands. You can use Change Printer... to select another printer from a list box that contains the names of the printers you have installed in Windows or to select a different option for the one you are using. The Repaginate... command displays page breaks (where one page ends and another begins) on the screen by placing a $>>$ in the left margin. Using the Repaginate... command allows you to check page breaks before printing.

The Edit menu

The Edit menu has six commands.

The first four commands have keyboard shortcuts. As on other menus we've seen before, the keyboard commands are listed to the right of the menu selections. As mentioned in Chapter 2 (and it's particularly apt for the keyboard-oriented activity of word processing with Write), even if you have a mouse, you may wish to use a keyboard command if your hands are already on the keyboard and it would be quicker to use the keyboard than to reach for the mouse.

Notice that the Undo, Cut, Copy, Paste, Move Picture, and Size Picture commands are dimmed, indicating that they are disabled. The Undo command is disabled until you carry out your first command. The Cut and Copy commands are disabled until you select something. Paste is disabled until you put something into the Clipboard. The Move Picture and Size Picture commands are disabled until you select a picture. When you select text or a picture, all of these commands become available.

```
Edit
Undo          Sh Esc

Cut           Del
Copy          F2
Paste         Ins

Move Picture
Size Picture
```

The Undo command reverses your last action. The command name changes and may appear as Undo Typing, Undo Editing, Undo Formatting, or simply Undo, depending on your last action. If your last action was Undo or you just began a new file, the command name will simply be Undo, and choosing it will reverse the Undo.

Cut, Copy, and Paste work the same in Write as they do in the desktop applications. Cut deletes the selected text and puts it into the Clipboard. Copy puts a copy of the selected text into the Clipboard. Once text or a graphic has been cut or copied to the Clipboard, you can use the Paste command and insert the stored text or graphic at the insertion point anywhere in your document.

The Move Picture command is used to move a picture horizontally on a page in a Write document. When you choose the Move Picture command, Write puts a move icon (actually the pointer with the size-box shape) on the picture and puts a dotted line around it. Then you can use the direction keys or the mouse to position the picture.

The Size Picture command works much like the Move Picture command. It puts a size icon on the picture and a dotted frame around the picture. You then use the direction keys or the mouse to move the size icon to the edge of the dotted frame and continue moving it until the frame is the size you want the picture to be.

The Search menu

The Search menu has four commands. Find..., Repeat Last Find, and Change... are the search and replace commands. You use the Find... command to search the entire document, starting at the insertion point, for instances of the text you specify. You use Change... if you wish to find and replace one text string with another, and Repeat Last Find to continue the search from the last Find... or Change... command.

The Find... command dialog box is shown here.

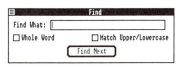

You can select the Whole Word box when you don't want Write to find instances of the search text embedded in other text. For example, if you told Write to search for the word *word* and did not check Whole Word, Write might identify the word *sword*. Write assumes you want to ignore capitalization when searching. If you want Write to find only those occurrences of the search text with the same capitalization as you specified in the search text, select the Match Upper/Lowercase box.

The Change... command dialog box looks as shown here.

Use this dialog box to specify the text you want to find and the text you want inserted in its place. Clicking the Find Next button finds the next occurrence of the specified text, but makes no change to the text currently selected. Clicking the Change Then Find button replaces the selected text with the new text and locates the next occurrence. Change makes the change, but does not continue the search. Change All changes all occurrences of the text automatically without asking you for confirmation.

The last command on the Search menu is the Go To Page... command. As its name indicates, this command allows you to go to a specific page in the document by typing the desired page number in a dialog box. The page numbers which are assigned when Write prints or when you choose the Repaginate... command from the File menu are displayed in the lower left corner of Write's work area. The Go To Page... command is helpful to move quickly to a specific page in a long document when scrolling would be too slow.

The Character menu

The Character menu has 12 commands. Commands on the Character menu are used to change the appearance of characters on the screen and the printed page.

The first command that's on the Character menu (Normal) is Write's default character style (plain text). The next three commands (Bold, Italic, and Underline) change the style of text you select. You

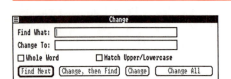

may choose more than one style in this group. Write puts a check mark in front of the styles you choose. If you change your mind, simply select the text in the style you wish to change, choose the command for the style you wish to remove, and Write will remove the check mark from in front of that style command and cancel that format.

The next two commands (Superscript and Subscript) are for those characters you want to appear slightly above or below the lines of text. Superscript and Subscript characters also appear in slightly smaller print. You can superscript footnote references[1], trademarks (PC XT™), and mathematical expressions ($c^2 = a^2 + b^2$). You can subscript chemical formulas, such as CO_2 and H_2O.

The last three groups of commands on the Character menu are for fonts. The term "font," as used in Windows, refers to the design of the characters on the screen or the page. Up to three font names appear on the menu. Some fonts provided with Windows are Courier, Helv (similar to the commonly used Helvetica), and Tms Rmn (similar to Times Roman). Whether or not you can use a particular font in your Write documents depends upon the printer you have installed. Write knows which type of printer you have installed and only displays fonts or styles that your printer can print. To change to a different font, you select the text you want to change and choose one of the fonts listed on the menu. There may be more than three fonts available for the current printer. If there are, they will be displayed when you choose the Fonts... command. For example, the fonts in the Fonts dialog box shown here are available for an Epson MX-80.

Two additional commands on the Character menu are Reduce Font and Enlarge Font. Most fonts have at least two sizes. You can quickly change from one size to another by using these commands or by using their keyboard shortcut commands: F9 for Reduce Font and F10 for Enlarge Font, which is quicker than using the Fonts... command.

Fonts

Font Name:
Helv

[Ok]
[Cancel]

Courier
Helv
Pica
Pica Compressed
Pica Expanded
Pica Expanded Compressed

8
10
12
Font Size:
10

The Paragraph menu

The Paragraph menu has commands that control the alignment, spacing, and indenting of paragraphs.

The Normal command can be used to restore Write's default paragraph format: With this, text is left-aligned, single-spaced, unjustified, and non-indented. The Left command aligns the paragraph on the left margin. The Right command aligns the paragraph on the right margin. The Centered command centers each line of the paragraph inside the current margins, and the Justified command aligns the paragraph both on the left and right margins by adjusting the spaces between words. When you choose one of these commands, it changes the format of the paragraph that currently has the insertion point, or, if several paragraphs are selected, it changes the format of the selected paragraphs.

The Single Space command puts a ⅙-inch space between each line of text. If different font sizes, superscripts, or subscripts are in the paragraph, spacing will change to accommodate the tallest font or the super- or subscript. The 1½ Space command sets the space between lines to ¼ inch. The Double Space command sets line spacing to ⅓ inch.

The last command on the Paragraph menu is the Indents... command. Choosing Indents... displays a dialog box that you can use to control how far a paragraph is indented from the left or right margin and the first line indent. The Indents... command only changes the indents of a paragraph or selected paragraphs; you'll need to use the Page Layout... command from the Document menu to change the margins of the page. You can also use the Indents... command to create a hanging indent, a paragraph whose first line extends farther to the left than the rest of the paragraph. To do this, you enter a positive number in the Left Indent text box and a negative number in the First Line text box.

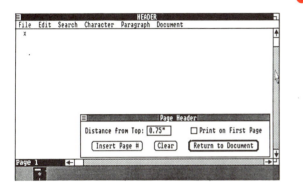

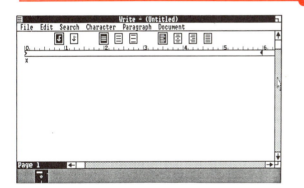

The Document menu

The document menu has five commands. They affect the entire document.

The first command (Header...) puts a line of text on the top of each page of a document as it is printed. You might, for example, use a header that includes the title of your article or chapter and the current page number. The Header... command takes over the entire screen. This is where you type the text for the header. The dialog box that appears when you choose the Header... command gives you the option to include page numbers.

To have a page number included, simply click the Insert Page # button. Write will insert the current page number when it prints. The dialog box has its own System menu box, containing commands that allow you to move or close the dialog box.

The Footer... command puts a line of text on the bottom of each page when the document is printed. The footer window takes over the entire screen, just as the header window does. You could use a footer to print your company name and the date on the bottom of each page of a proposal. If you wish, you may include a page number in the footer.

The Ruler On command displays a ruler at the top of the window. Once the ruler is displayed, Ruler On changes to Ruler Off, which allows you to remove the ruler. If you have a mouse, you can use the ruler to set tabs and change margins. You can drag the tab icons to the places you want them on the ruler. The first tab icon is a regular tab; the second one (the vertical arrow followed by a period) sets decimal tabs. You can select the text for which you wish to change the spacing by clicking on one of the spacing icons. You can also change the alignment of selected text. You can select a paragraph or paragraphs, and then click on the left-aligned, centered, right-aligned, or justified icons and the selected text will be aligned the way you specify. If you don't have a mouse, you can use the Tabs... and Page Layout... commands.

The Tabs... command lets you set tabs for lists and tables. Write has preset tabs every half inch. Tabs that you set on the ruler or with the Tabs... command override the preset tabs. If you want to change the preset tabs, you can set either left-aligned tabs or decimal tabs. Use decimal tabs to align a column of numbers on their decimal points.

The Page Layout... command is the place you specify any changes you want to make to the margins or starting page number. Write's default page layout has top and bottom margins of 1 inch, and left and right margins of 1.25 inches. Unless you specify otherwise, Write will start numbering pages with page 1.

Looking at all the commands on each menu is a lot of information to cover in a few short pages, but once you begin to use Write, you'll quickly learn the details of the commands you use regularly.

USING WRITE

To start using Write, let's type a short letter. In the following example, imagine that you are the marketing manager of a publishing house called Fictitious Publishing. You have regional sales managers you contact regularly. Right now, you're writing to one of your regional sales managers to inform her that one of your authors is making a publicity tour in her area. Publicity tours are always good sales opportunities, so you want her to contact her sales staff to be sure local stores will have plenty of this author's book, *Trivial Accomplishments,* available. In addition, you want your letter to include company sales figures for the last three months. Because you have Windows and Paint, and because Write lets you incorporate graphics right into the text, you think you'll try to construct a graphic that shows the sales figures rather than just presenting the numbers in the same old way.

We'll start by typing in the letter. If you haven't already done so, start Write.

M *Double-click on the file named WRITE.EXE.*

K *Select the file named WRITE.EXE with the direction keys and press Enter.*

With the insertion point at the upper left corner of the Write window (the place it is when you open Write and start a new document), type the date:

April 1, 1985

Proper business-letter form calls for the date to be right-aligned. To right align the date:

M *Choose Right from the Paragraph menu.*

K *Use Alt-Paragraph-Right.*

The date is automatically aligned at the right margin.

Press Enter to put a blank line under the date.

Notice that the insertion point is at the right margin. Write keeps the paragraph formatting of the previous paragraph.

You want to begin typing the body of the letter at the left margin, so you need to change the paragraph alignment back to normal—that is, left-aligned.

M *Choose Normal from the Paragraph menu.*

K *Use Alt-Paragraph-Normal.*

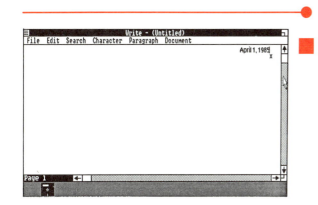

■ *Now type the rest of the letter:*

JoAnn Ingraham, Southwest Sales
Manager[Enter]
Fictitious Publishing[Enter]
5 Tradepress Road[Enter]
Santa Fe, New Mexico 87115[Enter][Enter]
Dear JoAnn:[Enter][Enter]
I wanted to let you know that Chris Peters,
author of Trivial Accomplishments, will be in
your area May 1–10 so you can alert your sales
staff. He'll appear on local television and radio
talk shows, and we're trying to get several
newspaper features. We'll send you his exact
schedule the last week of April. Prepublication
orders for the book look extremely
good.[Enter][Enter]
I also wanted to show you publication figures
for our three major books for the last three
months.[Enter][Enter]
Your group deserves much of the credit
for these figures. Keep up the good
work.[Enter][Enter]
Sincerely,[Enter][Enter][Enter][Enter]
Joe Readwell

Don't worry that there's not enough
room for the graphic. We'll take care
of it later.

You may want to make the book title italic. If
so, first select the title. Then choose the Italic
command. These formatting commands only work
on selected text.

M *Use the up scroll arrow, the scroll box, or the*
scroll bar, if necessary, to go back to the beginning
of the letter. Drag across the words Trivial Accomplishments *to select them.*

K *Use the direction keys to go back to the beginning*
of the letter. Hold down the Shift key and use the
direction keys to select the book title.

Choose the Italic command from the Character menu. Although the following examples don't include this option, you may use this or other font styles any time you wish.

If you make mistakes while typing, Write has ways to quickly move the cursor from one part of the letter to another. With the mouse, simply move the pointer to the character or word you wish to change. With the keyboard, you can use the left, right, up, and down direction keys to move character by character or line by line. But Write also has fast ways to move to the next word, sentence, or paragraph. As mentioned before, even if you have a mouse, you may find that it is easier to use the keyboard commands when your hands are already on the keyboard. To move to the next or previous word, press Ctrl-Right or Ctrl-Left (using the right and left direction keys). To move to the next or previous sentence, press the 5 key on the numeric keypad (the 5 key on the numeric keypad is called the GoTo key) and then press the right or left direction key. To move to the next or previous paragraph, first press the GoTo key (the 5 key on the keypad) and then press the up or down direction key. Once you learn these keyboard commands, you'll find they are really useful when editing.

Now we'll experiment with some of the different fonts and sizes and make a heading for the letter. Some of the time, you'll want to print formal letters on your own letterhead, but making a heading is a good alternative for quick, less-formal letters. And Write's fonts make it easy to design an attractive heading. By adding a heading, you can use the standard paper already in your printer and print a letter that looks better than one written on plain paper without a heading.

We'll design a heading for Fictitious Publishing that looks as shown here.

To create this heading, move the insertion point to the beginning of your letter.

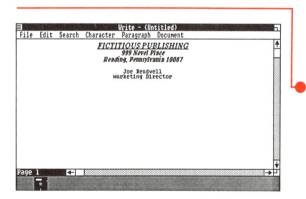

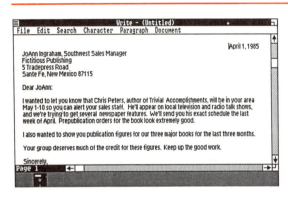

M   *Move the mouse pointer to the start of the first line and click.*

K   *Hold down the GoTo key and press the Home key.*

Notice that the insertion point is just to the left of the date in the upper right corner. It's not in the upper left corner, as you might expect it to be, because we aligned the date on the right margin.

■   *To make a blank line to begin the header, you press Enter.*

M   *Move the mouse pointer to the blank line at the top of the letter and click.*

K   *Press the up direction key to move back up to the blank line at the top of the letter.*

■   *Next, choose Center from the Paragraph menu so information you type in the heading will be centered.*

■   *Now type the first three lines of the heading:*

FICTITIOUS PUBLISHING[Enter]
999 Novel Place[Enter]
Reading, Pennsylvania 10087[Enter]

Notice how Write centers the first line you type. Then when you start the second line, Write keeps the paragraph formatting (in this case, centered) from the first line or previous paragraph until you choose another alignment.

■   *Press Enter for a blank line, and then type the text for the fourth line (your name) and for the fifth line (your title):*

Joe Readwell[Enter]
Marketing Director[Enter]

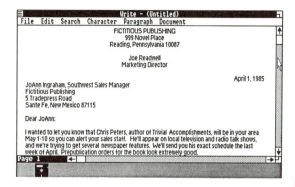

The heading is now at the top of the letter.

Now we'll select parts of the heading and experiment with different font types and sizes until you're familiar with Write's fonts and the heading looks just the way you want it. Remember, the fonts, font sizes, and character styles you have available depend on the printer you have installed. If you have different fonts displayed, experiment with the ones available. This example uses the fonts available on an IBM Proprinter.

To select the first line of the header:

M *Drag the mouse over the words* FICTITIOUS PUBLISHING.

K *Move the insertion point to just before the* F *in* Fictitious. *Hold down the Shift key and press the End key. This selects everything from the insertion point to the end of the line.*

Now we'll look at each of the fonts.

M *Choose the Courier font from the Character menu by pulling down the Character menu and changing the font to Courier.*

K *Use Alt-Character-Courier.*

Notice how the characters in *FIC-TITIOUS PUBLISHING* change. Write's default font on the IBM Pro-printer is Helv, a very plain font. We're looking for something a bit dressier.

When you select a font, you get that font in a particular size. Most fonts come in several sizes, depending on what capabilities your printer has, and you can change the default size without changing the font. If you want to check the sizes you have, use the Font... command.

Choose the Enlarge Font command from the Character menu.

Use Alt-Character-Enlarge Font (or press F10, the keyboard shortcut for the Enlarge Font command).

FICTITIOUS PUBLISHING is now larger, more the size that suits a heading.

Let's look at the other two fonts on the Character menu to see which one looks best.

With FICTITIOUS PUBLISHING *still selected, pull down the Character menu and choose the Helv font.*

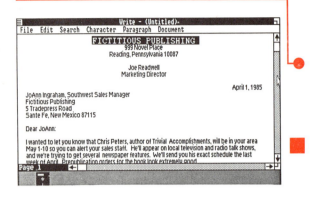

The first line of the heading changes to look as shown here.

Now try the third font.

Pull down the Character menu and choose the Tms Rmn font.

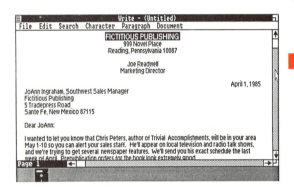

Of the three headings, let's say you decide on Tms Rmn, but think that perhaps you could make it more distinctive by adding some additional character styles.

To make the heading stand out even more, we'll make it bold and underline it. Then we'll make it italic because the slanted type seems to fit the name FICTITIOUS.

With FICTITIOUS PUBLISHING *still selected, choose the Bold command, then the Italic command, then Underline, all three from the Character menu.*

Your heading now looks as shown here.

As you can see, Write lets you have more than one format at a time for selected text.

Format the next two lines of the heading in the same way.

Select the next two lines, the address. Choose the Tms Rmn font and then choose the Enlarge Font command. Next choose Bold, and then Italic. When you're finished, move the insertion point to the beginning of the line containing your name so you can clearly see these changes.

We won't underline the address.

Now all that's left is to format your name and title. You want this to be a bit less obtrusive, and think the Courier font in a small size might work well with the Tms Rmn font.

Select your name and title. Choose the Courier font from the Character menu.

If the font size is too large:

M *Choose the Reduce Font command from the Character menu.*

K *Press F9, the keyboard shortcut for the Reduce Font command.*

That's all there is to creating the heading.

Before we work with Paint and create a graphic for this letter, let's save it.

Choose the Save... command from the File menu.

You'll see a dialog box like the one shown here.

Write - (Untitled)

File   Edit   Search   Character   Paragraph   Document

FICTITIOUS PUBLISHING
999 Novel Place
Reading, Pennsylvania 10087

Joe Readwell
Marketing Director

April 1, 1985

JoAnn Ingraham, Southwest Sales Manager
Fictitious Publishing
5 Tradepress Road
Sante Fe, New Mexico 87115

Dear JoAnn:

I wanted to let you know that Chris Peters, author of Trivial Accomplishments, will be in your area May 1-10 so you can alert your sales staff. He'll appear on local television and radio talk shows, and we're trying to get several newspaper features. We'll send you his exact schedule the last week of April. Prepublication orders for the book look extremely good.

Page 1

Write - (Untitled)

File   Edit   Search   Character   Paragraph   Document

FICTITIOUS PUBLISHING
999 Novel Place
Reading, Pennsylvania 10087

Joe Readwell
Marketing Director

April 1, 1985

JoAnn Ingraham, Southwest Sales Manager
Fictitious Publishing
5 Tradepress Road
Sante Fe, New Mexico 87115

Dear JoAnn:

I wanted to let you know that Chris Peters, author of Trivial Accomplishments, will be in your area May 1-10 so you can alert your sales staff. He'll appear on local television and radio talk shows, and we're trying to get several newspaper features. We'll send you his exact schedule the last week of April. Prepublication orders for the book look extremely good.

Page 1

Save Current Document As: C:\WINDOWS

[   ]   [Save]

☐ Text Only   ☐ Make Backup   [Cancel]

■ *Type a name for the letter in the typing box (something like INGRAHM).*

M *Click the Save button.*

K *Press Enter.*

Don't select the Text Only and Make Backup options. If you choose Text Only, Write saves the document without any formatting (no boldface, underlining, italics, and special fonts). We want to save our formatting and font information with the letter. An X in front of Make Backup tells Write to save a copy of the previous version of your document with the .BAK extension. This is a good safety measure, but we have no previous version.

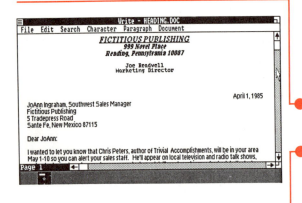

You may wish to save the heading of this letter in a separate file so you can use it on other letters. That way, you won't have to recreate it each time you write a letter with this heading. To save the heading, just save another copy of this letter with a name like HEADING. When you do this, the title bar will change and display the most recent title.

Select the text of the letter—everything but the heading—and choose the Delete command from the Edit menu. And don't worry—you still have a copy of the complete letter in the file named INGRAHM.

Choose the Save. . . command again and it will save this document, which is now only the heading. Next time you want to use the heading on a letter, instead of opening a new Write file, open the one named HEADING. Type your letter and save it under its own name. Saving under a different name leaves the HEADING file unchanged, so you can use the heading for other letters. You can now close Write, if you want to.

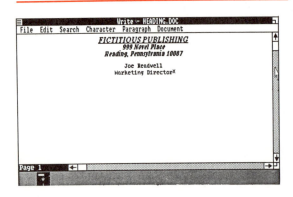

PAINT

You've learned about Write and know how to use it to write a business letter. If you've worked with word processors before, you're probably not amazed with Write (with the exception of Write's fonts); it's a good word processor and easy to use, but you already know the advantages of word processing over typing. But once you learn to use Paint and then how to copy graphics from Paint to Write, you WILL be amazed. The graphic interface Windows provides these tools and the way they work together is truly remarkable. They have the ability to transform the appearance of your documents. In your next task, you'll see how this works. You'll learn to use Paint and then construct a simple graphic to accompany the letter.

When you start Paint from the MS-DOS Executive window, you'll see the initial Paint screen, which looks like the one shown here.

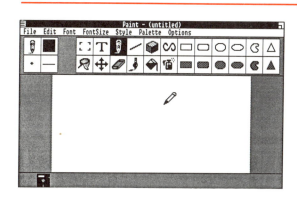

It has the title bar and menu bar just like all Windows applications. The work area is divided into two parts: the canvas, which is the entire drawing area (the large white area on the screen), and the drawing window (the part of the work area that frames the canvas).

You'll work on Paint's electronic canvas with tools such as a paintbrush, pencil, straightedge, and eraser—tools that are similar to those a real artist uses. You can use these tools (draw with the pencil, for example) either with a mouse or with the keyboard, but using a mouse seems more natural. Drawing with the mouse and pencil tool is more like drawing with a real pencil or pen.

The four boxes in the upper left corner of the screen, just below the menu bar and above the canvas, are current status boxes. They show the tool, paint pattern, brush shape, and line width Paint will use when you draw. Each time you change tools (for example, from the pencil to the paintbrush) the change is reflected in the status box.

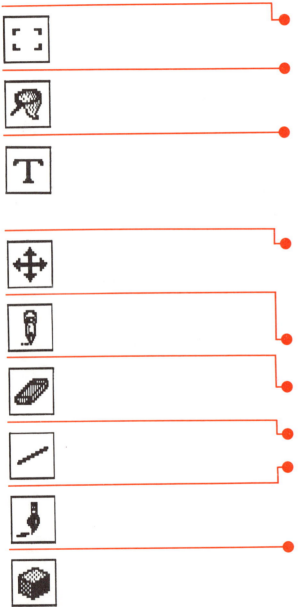

The two rows of boxes to the right of the current status boxes contain the tools and shapes you'll use to draw and refine your artwork. Let's look briefly at each tool now (you'll learn more about the tools later in this chapter when we actually use them).

The first tool (in the box at the upper left corner of the tool and shape palette) is the selection rectangle. You'll use it to select portions of your drawing so you can move or copy them.

Just below the selection rectangle is the selection net. You use it instead of the selection rectangle when the shape you want to select to move or copy is nonrectangular.

To the right of the selection rectangle is the text tool. You use it when you want to add text to your drawings. You choose the text tool, move the I-beam pointer with the direction keys or mouse where you want the text to go, click or press the Spacebar for an insertion point, and then type the text in from the keyboard. You can add text in many fonts and sizes.

Beneath the text tool is the scroll tool. You use it to move the canvas up and down in the drawing window. (The canvas is larger than what you see in the drawing window—you can see how much larger it is by choosing the Zoom Out command from the Options menu.)

Next to the text tool is the pencil. You can use the pencil to sketch, much as you would use a standard pencil.

Beneath the pencil is an eraser. You can use it to erase mistakes or parts of a drawing that you no longer want.

Next to the pencil is the line tool. You use the line tool to draw straight lines.

Beneath the line tool is the paintbrush. You can use it to paint in the current pattern with any of Paint's 24 brush shapes.

Next to the line tool is the 3-D tool, which helps you draw three-dimensional shapes by displaying axes that can help you judge perspective.

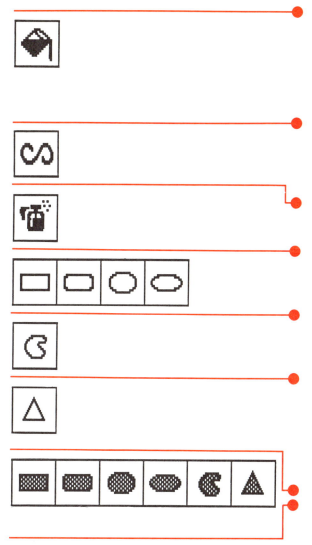

Beneath the 3-D tool is the fill tool. When you choose this tool, which looks like a paint bucket, you can fill an enclosed space with the pattern shown in the current-pattern status box. Paint provides 36 patterns to choose from and you can also create your own.

The next tool, which resembles a sideways S, is the curve tool. You can use it to create a curved line. First, use the curve tool in order to draw a straight line. When you click or press the Spacebar on either side of the line, the line will curve in the direction you indicated.

Below the curve tool is the airbrush. You can use the airbrush to spraypaint in the current pattern.

The next four figures on the top row are the rectangle, rounded box, circle, and oval. You select one of these shapes and then drag or use the direction keys to draw it.

The kidney-shaped icon next to the oval is called the freehand polygon. You drag or use the direction keys to draw the shape you want. Paint draws a straight line to close the polygon.

The icon that looks like a triangle is called the polygon. You can use it to make shapes with straight sides. You simply click or press the Spacebar to mark corners and Paint draws the sides. When you double-click or press Enter, Paint draws a line between the last two corners to complete the shape.

Just below these shapes are the same shapes filled. If you choose one of these shapes and draw it, it will be filled with the current pattern.

As you can see, Paint provides a variety of tools—many more than most of us who are not graphic artists have on our desks. With these tools, those of us who are only marginal artists have a better chance of producing creditable art.

Now let's look at Paint's menus to see what commands are available to use with the tools to create and edit illustrations. Paint has seven menus: File, Edit, Font, FontSize, Style, Palette, and Options.

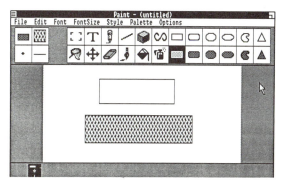

```
File
New
Open...
Save
Save As...
Print
```

```
Edit
Undo        Sh Esc

Erase

Cut         Del
Copy        F2
Paste       Ins
Clear

Invert
Trace Edges
Flip Horizontal
Flip Vertical
```

The File menu

The File menu has five commands. They work the same as corresponding commands on File menus of all Windows applications.

You use the New command to open a new Paint file, and the Open... command to open an existing Paint file. Paint files are named with the .MSP (for Microsoft Paint) extension. You can use the Save command to save an existing (previously named) Paint file or a new Paint file, and the Save As... command to name a new Paint file or to save an existing file under a different name. The Print command calls the Spooler to print a Paint canvas.

The Edit menu

The Edit menu has 10 commands.

Undo—the first command on the Edit menu—can be a real lifesaver when you're first learning to use Paint. It cancels your most recent drawing action or series of steps in a selected area. When you first start with Paint, a tool may do something unexpected. If you don't like the result, you can simply choose the Undo command and cancel what you last did. The second command, Erase, is an even more dramatic way to take care of unwanted drawings. The Erase command erases the entire canvas. A shortcut to erase the canvas is to double-click the eraser tool.

The next group of commands—Cut, Copy, and Paste—works the same way in all Windows applications. Cut deletes the selection and puts it in the Clipboard; Copy makes a copy of the selection and puts it in the Clipboard; and Paste copies the contents of the Clipboard to the middle of the canvas. The last command in this group, Clear, clears the selection. You use Erase to clear the entire canvas and Clear to erase only the selected area.

The commands in the last group on the Edit menu—Invert, Trace Edges, Flip Horizontal, and Flip Vertical—are called special-effects commands. The Invert command reverses the color of the images on the canvas; it turns black to white and white to black. Trace Edges draws a slightly enlarged outline around selected text, patterns, and shapes. Flip Horizontal flips the selected object

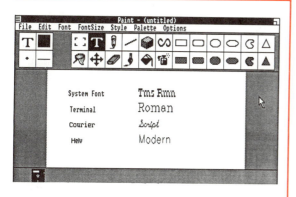

from left to right. Flip Vertical flips the selected object from top to bottom. Flip Horizontal and Flip Vertical can be useful when drawing objects with two similar parts, such as the two halves of a pair of scissors. You can simply draw one half of the scissors, copy it to the Clipboard, paste it in next to the first half, and choose the Flip Horizontal command. You'll have a complete pair of scissors with both parts matching perfectly, with little more effort than it took to draw the first half.

The Font menu

The Font menu has some of the same fonts you saw on Write's Character menu, as well as some additional Paint fonts.

Choose a font from this menu and then pick up the text tool. The characters you type will be displayed in the font you selected. You can experiment with other fonts. Choose another font from the menu and the text you've just typed will be displayed in the new font. You can continue changing fonts until you either click in the drawing window to deselect what you have just typed or select another tool.

The advantage of Paint's fonts is that, unlike Write fonts, they are all printable on a printer that can print graphics because they are graphic images. But this also means that you can't edit text you create with them once you paste this text into another application, such as Microsoft Write.

Samples of the fonts on the Font menu look as shown here.

The FontSize menu

You use the FontSize menu to determine the size of your text. You can experiment with font sizes in the same way you tried out different fonts. Choose a font and size, then pick up the text tool and begin to type. Experiment with different fonts and sizes until your text looks exactly the way you want it to.

The Style menu

The first six commands on the Style menu change the appearance of text.

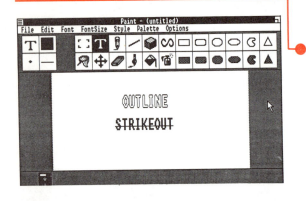

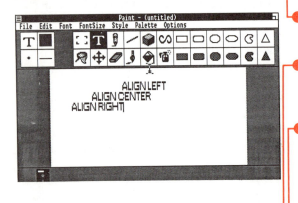

Plain (the default style), Bold, Italic, and Underline are the same as on Write's Character menu. The Outline and Strikeout commands produce text that looks like the text shown here.

You can give your text more than one style from this group of commands.

The next three commands—Align Left, Align Center, and Align Right—align the text you type by using the text-tool pointer as an invisible alignment column. What you do is choose one of the alignments (Align Left is the default), click the mouse button or press the Spacebar to mark the location of the invisible column, and then type the text. It will automatically be aligned according to the alignment of your choice.

The Palette menu

The Palette menu has four commands.

The dialog box that's displayed when you choose the Patterns... command is the place where you choose Paint patterns from a palette that looks like the one shown here.

You can use the pattern you select to fill in parts of your drawings. For example, we'll use a different pattern for each bar in the bar chart that we're about to draw.

Click on a pattern to select it. Your selection is surrounded by a black border on the palette and is displayed in the current status box in the upper left corner of the Paint window.

The dialog box displayed when you choose the next command, Line Widths..., gives you a choice of width of the line drawn with the line, 3-D, curve, and six shape tools. You simply choose a line width from the palette (the choice is reflected in the current status box) and when you pick up the line tool, for example, the line you draw will be the width of your choice.

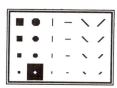

The third command, Brush Shapes..., is similar to Line Width..., but works with the paintbrush tool. You choose a brush shape from the palette shown here.

The last command, Tools..., displays the tools that are shown at the top of the Paint work area.

If a tool you need is concealed by another drawing window, you can choose tools using the direction keys with this command. Using the mouse, just click on the tool you want to use. (You can change tools with the keyboard without the Tools... command by pressing Tab to move top to bottom, left to right through the tool icons or Shift-Tab to move bottom to top, right to left.)

The Options menu

The last of Paint's menus is the Options menu.

The Zoom In command gives you a magnified view of a portion of the canvas so you can edit with greater detail. It zooms in on the area of your canvas where you last clicked the mouse button or pressed the Spacebar, or returns a zoomed-out window to its normal size. You could use it to zoom in and erase a mark too small to erase accurately in the drawing window. The zoomed-in window has a small box in the upper left corner called the view finder, which displays a miniature version of the portion of the drawing you're zoomed in on. You can use the view finder to confirm that, in fact, you've zoomed in on the portion of the canvas you want to edit, and to see the results of your editing. Zoom Out returns the drawing window to its normal size if you are currently zoomed in or displays the entire canvas with the current drawing window outlined if you are in normal size.

The commands in the next group are the grid commands. Paint's default is No Grid. If you choose Fine Grid, Medium Grid, or Coarse Grid, Paint puts an invisible network of horizontal and vertical lines on the canvas. You can use this to more easily align shapes and lines. As you move a shape on this grid, rather than moving randomly, Paint moves the shape from one intersection to the next on the grid. (You can't position a shape between intersections.)

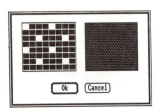

The next command, Edit Pattern..., gives you the capability to customize a pattern. If you can't find a pattern that's exactly what you want from the 36 pattern choices in the Palette menu, create your own by choosing the Edit Pattern... command.

Redesign the current pattern by clicking the squares in the box on the left part of the Edit Pattern... overlay. If you're using a keyboard, manipulate the magnified pattern by using the Spacebar and direction keys. In each case, the box on the right of the Edit Pattern... overlay displays the updated pattern. When you're satisfied, indicate OK and it will be saved and selected for your use.

The last two commands provide you with a choice as to how the images you create will be understood by Paint. Choosing the For Screen command puts no restrictions on those images; For Printer (the default) creates images so they will be interpreted correctly by the printer. These commands may be used only before you draw on the canvas.

Even though Paint has quite a few commands and menus, you will find that it's easy to use. Most of the time, you will be able to simply pick up a tool and use it.

USING PAINT

Now we'll use Paint to make the sales graphic to accompany the letter. We'll draw a simple bar chart that shows the last three months' sales for three of Fictitious's books.

With Paint's tools, this is not difficult. Here's how you do it.

First, start Paint.

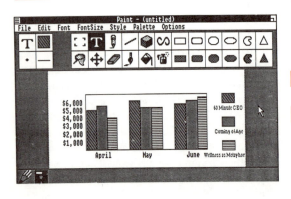

M *Drag the MS-DOS Executive icon into the work area.*

K *Press Alt-Tab to select the MS-DOS Executive icon. Use Alt-Spacebar-Move and then press Enter.*

The MS-DOS Executive window takes over the work area and Write automatically becomes an icon in the icon area.

M   *Double-click on the file named PAINT.EXE in the MS-DOS Executive window.*

K   *Use the direction keys to select the file named PAINT.EXE in the MS-DOS Executive window and press Enter.*

You'll see Paint's initial screen with an empty canvas.

■   *Before drawing the chart, choose the Fine Grid command from the Options menu.*

This puts an invisible grid on the screen that will make it easier to align the parts of the bar chart. If you pull down the Options menu now, you'll see that Paint has put a check mark in front of Fine Grid in the menu to show that it is selected.

First, we'll choose the unfilled rectangle tool to draw the box for the outside of the bar chart.

M   *Select the unfilled rectangle by clicking on it in the tool palette.*

K   *Use the Tab key to move the selection to the unfilled rectangle tool.*

The pointer shape changes to a cross and the tool in the current status box is now the unfilled rectangle.

To draw the box, we'll first position the pointer in the upper left part of the screen.

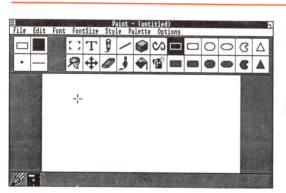

M   *Position the mouse pointer where you want the upper left corner of the box to be. Hold down the mouse button and drag down and to the right. (As you drag, notice Paint drawing a rectangle.)*

K   *Use the direction keys to position the pointer where you want the upper left corner of the box to be. Hold down the Spacebar and use the down and right direction keys to move the pointer to where you want the lower right corner of the rectangle to be. (As you press the direction keys, Paint draws a rectangle.)*

Release the mouse button or the Shift key when your rectangle looks as shown here.

The next step is to add values to the Y-axis, the vertical axis of the chart. To add text to this Paint canvas, we'll use the text tool.

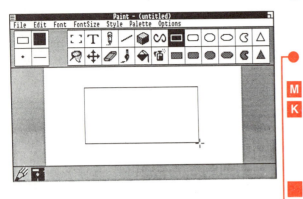

M *Click on the text tool to select it.*

K *Use the Tab key or Shift-Tab to move the selection to the text tool.*

The pointer changes to an I-beam.

Move the pointer to the left of the upper left corner of the rectangle.

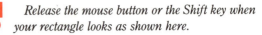

M *Click the mouse button.*

K *Press the Spacebar.*

An insertion point appears.

Type the first value:

$6,000

If you don't like the position of the text, you can use the Backspace key to delete it, position a new insertion point, and type it again.

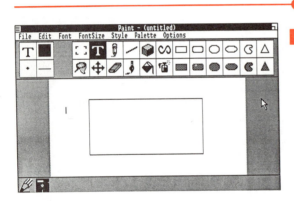

We want to space the values ($6,000, $5,000, $4,000, $3,000, $2,000, and $1,000) evenly along the Y-axis. This will be easy if we simply press Enter at the end of each line.

Press Enter.

Type the second value:

$5,000

Continue entering the Y-axis values until your chart looks as shown here.

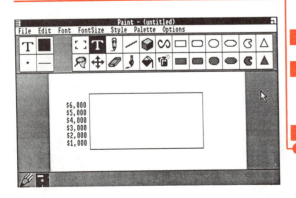

Next, we'll draw the actual bars in our chart. To do this, we can use the same unfilled rectangle we used to draw the outside box. With the Fine Grid turned on it will be easier to align these boxes and make them similar widths. We'll start by drawing the first bar to represent sales of $5,000.

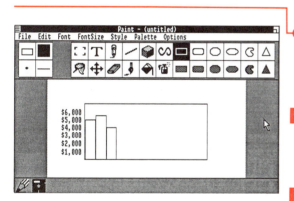

Choose the unfilled rectangle tool. Then position the pointer at the left edge of the rectangle at the $5,000 point.

Drag the pointer down and right until the rectangle that is drawn is about a quarter of an inch wide and touches the bottom of the outside box.

Hold down the Spacebar and use the direction keys until the rectangle drawn is about a quarter of an inch wide and touches the bottom of the outside box.

Draw a second rectangle next to the first one with a starting value of $5,500, and then draw a third rectangle contiguous to the second with a starting value of $4,000.

These rectangles represent April sales for each of three books.

Next, draw three more rectangles for May book sales. The first rectangle has a starting value of $6,000. The second and third have starting values of $5,500.

Now draw the last three rectangles, the ones that represent June sales for three of Fictitious's books. The first book has a starting value of $5,075, the second $6,000, and the third $6,025.

Don't worry if there is too much space between the last bar and the right side of the outside box.

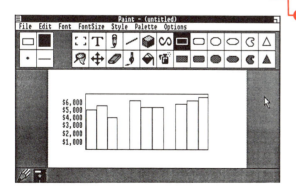

If you need to change the right side of the outside of the chart so it's closer to the last bar, you could use the eraser. But it's difficult to be accurate in tight spots with the eraser. It's easy to slip and accidentally erase a corner that's hard to redraw. An easier way to erase the unwanted part of the graph is to choose the filled rectangle with the white pattern and the smallest (invisible) line width. Just drag the rectangle over the part of the graphic you want to erase (in this case, the right side).

If you should accidentally erase part of the graph, Paint, like Write, has an Undo command that undoes your last action. Just choose Undo from the Edit menu. Paint will redraw the line you just erased, and you can try erasing again.

Now it's time for the fun part—filling in the bars with different patterns, one for each book. To do this, we'll choose a pattern from the Palette menu and then use the fill tool.

> *Choose Patterns... from the Palette menu.*

M *Click on the pattern that will represent the bar for the first book.*

K *Use the direction keys to select the pattern that will represent the bar for the first book. Press Enter to choose the selected pattern.*

In our example, we chose the dark pattern with white diagonal lines for the first bar.

> *Choose the fill tool.*

> *Position it so the tip of the stream of paint pouring out of the can is inside the first bar.*

M *Click the mouse button.*

K *Press the Spacebar.*

Magically, the bar is filled with the pattern of your choice.

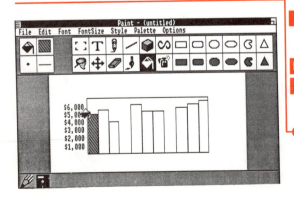

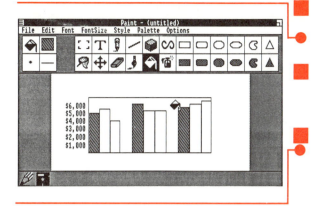

Continue by filling in the first bar in the second group and the first bar in the third group with this same pattern.

Now choose a second pattern from the Patterns... command on the Palette menu and fill the second bar in each of the three groups with this pattern.

Choose a third pattern for the third bar in each of the groups and fill these bars in the same way.

Finally the chart is starting to look like a real bar chart. The last steps are to add some text to label the X-axis and then to add a legend to identify the individual bars.

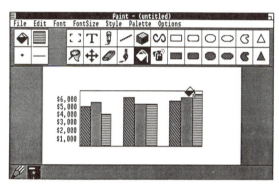

Choose the text tool and choose Align Center from the Paragraph menu. Position the I-beam underneath the middle bar in the first group on the chart. Click or press the Spacebar for an insertion point, then type the text:

April

These three bars represent April sales figures for the three books.

Now add the text May *and* June *under the next two groups of bars.*

The last task is to add a legend so anyone looking at the chart will know which bars represent which books. We'll use the unfilled rectangle to draw boxes for each pattern. Then we'll label each box in the legend with the book title.

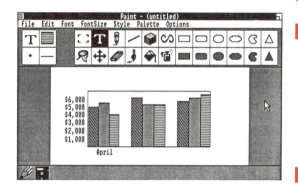

Choose the unfilled rectangle tool. Position it on the canvas and draw one rectangle.

Choose the Selection tool.

Select the rectangle you just drew by starting at the upper left corner of the box and moving diagonally down and to the right.

Choose Copy from the Edit menu and the rectangle will be copied to the Clipboard.

Choose Paste from the Edit menu.

A duplicate rectangle will be copied to the center of the canvas.

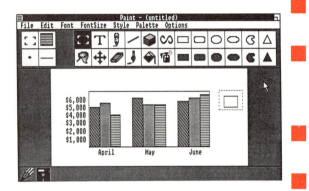

Use the direction keys or mouse to move the new rectangle to just below the first rectangle.

Choose Paste again.

Another copy of the rectangle will be copied to the center of the canvas.

Move the next rectangle to just beneath the second rectangle.

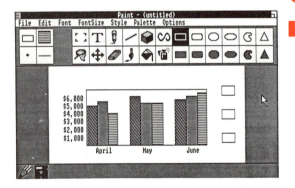

Choose the pattern you used to fill the first bar, pick up the fill tool, and fill the top box in the legend. Then fill the second box with the second pattern and the third box with the third pattern.

Another way this could have been done is by using a filled rectangle and individually drawing each box with a different pattern. As with many of Paint's options, you can choose the way that works best for you.

Now all that's left is to label the boxes with book titles. We'll first choose the font type and size we want. That way, we won't have to make changes after typing the text.

Transparent patterns

If you hold down the Shift key when painting with the paintbrush or spray can, the pattern will be transparent. When you paint over a figure with a transparent pattern, only the area that's behind the figure will be affected and the lines of the original figure will remain unmarked.

Choose the Tms Rmn font from the Font menu.

> There's not much room for our titles, so we want the smallest font that's available.

Pull down the FontSize menu and choose 6, the smallest size.

Choose Align Center from the Style menu to automatically align the title under the rectangles.

Pick up the text tool and position the I-beam under the center of the top box and click or press the Spacebar for an insertion point.

Type the title of the first book:

60 Minute CEO

Position the I-beam under the second box, click or press the Spacebar for an insertion point, and type part of the second title:

Coming of Age

> The full title of the book is *Coming of Age in Silicon Valley.* But there's not enough room, so leave off *in Silicon Valley.*

Follow these steps and type the third title:

Wellness as Metaphor

> Your screen should now look as shown here.

That's all there is to using Paint to make a professional-looking bar chart. If you, like me, are not a graphic artist, this chart made with Paint's tools is most likely more professional than one you could draw by hand—and it took a fraction of the time.

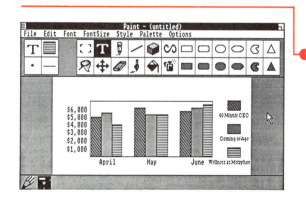

You can also use Microsoft Chart or Lotus 1-2-3 to draw a chart for you, copy it into the Clipboard, and then paste it into Paint to edit it so it's exactly what you want. This might give you an even more professional-looking chart and would be easier than using Paint's tools. But before you do this, draw the chart described above. Using Paint to draw your own chart at least once is the best way to learn to use Paint.

COPYING FROM PAINT TO WRITE

Now that we have a professional-looking chart in Paint, we can select it, copy it to the Clipboard, and paste it into the letter.

To select the chart:

■   *Pick up the selection tool and position it just to the left and above the chart.*

M   *Drag the selection rectangle down and right until the dotted box that Paint draws as you drag surrounds the entire chart and legend.*

K   *Hold down the Spacebar and use the direction keys to expand the selection rectangle Paint draws until it surrounds the entire chart and legend.*

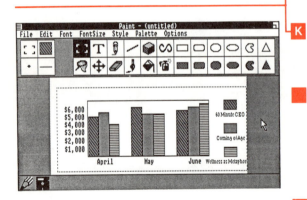

■   *Choose Copy from the Edit menu.*

This copies the selected chart to the Clipboard.

Before leaving Paint, save the completed chart.

■   *Choose the Save As... command from the File menu. Name the chart something like INGCHART and click the Save button or press Enter.*

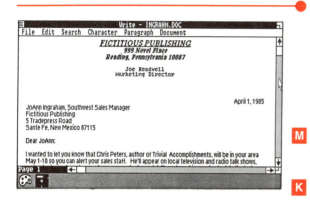

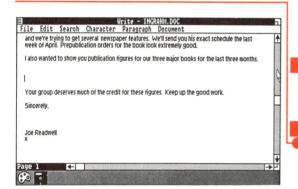

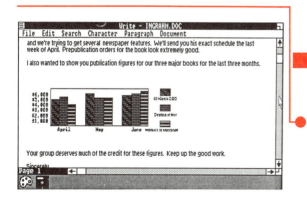

M *Drag the Write icon into the work area.*

K *Use Alt-Tab to select the Write icon. Use Alt-Spacebar-Move and press Enter.*

This time, Write takes over the window, the letter is on the screen, and Paint is reduced to an icon.

Now we need to position the insertion point exactly where we want Windows to paste the chart. We'll leave a few blank lines above the chart. Once the chart is pasted in you can size it and move it left or right, but not up or down.

M *Use the bottom scroll arrow, the scroll bar, or the scroll box until you can see the bottom half of your letter.*

K *Press PgDn so that you can see the bottom half of your letter.*

Now you can see where we'll paste the chart.

Move the insertion point to just before the Y in Your group. *Press Enter twice to make extra space between the last sentence and the top of the chart.*

Position the insertion point exactly where you want the upper left corner of the chart to be.

It's important to leave enough room between the last line of text and the insertion point. This is the only dimension you can't change once the chart is pasted in.

Choose Paste from the Edit menu.

Windows copies in the chart from the Clipboard, putting the upper left corner at the insertion point.

Right now, it looks a bit strange. Write has scaled the picture for your printer. But after you move and size it, it will look better. First, center the chart on the page.

M   *Click on the chart to select it.*

K   *Use the direction keys to move the insertion point up until the chart is selected.*

Choose Centered from the Paragraph menu.

Now we'll use the Size Picture command to make the chart a little larger so we can read the numbers and text more easily.

Select the chart and choose the Size Picture command from the Edit menu.

A dotted frame surrounds the chart and an icon appears in the center.

You can make the chart wider by sizing it from the right edge, you can make it longer by sizing it from the bottom, or you can size in both directions at once from the lower right corner. We'll size this chart in both directions at once. When you choose the Size Picture command, Write puts two numbers in the lower left corner of the window that show you the relative size of each dimension. As you size the chart, these numbers will change.

M   *Without pressing the mouse button, move the icon (the pointer becomes an icon) to the lower right corner of the chart. Move the icon down and right. The frame expands, showing you the size the chart will be. When the frame is the size you want the chart to be, click the mouse button. Our example has the numbers 1.4X/1.4Y in the lower left corner.*

K   *Use the direction keys to move the icon to the lower right corner of the chart. Use the down and right direction keys to enlarge the chart. The frame expands, showing you the size the chart will be. When the frame is the size you want the chart to be, press Enter. Our example has the numbers 1.4X/1.4Y in the lower left corner.*

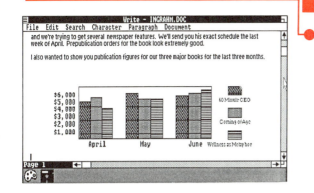

Now select the redrawn chart (if it isn't already selected), choose the Centered command from the Paragraph menu, and the chart will be centered.

That's all there is to copying in artwork from Paint. The Clipboard works the same way when you're transferring between Write and Paint as it does when you're transferring between any Windows application: You select what you want, copy or cut it to the Clipboard, and then simply paste it into the application exactly where you want it.

Now let's print the memo so we can see what the finished product looks like.

Choose Print... from the File menu.

You'll see a dialog box like the one shown here.

Click OK or press Enter to accept Write's defaults and Windows will send the letter to the Spooler.

A dialog box appears and gives you a little time to cancel printing if you change your mind. If you don't click the Cancel button, the dialog box disappears and your letter begins to print on your printer. The finished copy is shown here.

Write and Paint are two examples of Windows applications that are more sophisticated and have many more features than the desktop applications. Like all Windows applications, they share memory and they work with the resources that are currently part of your system, such as your printer and graphics card. But most important, these applications have the same graphic interface. This is what allowed us to put together a pretty impressive memo—one with a heading that took advantage of Write's fonts and with a graphic from Paint incorporated directly into the text. Later chapters show how to combine information from even more applications, both from Windows applications and from standard applications.

6

PUTTING IT ALL TOGETHER WITH WRITE, PAINT, AND DESKTOP APPLICATIONS

If you've worked through Chapter 5, you know the basics of Write and Paint. You've used Write to draft a letter and Paint to make a graphic to accompany the letter, and you know how to transfer information between these applications.

This chapter doesn't show you any new applications. Instead, it shows you how to use all of the Windows tools together—Write, Paint, and the desktop applications—to accomplish a task.

The sample task we'll use in this chapter assumes you're an office-automation consultant who has been contacted by the office manager of a medical clinic for help. A year ago you were hired to recommend and install computers for the clinic. The clinic currently uses these computers for accounts receivable and word processing. Now the manager wants your expertise again to help computerize another function: management of the pension and profit-sharing accounts. Your job is to write a proposal recommending the software and other services the clinic will need, including installation, customization, training, and support.

You'll use Write to put together the proposal, incorporating some boilerplate text you have in a second Write file. (Boilerplate refers to standard words and phrases used over and over—in this case, some standard paragraphs you use in the proposals you write.) Every client wants his or her job to be your highest priority, to be done right away. So you think a project schedule, in the form of a Gantt chart (a chart displaying the state and duration of activities), would be useful to graphically display the steps involved and the time required for each step. You'll use Paint to construct this chart. And you'll use Terminal to contact an information service for some details you need for the proposal. Then you'll print copies of the proposal and send a copy to each of the doctors and the manager at the clinic, all of whom are listed in Cardfile.

In addition to writing the proposal, you want to track your time. You want to see how long it takes to do the research necessary to put together a proposal and then how long it takes to actually assemble the proposal, so you can factor in these costs. Notepad has a log feature that will make tracking time easier.

So, let's get started. As you work on this task, you'll see that Write, Paint, and the desktop applications are powerful, easy-to-use, and readily available tools, not just for this task, but for much of the work you do daily.

TRACKING TIME WITH NOTEPAD'S LOG FEATURE

If you open a Notepad file and type the four characters *.LOG* at the beginning of the file, each time you open that Notepad file, Windows will stamp it with the current time and date. You'll open a Notepad file containing *.LOG* each time you start working on the proposal and then again at the end of your work (or each time you need to leave this project to work on something else); you'll add a few simple identifying notes so that you'll have a log that tracks the amount of time spent on this proposal and later on the project.

■ *Start Windows and start Notepad.*

> When a new Notepad opens, it opens with the blinking insertion point in the upper left corner.

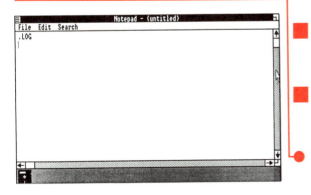

■ *Type:*

.LOG

■ *Press Enter.*

> You must type *.LOG* in capital letters as the first four characters in the file or the log feature won't work.

Chapter 6: Putting It All Together with Write, Paint, and Desktop Applications

Now save this file, close Notepad, and open it
again so you can see how the log feature works and
how to open a file and start an application in one
operation.

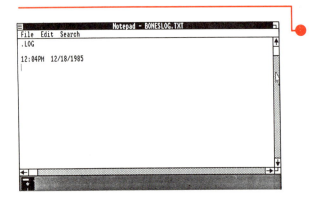 *Choose the Save As... command from the File
menu. Type the name of the file. (In this example,
we'll name the file BONESLOG, because Bones is
the name of the clinic.)*

M *Click the Save button.*

K *Press Enter.*

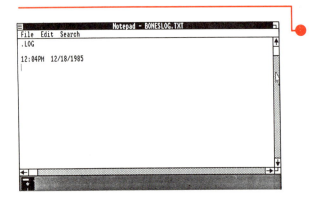 *Now close Notepad.*

Notepad closes and the MS-DOS
Executive window takes over the
work area.

Now to see how the log feature works:

M *Start Notepad and open the BONESLOG file by
double-clicking on the file named BONESLOG.TXT.*

K *Start Notepad and open the BONESLOG file by
selecting the file named BONESLOG.TXT using the
direction keys, and then pressing Enter.*

Windows has the nice feature of
letting you open a file (in this case,
BONESLOG) and the application it
works with (in this case, Notepad)
simply by starting the file.

The BONESLOG file opens and is automatically
stamped with the current time and date.

Instead of closing Notepad and
starting BONESLOG from the
MS-DOS Executive, you could use
the Open... command to start
the BONESLOG or any other
Notepad file.

Notepad automatically stamps the time and date in files beginning with .LOG each time they are opened. If the Notepad file is an icon and you start it by moving it into the work area, the log feature won't work. But you can use the F5 key to enter the time and date.

Let's add a brief note under the date to indicate we're starting our preliminary work on the proposal.

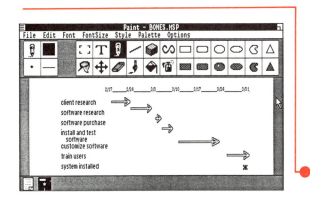

Press Enter to leave a blank line between the date and the text you're about to type.

Now type:

Start preliminary work for Bones proposal[Enter][Enter].

This is all you need Notepad for right now. Leave it as an icon so it will be easy to use again when you finish work on the next phase of the proposal and want to make another entry in the log.

To make Notepad an icon and open the MS-DOS Executive in one step:

M *Drag the MS-DOS Executive icon into the work area.*

K *Press Alt-Tab until the MS-DOS Executive icon is selected. Use Alt-Spacebar-Move and press Enter.*

MAKING A PROJECT SCHEDULE IN PAINT

As mentioned earlier, you've decided that it would be useful to graphically depict the steps involved in this project and the amount of time each will take as part of your proposal. Using the tools in Paint, it is not difficult to make a graphic schedule. And copying the schedule to Write to make it part of the proposal will give the client a visual representation of the project, which will provide the information you need to negotiate both price and time.

You'll use Paint to make a Gantt chart of the schedule that looks something like the one that's shown here.

Chapter 6: Putting It All Together with Write, Paint, and Desktop Applications

Since you've used Paint in Chapter 5 to make a bar chart, rather than giving specific directions in this chapter, I'll just give a general outline and you can experiment and draw the chart on your own.

Start by using the line tool to draw a straight line across the top of the canvas. This is the time line. Then, add the dates, spaced at one-week intervals beginning on February 17 and ending March 31. I used the text tool and 6-point Tms Rmn font for the dates.

Then, add the tasks on the left side of the chart. I used 8-point Helv for the tasks.

Then, draw the arrows that indicate the duration of each task. Use the line tool for the arrow shaft and the filled polygon with the black pattern for the tip (the polygon is the tool that looks like a triangle). Making the arrow tips is an example of a situation where you may prefer using the keyboard instead of the mouse. The keyboard moves the tool pixel by pixel, so it's easier to be accurate; the mouse is more difficult to control for fine movements. After drawing one arrow, you may wish to select the part of the arrow you need for the second task, copy it to the Clipboard, and then paste it where you want it to represent the time for the second task. Copying one arrow will take a fraction of the time it would take to draw each of the six arrows individually. After all the arrows are drawn, select them and use the Trace Edges command from the Edit menu. This transforms them from ordinary arrows into more distinguished models. Use an asterisk rather than an arrow to represent the last task because it has no duration.

As you work, if you need to see more detail (for example, to fix a slight irregularity in your arrow tip), remember the Zoom commands. Move the pointer to the part of the chart you wish to modify and click the mouse or press the Spacebar. Then choose the Zoom In command from the Options menu. Paint will zoom in on that area of the chart. Then make your changes and choose the Zoom Out command to return to a normal-size canvas.

Chapter 6: Putting It All Together with Write, Paint, and Desktop Applications

Create a Gantt chart in Paint and save it in a file called BONES.

> Paint adds the .MSP extension, so you'll be able to recognize it as your graphic for the Bones clinic proposal.

That's all there is to creating the scheduling chart. When pasted into the proposal, it will help the client more clearly understand the tasks and the time required for each.

If you wish, before making the cost schedule, pull Notepad into the work area. This will automatically shrink Paint to an icon. You should see your BONESLOG file in the Notepad window. Windows did not stamp the time and date this time because you didn't open the file: BONESLOG was already open and running as an icon. But you can still stamp it by choosing the Time/Date command from the Edit menu or by pressing F5.

M *Choose Time/Date from the Edit menu.*

K *Press F5.*

After the time and date, press Enter, then type:

Chart completed[Enter][Enter]

Save the updated BONESLOG Notepad file.

> That way, you'll know how long this part of the proposal took. On future proposals it will be easier to decide whether or not you have time to construct a chart like this.

ABOUT...

For Screen vs For Printer

Two of the commands from the Options menu in Microsoft Paint are For Screen and For Printer. When For Printer is selected (the default), the canvas is the size that matches your printer's features. When For Screen is selected, the canvas fills the entire work area and the images may not be displayed as they'll be printed. You can select For Screen only before you use a tool to work on the canvas.

MAKING THE COST SCHEDULE

Now you'll use Write to construct a cost schedule, another module of your proposal. After this, you'll construct the rest of the proposal around the cost schedule. Instructions in the following section are less detailed than the instructions for using Write in Chapter 5, since you now know the basics.

■ *Start Write from the MS-DOS Executive or by dragging its icon up from the icon area if it's already loaded.*

■ *Choose Centered from the Paragraph menu and type the title in all capital letters:*

COST SCHEDULE

Make all your titles boldface so they stand out.

■ *Select the title* COST SCHEDULE, *and choose the Bold command from the Character menu.*

M *Click to get an insertion point at the end of the line containing the title.*

K *Press the End key to move the insertion point to the end of the line containing the title.*

■ *Press Enter twice for two blank lines under the line containing the title.*

■ *Choose Normal from the Paragraph menu to change the paragraph alignment from centered and choose Normal from the Character menu to change the font style from Bold.*

Now you need to set tabs and then enter the cost-schedule information. (Instructions for setting tabs are given here in detail because tabs were not covered in Chapter 5.)

■ *Choose Tab... from the Document menu.*

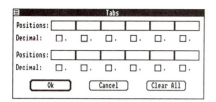

You'll see a dialog box like the one shown here.

You need to enter two tabs, a normal (left-aligned) tab at .5 inches and a decimal-aligned tab at 4.5 inches. Decimal tabs line up numbers on the decimal point. Notice that the blinking insertion point is in the first Positions box.

■ *Type:*

.5

This is the number of inches from the left margin you want the first tab to be set.

Underneath the first Position box is a Decimal box. The first tab will be a standard left-aligned tab, so you can bypass the Decimal box.

M *Click in the second Position box.*

K *Press the Tab key twice to move to the second Position box.*

■ *Type:*

4.5

This is the number of inches from the left margin that you want the second tab.

The second tab stop is a decimal tab (you want the numbers aligned on their decimal points).

M *Click in the decimal box beneath the 4.5. Then click the Ok button.*

K *Press the Tab key to move to the Decimal box. Press the Spacebar to choose Decimal. Press Enter.*

Now that the tabs are set where you want them, it will be easy to enter the cost-schedule information (all but the subtotals and total, which you'll calculate and enter a little later).

■ *Start by entering the following cost-schedule information:*

> *Software[Enter][Enter]*
> *[Tab]Microsoft Windows[Tab] 99.00[Enter]*
> *[Enter]*
> *[Tab]Closed Systems accounting*
> *software[Enter]*
> *[Tab]General Ledger[Tab]*
> *1,065.00[Enter][Enter]*
> *[Tab]Subtotal:[Enter][Enter][Enter] Subtotal*
> *Software Support[Enter][Enter]*
> *System installation[Tab] included[Enter]*
> *[Tab]System customization (80 hours)[Tab]*
> *5,200.00[Enter]*
> *[Tab]Software training (40 hours)[Tab]*
> *1,600.00[Enter]*
> *[Tab]Travel (Sun Valley)[Enter]*
> *[Tab]Telephone support (6 months)[Tab]*
> *included[Enter][Enter]*
> *[Tab]Subtotal:[Enter][Enter] subtotal*
> *TOTAL Software and Support:[Enter]*

■ *Make the last line boldface so the "bottom line" stands out.*

There is one figure we need before we can add up the costs: the airfare to Sun Valley. Instead of calling a travel agent, let's use Windows' Terminal program and dial the Official Airline Guide (OAG) to find the best fare.

Using the OAG

The OAG is a specialized electronic service that provides airline fare and schedule information. You can access it directly or through another service, such as NewsNet. Like NewsNet, the OAG requires a password and an identification number. If you have a NewsNet password and identification number, but not OAG ones, use your NewsNet account. If you have a separate OAG account, it's better to use that. That way, you won't have to pay both NewsNet and OAG charges.

Run Terminal on the right half of the screen and keep Write on the left half, so you can see both the OAG information and part of the Cost Schedule at the same time.

■ *Start Terminal by positioning its icon on the right border of Write's work area.*

■ *After dialing the OAG, you will be prompted for your identification number and password.*

■ *After you see the opening instructions, type:*

/S

■ *Press Enter to see schedule information.*

OAG will prompt you for the rest of the information it needs: departure city (in this example, Seattle), destination city (in this example, Sun Valley), and departure date (in this example, 3/17/86).

■ *When prompted for a return date, you can type 3/31 (and cross your fingers that you will actually finish on target), or press Enter to leave the departure date open.*

OAG will display a list of available flights.

If you'd like further information about any item, type *X* and the number of the line you'd like expanded on. In this example, if I wanted to see expanded information for the 7:00 flight, I'd type *x1* and press Enter to have OAG display this information.

■ *Now, to see fares associated with these flights, type:*

F

■ *Press Enter.*

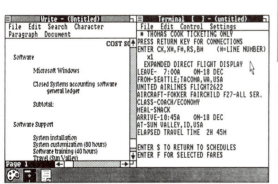

SECTION 3
Chapter 6: Putting It All Together with Write, Paint, and Desktop Applications

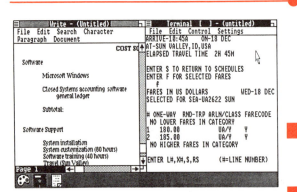

■ *Respond to the prompts indicating what types of fares you're interested in.*

OAG will then display fare information.

It looks like the one-way fare from Seattle to Sun Valley will be $185, so include a round-trip cost of $370 in the Cost Schedule. (There are no round-trip fares for this destination.)

That's all you need from the OAG.

■ *Type:*

/Q

■ *Press Enter to quit.*

This disconnects you from the OAG, but you still need to leave the network, if you're using one.

■ *Choose the Connect... command from the Controls menu and, when you see the dialog box with the "Are you sure you want to disconnect?" message, click Yes or press Enter.*

Now that you have the information you need, leave Terminal, add the airfare to the cost schedule, and total the costs.

■ *Close Terminal.*

Write expands to fill the work area.

■ *Now add the airfare ($370) to the cost column.*

This is the price of a round-trip ticket to Sun Valley.

Now all that's left to complete the Cost Schedule is to total the costs. You can use Calculator for this.

■ *Open Calculator on the left half of the screen.*

M *Click in the Write window to make it active.*

K *Press Alt-Tab until the title bar at the top of the Write window turns dark.*

Now Write is the active Window.

You need to scroll this window to the right until you can see the column of figures you want to total.

M *Click the horizontal scroll arrow in the lower right corner of the Write window until you can see the cost column.*

K *Continue pressing the right direction key until you can see the cost column.*

Your screen should look something like the one shown here.

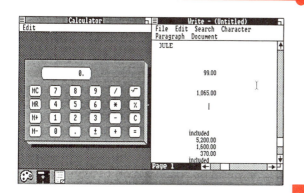

You can enter these numbers into Calculator as before by using the mouse or the numeric keypad. But a quicker way is to select the number from the proposal, choose the Copy command to copy it to the Clipboard, and then paste it into Calculator with the Paste command on Calculator's Edit menu. Then use the + key (on the screen or on the keyboard) and copy in the next value. When you're finished, use the = key for a total.

■ *Make the Calculator window active.*

■ *Subtotal the software amounts.*

Calculator displays the result.

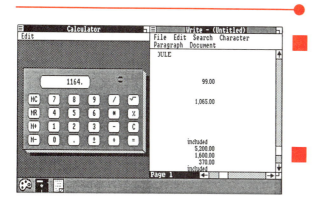

■ *Make the Write window active. Enter this subtotal:*

$1,164.00

You can enter this figure by typing it or by pasting it from the Clipboard.

■ *Add a dollar sign, the comma, and the zeroes after the decimal point. Then select the number and make it boldface.*

Use Calculator to compute the Software Support subtotal. Copy the total ($7,170.00) into the appropriate place in the cost column. Then select it and make it boldface.

Now use Calculator one last time to get the total software and support costs. The support costs are still displayed in Calculator. Simply press the plus key, enter the software costs (1164), and press the equal sign key.

Calculator displays the grand total.

Copy the grand total into the bottom line of the proposal TOTAL Software and Support. *Press Tab to move to the cost column and type the grand total:*

$8,334.00

Give the grand total both the boldface and underline formats so it's easy to locate.

Now the Cost Schedule part is completed.

Close Calculator and then save the proposal as BONESPRO.

You might also wish to update the time log in Notepad so you know how long the Cost Schedule took. To do this:

Position the Notepad icon in the middle of the Write work area. Notepad expands and fills the screen. Your Write file BONESPRO is now an icon.

M *Choose Time/Date from the Edit menu.*

K *Press F5 to add the time and date.*

Type:

Cost Schedule completed

Your screen should now look like the one shown here.

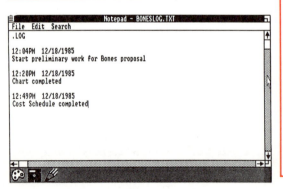

■ *Then return the Notepad to an icon.*

We'll use Notepad one last time when we finish the proposal.

The last major task is to assemble the other parts of the proposal. The Bones proposal will have these seven parts:

Hardware Description
Software Description
User Training
Conversion Support
Testing, Installation, and Customization
Project Schedule
Relevant Andrews and Goodman Experience

Some of the information for a proposal, particularly the hardware and software descriptions, is unique to each proposal, and you'll have to construct these parts for each one. But information in four sections (User Training; Conversion Support; Testing, Installation, and Customization; and Relevant Andrews and Goodman Experience) really doesn't vary too much from proposal to proposal. So it's best to have these boilerplate paragraphs in another Write file called PROPOSLS.DOC. Then, when you assemble a proposal, you can just copy in the relevant paragraphs at the proper places, and your proposal will be finished much more quickly than if you had to enter each part by hand. If you actually had a consulting business like Andrews and Goodman, you would probably already have a PROPOSLS.DOC file. So, for the sake of our example, create this file now and you will be ready to add it to the body of the proposal.

■ *Open a new Write file and type the following:*

USER TRAINING[Enter][Enter]
User training is perhaps the most important factor in the success of any computer installation. This training involves how to use the application software. It is facilitated by

the teaching materials prepared by Andrews and Goodman and the software vendors.
[Enter][Enter]

Andrews and Goodman personnel will conduct all training sessions. The general training approach is to introduce users to a subject area, include any relevant teaching aids, and then allow users to work at their own pace until the material is familiar. Training concludes with a follow-up session to answer questions and reinforce the material. Andrews and Goodman feel that hands-on training is the most valuable; consequently, all the training will be hands-on.
[Enter][Enter]

To further assist with the training and support, Andrews and Goodman will prepare a procedures manual specifically for you. This will serve as an overall guide to using this system. When appropriate, Andrews and Goodman will also provide teaching aids to supplement the documentation provided with the software.
[Enter][Enter][Enter]

CONVERSION SUPPORT[Enter][Enter]

It is extremely important to plan the conversion from the manual system carefully. This includes developing and documenting manual procedures, preparing conversion forms, ordering any required pre-printed forms, monitoring the conversion effort, and checking the results of the first period of processing.
[Enter][Enter]

Andrews and Goodman personnel will work closely with your designated employees in all phases of the conversion effort to ensure an orderly transition to the new system.
[Enter][Enter]

After the conversion, it is essential that the software be supported. This includes answering user questions and assisting with troubleshooting. Normally, most of the support is needed during the first few weeks after the conversion. The software fee paid to Andrews and Goodman includes complete ongoing

SECTION 3
Chapter 6: Putting It All Together with Write, Paint, and Desktop Applications

support for a period of six months. Subsequent
software support, if desired, is available for
$875.00 per year.[Enter][Enter][Enter]
TESTING, INSTALLATION, AND
CUSTOMIZATION[Enter][Enter]
Both before and after installation, the software
will be thoroughly tested by Andrews and
Goodman. Then they will customize it to
the specifics of your organization.
[Enter][Enter][Enter]
RELEVANT ANDREWS AND GOODMAN
EXPERIENCE[Enter][Enter]
An important factor in selecting a system is
the experience of the vendor with similar
installations. Andrews and Goodman has
extensive experience with systems similar to the
one in this proposal. All of our installations have
been very successful. A list of Andrews and
Goodman references will be furnished upon
request.[Enter]

■   *Center and boldface the headings.*

■   *Choose Save As... from the File menu and, for a*
name, type:

PROPOSLS

We'll start the Bones proposal by making the
title page. We'll build the proposal above the Cost
Schedule section of the BONESPRO Write file, and
when we finish, the Cost Schedule will be our proposal's last page.

■   *Drag the Write icon above the icon area and*
expand the BONESPRO window.

■   *Type the name and address of the consulting firm*
at the top of the title page:

ANDREWS AND GOODMAN   1111-3rd Avenue
Seattle, WA 98101

■   *Change the name of the firm to a larger font size so*
it stands out.

Chapter 6: Putting It All Together with Write, Paint,
and Desktop Applications

■ *Next, select the entire top line, choose Bold from the Character menu, then choose Center from the Paragraph menu.*

Boldface lettering will give the cover a more distinctive look.

■ *Now press the Enter key eight times for seven blank lines and type the first part of the proposal title:*

Proposal for:

■ *Then press Enter twice for a blank line and type:*

Bones Orthopedic and Fracture Clinic[Enter]
4301 Skilift Road[Enter]
Sun Valley, Idaho 87111[Enter][Enter][Enter]
[Enter][Enter][Enter][Enter]

■ *Center these five lines.*

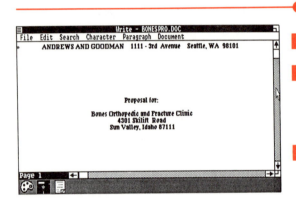

Your title page looks as shown here.

■ *Enlarge the title and make it bold.*

■ *Next, type the table of contents.*

This is a short proposal, so the table of contents will fit on the title page.

■ *Type:*

CONTENTS[Enter][Enter]

Notice that the word *CONTENTS* is centered. Write keeps the same alignment until you change it.

■ *Make CONTENTS bold.*

■ *Change the alignment back to Left.*

■ *Type the text for the table of contents:*

[Tab]Hardware Description[Enter][Enter]
[Tab]Software Description[Enter][Enter]

Chapter 6: Putting It All Together with Write, Paint, and Desktop Applications

[Tab]User Training[Enter][Enter]
[Tab]Conversion Support[Enter][Enter]
[Tab]Testing, Installation, and
Customization[Enter][Enter]
[Tab]Project Schedule[Enter][Enter]
[Tab]Relevant Andrews and Goodman
Experience[Enter][Enter]
[Tab]Cost Schedule

We'll add the page numbers when we
finish the proposal and know where
the page breaks are.

You want a new page to start when you begin the
body of the proposal, the next section.

After you've typed the last entry (Cost Schedule),
hold down the Ctrl key and press Enter to specify a
page break.

This is the end of the title page.
Write puts a dotted line on the
screen, indicating the page break.

Next, you need to type the Hardware Description
and Software Description sections.

Enter the following hardware and software
descriptions:

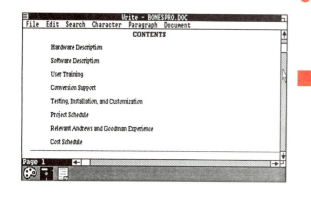

HARDWARE DESCRIPTION[Enter][Enter]
Andrews and Goodman will use Bones Clinic's
existing hardware, a single-user system with
adequate disk storage both for existing
applications and the application included in
this proposal.[Enter][Enter][Enter]
SOFTWARE DESCRIPTION[Enter][Enter]
The following software is proposed:
[Enter][Enter]
[Tab]Microsoft Windows[Enter]
[Tab]Closed Systems general-ledger
accounting software for pension accounting
[Enter][Enter][Enter]
Microsoft Windows[Enter][Enter]
Andrews and Goodman recommends Microsoft

SECTION 3
Chapter 6: Putting It All Together with Write, Paint,
and Desktop Applications

Windows. Microsoft Windows is necessary to run the Closed Systems accounting software. And Windows makes this software easier to learn and use.[Enter][Enter]
Previous software installed by Andrews and Goodman will run with Microsoft Windows. [Enter][Enter][Enter]
Pension Accounting Software[Enter][Enter]
The proposed accounting software is Closed Systems, which is one of the most widely used accounting packages on several minicomputers. Four years ago, it was converted to run on several microcomputer systems, including yours. Just this year, it was redesigned to run with Microsoft Windows. This software has a large installed base (over 20,000) and is extremely well tested and documented. It is very flexible and suited to a wide range of organizations.[Enter][Enter]
The following modules are currently available: general ledger, accounts payable, accounts receivable, payroll, sales order, inventory, and job costing.[Enter][Enter]
The Closed Systems general-ledger software meets all the requirements for your pension accounting system.[Enter]

■ *Center the titles* HARDWARE DESCRIPTION *and* SOFTWARE DESCRIPTION *and make them boldface.*

■ *Press Ctrl-Enter to put a page break at the end of this section.*

That way, the next section will start on a new page.

The next group of sections (User Training; Conversion Support; Testing, Installation, and Customization; and Relevant Andrews and Goodman Experience) are the boilerplate sections you can take directly from the file named PROPOSLS.DOC you created earlier. Windows will let you have more than one Write window open at the same time, so you can select from the PROPOSLS file, copy to the

SECTION 3
Chapter 6: Putting It All Together with Write, Paint, and Desktop Applications

Clipboard, and paste into the BONESPRO file without having to open and close applications in the middle of copying and pasting. It's easiest if you first move the insertion point to just below the page break. That way, it will be in the right position when you paste; you won't need to move it first.

Move the MS-DOS Executive icon to the bottom border of the Write window to open the MS-DOS Executive window.

Start the Write file named PROPOSLS.DOC.

You want all the information in this file in your proposal, so you can copy in the entire file at once. If you didn't want all the information in a boilerplate file, you would select the sections you wanted one by one and copy them in the order you wanted them in the proposal.

To select the entire document:

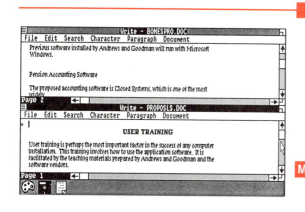

M *Move the mouse to the left edge of the PROPOSLS window. When the I-beam pointer becomes an arrow pointer, hold down the Ctrl key and click. This selects the entire document.*

K *Press the GoTo and Home keys to move the insertion point to the beginning of the document. Hold down the Shift key and press the GoTo key and then the End key. This selects the entire document.*

Choose the Copy command from the Edit menu to copy this document into the Clipboard.

Make the BONESPRO window active and choose Paste from the Edit menu.

Windows copies the information from the Clipboard (in this case, the PROPOSLS document) into the active document starting at the insertion point—a fairly easy way to add an entire section of information to the proposal.

You're finished with the PROPOSLS file.

SECTION 3
Chapter 6: Putting It All Together with Write, Paint, and Desktop Applications

■ *Close the PROPOSLS file to free up the memory it requires and to give the entire work area to your current proposal.*

Now you need to add one sentence to the boiler-plate text to customize it for the Bones Clinic job. Then you'll add the project schedule you created earlier in Paint.

■ *Move the insertion point to the end of the Testing, Installation, and Customization paragraph and add this sentence:*

They will set up and install the general ledger to meet your specific pension accounting needs.

■ *Press Ctrl-Enter to add a page break after this sentence. The project schedule will appear on the next page.*

■ *Type the title of this section in all capital letters:*

PROJECT SCHEDULE

■ *Center the title and make it bold. Then press Enter twice and change the alignment option from Centered back to Left.*

Now you need to open Paint, select the schedule, copy it to the Clipboard, and then paste it into the proposal right here. Because Paint allows you to select only what you can see on the canvas, you need to let Paint have the entire work area, select the schedule, then close Paint and use Write again.

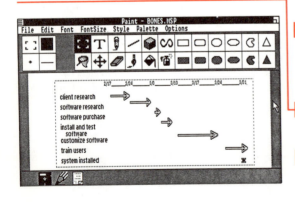

■ *Start the Paint file, BONES.MSP.*

Paint opens with the schedule on the screen and Write becomes an icon.

■ *Select the schedule with the selection rectangle. Copy it to the Clipboard.*

■ *Close Paint and move the Write icon back into the work area to restart Write.*

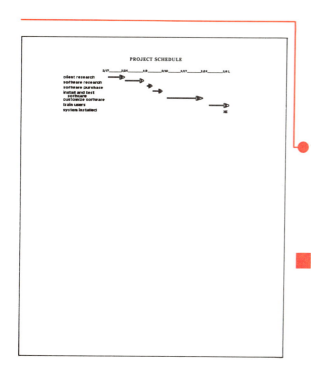

The insertion point should be two lines below the title *PROJECT SCHEDULE*. This is where the upper left corner of the schedule will be pasted.

■ *Choose Paste from the Edit menu.*

> In a few seconds, your schedule will be pasted in.

The schedule looks a little squashed, but it is the size it will be when printed, and you may adjust it with the size Picture command from the Edit menu if you wish. Select the schedule and center it. If you printed it on a laser printer, it would look like the one shown here.

Now the proposal is just about finished. You can add a header with page numbers and a footer with the name of the firm and the date, add page numbers to the table of contents, and you'll be ready to print the entire proposal.

■ *Choose the Header... command from the Document menu.*

> As the dialog box appears, the Write window is replaced by the Header window (notice that the title bar now reads *HEADER*). The Header window is the place you type the text of the header.

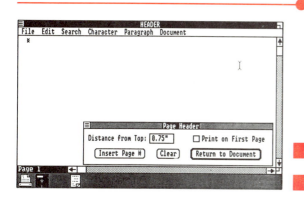

All you want in the header this time is the word *Page* and the correct page number. You want this information right-aligned. The blinking insertion point is in the upper left corner of the Header window. To make the headers match the text, make them Tms Rmn.

■ *Choose Tms Rmn from the Character menu.*

■ *Type:*

Page

Type a space. Choose the Right command from the Paragraph menu and Write will align the page number on the right margin.

Now you need to complete the necessary information in the dialog box. Don't put a check mark in the Print On First Page box because you don't want this header on the title page. Accept Write's default placement for the header of .75 inches from the top.

M *Click the Insert Page # button. (Notice that Write adds (page) to your header. When your document is printed, Write will replace this word with the current page number.) Click the Return To Document button.*

K *Press Alt-Tab to make the header dialog box active. Press the Tab key until the blinking underscore is under the Insert Page # button. Press the Spacebar, and Write will add (page) to the header and replace this with the current page number when the document is printed. Press the Tab key two more times until the blinking underscore is beneath the Return To Document button, and press Enter.*

Write takes you back to the proposal and will take care of the details of the header when it prints.

Now you'll add a footer with the name of the firm and the date.

Choose the Footer... command from the Document menu.

Just as with the Header... command, a dialog box similar to the Header dialog box appears and the Write window becomes the Footer window.

As with the header text, you want the footer text to match the body of the proposal.

Choose Tms Rmn from the Character menu.

■ *Type the footer:*

Prepared by Andrews and Goodman[Tab]
[Tab][Tab] January 1986

■ *Complete the dialog box as shown here.*

Write will place this text on the
bottom of every page, including the
first page, when it prints.

Now all that's left before printing is to add page
numbers to the table of contents.

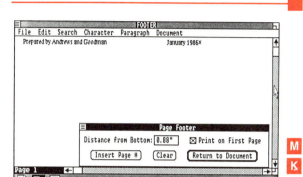

M

K *Scroll up until you can see the table of contents.*

*Press the GoTo key and then the Home key to move
to the beginning of the proposal. Press PgDn so you
can see the table of contents.*

You need to set one more tab so you can line
up the page numbers closer to the right margin.

■ *Choose the Tabs... command from the Document
menu. Make the third tab 5.5 inches, then click Ok
or press Enter.*

This third tab can be a regular rather
than a decimal tab.

■ *Move the insertion point to just after the first entry
in the table of contents, press the Tab key twice, and
type the page number for Hardware Description:*

2

■ *Continue adding these page numbers:*

Hardware Description   2
Software Description   2
User Training   3
Conversion Support   3
Testing, Installation, and Customization   3
Project Schedule   4
Relevant Andrews and Goodman Experience   4
Cost Schedule   4

SECTION 3
Chapter 6: Putting It All Together with Write, Paint,
and Desktop Applications

Your proposal is complete and ready to print.

■ *Choose the Save command from the File menu to save these additions.*

Before printing it, you may wish to make one last entry in the BONESLOG file, indicating the time. Then you'll have a record of the total time it took you to put together the proposal, and a breakdown of the time spent on each part.

■ *Move the Notepad icon from the icon area into the work area and press Enter twice.*

M *Choose Time/Date from the Edit menu.*

K *Press F5 to have the time and date inserted.*

■ *Type this text:*

Proposal assembled and ready to print

Now, if you wish, you can compute total elapsed time, or, if you're really eager to see the printed proposal, you can leave the computations for later. Once the proposal is accepted and you begin working on the job, you can use the log in the same way to track hours worked. You can use the information to be sure your bids cover proposal development time, as well as actual project work. That way, you can make necessary revisions on future bids.
Now to print the proposal:

■ *Move the Write icon back into the work area. Be sure your printer is ready to go, and choose the Print... command from the File menu.*

If you printed it on a laser printer, your completed proposal, which you've assembled using many of Windows' tools, would look like the one shown on the next page.

Page 1

ANDREWS AND GOODMAN   1111 - 3rd Avenue   Seattle, WA 98101

Proposal for:

Bones Orthopedic and Fracture Clinic
4301 Skillift Road
Sun Valley, Idaho 87111

CONTENTS

Prepared by Andrews and Goodman   January 1986

Page 2

HARDWARE DESCRIPTION

Andrews and Goodman will use the Bones Clinic's existing hardware, a single-user system with adequate disk storage both for existing applications and the application included in this proposal.

SOFTWARE DESCRIPTION

The following software is proposed:

    Microsoft Windows
    Closed Systems general-ledger accounting software for pension accounting

Microsoft Windows

Andrews and Goodman recommend Microsoft Windows. Microsoft Windows is necessary to run the Closed Systems accounting software. And Windows makes this software easier to learn and use.

Previous software installed by Andrews and Goodman will run with Microsoft Windows.

Pension Accounting Software

The proposed accounting software is Closed Systems, which is one of the most widely used accounting packages on several minicomputers. Four years ago, it was converted to run on several microcomputer systems, including yours. Just this year, it was redesigned to run with Microsoft Windows. This software has a large installed base (over 20,000) and is extremely well-tested and documented. It is very flexible and suited to a wide range of organizations.

The following modules are currently available: general ledger, accounts payable, accounts receivable, payroll, sales order, inventory, and job costing.

The Closed Systems general-ledger software meets all the requirements for your pension accounting system.

Prepared by Andrews and Goodman   January 1986

Page 3

USER TRAINING

User training is perhaps the most important factor in the success of any computer installation. This training involves how to use the application software. It is facilitated by the teaching materials prepared by Andrews and Goodman and the software vendors.

Andrews and Goodman personnel will conduct all training sessions. The general training approach is to introduce users to a subject area, include any relevant teaching aids, and then allow users to work at their own pace until the material is familiar. Training concludes with a follow-up session to answer questions and reinforce the material. Andrews and Goodman feel that hands-on training is the most valuable; consequently, all the training will be hands-on.

To further assist with the training and support, Andrews and Goodman will prepare a procedures manual specifically for you. This will serve as an overall guide to using this system. When appropriate, Andrews and Goodman will also provide teaching aids to supplement the documentation provided with the software.

CONVERSION SUPPORT

It is extremely important to plan the conversion from the manual pension system carefully. This includes developing and documenting manual procedures, preparing conversion forms, ordering any required pre-printed forms, monitoring the conversion effort, and checking the results of the first period of processing.

Andrews and Goodman personnel will work closely with your designated employees in all phases of the conversion effort to ensure an orderly transition to the new system.

After the conversion, it is essential that the software be supported. This includes answering user questions and assisting with troubleshooting. Normally, most of the support is needed during the first few weeks after the conversion. The software fee paid to Andrews and Goodman includes complete ongoing support for a period of six months. Subsequent software support, if desired, is available for $875.00 per year.

TESTING, INSTALLATION, AND CUSTOMIZATION

Both before and after installation, the software will be thoroughly tested by Andrews and Goodman. Then they will customize it to the specifics of your organization. They will set up and install the general ledger to meet your specific pension accounting needs.

Prepared by Andrews and Goodman   January 1986

Page 4

PROJECT SCHEDULE

RELEVANT ANDREWS AND GOODMAN EXPERIENCE

An important factor in selecting a system is the experience of the vendor with similar installations. Andrews and Goodman has extensive experience with systems similar to the one in this proposal. All of our installations have been very successful. A list of Andrews and Goodman references will be furnished on request.

COST SCHEDULE

Software	
Microsoft Windows	99.00
Closed Systems accounting software	
general ledger	1,065.00
Subtotal:	**$1,164.00**
Software Support	
System installation	included
System customization (80 hours)	5,200.00
Software training (40 hours)	1,600.00
Travel (Sun Valley)	370.00
Telephone support (6 months)	included
Subtotal:	**$7,170.00**
TOTAL Software and Support:	**$8,334.00**

Prepared by Andrews and Goodman   January 1986

The completed proposal for the Bones Clinic

Working with Windows like this makes assembling a proposal or any other document much easier than if you started at the beginning and typed in everything by hand. Using Terminal and the OAG for airfare information is quick and easy, and you can do it without ever closing the window containing the proposal. Using Calculator to total expenses is handy. Keeping standard boilerplate paragraphs in a separate Write file is a good idea for anyone who puts together information with similar parts. And adding a graphic (in this case, a visual schedule), which is easy to do with Paint, makes the proposal more informative and better looking.

There is one last Windows tool you could use. If you have a client list in Cardfile, all you need to do is bring the card for this client to the front of the cards. Then you could print this card, write a cover letter to accompany the proposal, and mail a proposal and cover letter to the clinic manager and each of the doctors and you're finished.

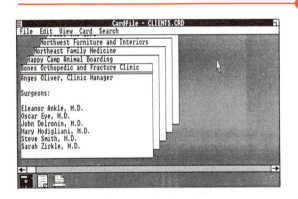

SECTION 3
Chapter 6: Putting It All Together with Write, Paint,
and Desktop Applications

7

RUNNING ADVANCED WINDOWS APPLICATIONS

This chapter previews several different types of Windows applications: a drawing program, a spreadsheet, a filing program, a desktop-publishing program, a typesetting program, a program used to design information-processing systems, and a testing program for manufacturers of electronic products. We'll take an in-depth look at one of these programs: Micrografx's In·a·Vision, a sophisticated drawing program. This is not an exhaustive list of all the Windows products that are currently available or that will be available in the near future. Several major software developers, including Lotus Development Corporation and Living Videotext, Incorporated, have announced that they support Windows and are developing Windows products. Rather, it is a sampling of different types of products which demonstrates a variety of ways the Windows interface can be used.

MICROGRAFX'S IN·A·VISION

First let's take a close look at a Windows application: In·a·Vision by Micrografx. In·a·Vision is a sophisticated computer-aided drawing package. In·a·Vision is described by Micrografx as a state-of-the-art drawing/CAD (computer-aided design) program. Designed around Windows' graphic interface, it is intended to be easy enough for business people to use for creating organizational and flow charts, but sophisticated enough for architects and engineers.

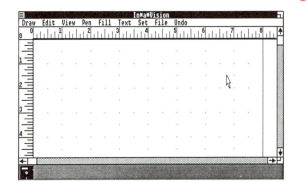

Graphic user interface

When you start In·a·Vision, you see an initial screen that looks as shown here. You'll notice that In·a·Vision conforms to the Windows graphic user interface. It has the title bar at the top of the window, the menu bar, the work area surrounded by scroll bars, and the icon area below.

This graphic user interface is the same as the other Windows applications you've already used (Microsoft Write and Paint and the desktop applications), which should make In·a·Vision easy for you to learn and use.

Getting an overview

It's easy to get an overview of a Windows application by looking at the commands on its menus. Spend a few minutes pulling down In·a·Vision's menus. Experiment by using some of the tools and patterns and making some practice drawings to get a feel for the program. If you find a command you can't figure out, the In·a·Vision manual has an excellent command reference section; it's easy to locate information you need for a specific command.

You may have noticed two more obvious places where In·a·Vision differs from other Windows applications we've used. The File menu (which has the standard File menu commands to load, save, and print a file) is not the leftmost menu; it's second from the right. And it contains Cut, Paste, and Copy commands, which are usually found on the Edit menu. On the far right is the Undo menu, which is really more of a button than a menu. Clicking on it undoes your last action.

Using In·a·Vision

After you've experimented a bit, you're ready for a simple project. Let's say you've agreed to give a short talk about Windows to an informal users' group at your company tomorrow. The group is made up largely of programmers, and they want some technical information. You'd like to talk without extensive notes, but think if you had some overhead transparencies, you could use them to stay on track and they would add some visual interest, as well. You can use some of In·a·Vision's simpler features to make these transparencies quickly and easily. We'll make two transparencies that look like the ones shown here.

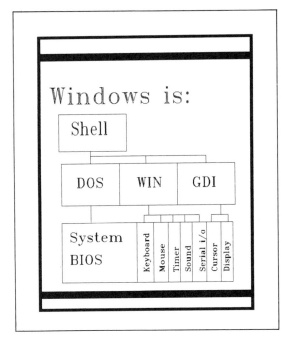

■ *Start In·a·Vision.*

First we'll make the frames or borders for the transparencies. It's easier to do this if we can see the entire page.

■ *Choose Current Page from the View menu.*

The display changes to show two pages.

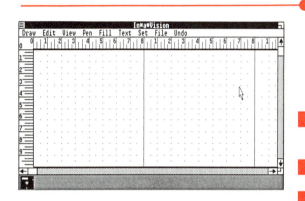

We'll draw the border with the Rectangle command from the Draw menu. Then we'll add the decorative stripe at the top and bottom. Then we can select this frame and copy it for the second page.

■ *Choose the 1/10 in. wide pen-width command from the Pen menu.*

■ *Choose Rectangle from the Draw menu.*

■ *Start in the upper left corner of the page and draw a rectangle that just surrounds the outside grid marks.*

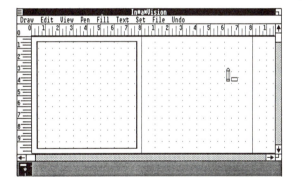

You draw In·a·Vision rectangles the same way you draw rectangles in Paint. If you have a mouse, you start in the upper left corner, hold down the mouse button, and then drag down and right. With the keyboard, you hold down the Spacebar and use the direction keys to expand the rectangle. A nice feature in In·a·Vision for keyboard users is the ability to move diagonally with the direction keys. To move diagonally, press one of the keys on the corners of the numeric keypad (Home, PgUp, PgDn, and End).

Now copy this rectangle so the second transparency will have an identical frame.

M *Click anywhere inside the rectangle to select it.*

K *Move the pointer inside the rectangle and press the Spacebar to select it.*

Choose the Copy command from the Edit menu.

M *Hold down the mouse button and drag the selected rectangle to page two. Position it where you want it.*

K *Hold down the Spacebar and use the direction keys to move a copy of the rectangle to page two. Position the rectangle where you want it.*

Now draw the stripes, using a wider pen width.

Choose ¼ in. wide from the Pen menu. Choose Horz/Vert Line from the Draw menu.

The Horz/Vert Line command makes it easy to create horizontal and vertical lines without precise mouse movements.

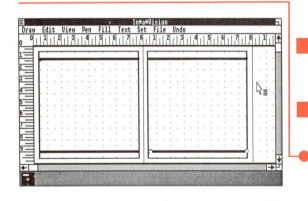

Position the pen on the 1-inch horizontal grid line and draw a stripe across the top of the first page about ¼ inch below the top border.

Now draw a stripe across the bottom of the page on the 9-inch grid line and then either draw two more stripes across the top and bottom of page two or copy the stripes just as you copied the rectangle.

Next, type the text for the first page.

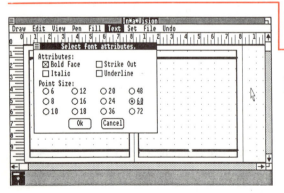

Choose the Set Attributes... command from the Text menu. Complete the dialog box by indicating Bold Face text in 60-point size.

Choose the Text command from the Draw menu, place the pointer approximately where you want the W of Windows to go, and click the mouse button or press the Spacebar.

■ *Type this text:*

Windows is:

In·a·Vision's default font is the Roman graphic font. Using a graphic font allows you to select text, move it, and size it, just as if it were an object you had drawn.

M *Select the text you just typed by clicking on it.*

K *Select the text you just typed by moving the pointer anywhere in the text and pressing the Spacebar.*

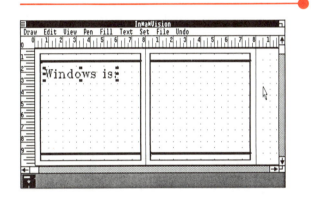

Notice that In·a·Vision puts dots around the selected text or object. These are called handles. (You can remove the handles by clicking the mouse button when the pointer is in a blank area of the screen or pressing the Spacebar.)

You can move this text around by holding down the mouse button and dragging it or by holding down the Spacebar and using the direction keys. You can also use the handles to size the selected text. If you drag it from one of the bottom handles, it will grow longer. If you use one of the side handles, it will grow wider, and if you use a corner handle, it will grow or shrink proportionally in both directions.

■ *Use the handles to position and size the text until it is exactly the way you want it.*

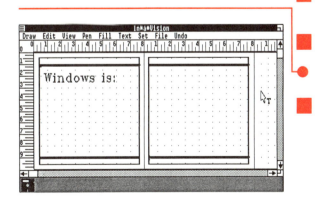

■ *Click or press the Spacebar while the pointer is in a blank area of the screen to deselect this text and remove the handles.*

■ *Choose the Set Attributes... command from the Text menu and choose a smaller font size, 36 point, for the next part of the transparency.*

Now choose the Text command from the Draw menu and type these three lines below the line that reads Windows is:

A User Friendly Shell[Enter][Enter]

OS Extensions[Enter][Enter]

An Extended BIOS

Select each line, position it properly, and, if you wish, change its size.

When you complete the first transparency, your screen will look something like the one shown here.

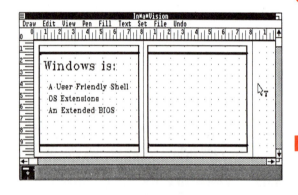

Now make the boxes and text for the second transparency.

The text at the top of the second transparency is the same as the text on the top of the first one, so instead of retyping it, simply select it and copy it to page two.

Select the text that reads Windows is:. *Choose the Copy command from the Edit menu. Use the mouse or the Spacebar and direction keys to position the text on the top of the second page.*

You can also hold down the Shift key and drag an object to copy it.

Next, draw the three large rectangles. Sizing and positioning them is easy because of the visible grid. You can use the horizontal/vertical line tool to divide them later.

Choose Fine from the Pen menu to have the rectangles drawn with the default fine-width line.

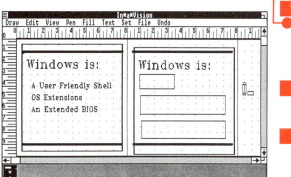

Choose Rectangle from the Draw menu.

The keyboard shortcut for the Rectangle command (In·a·Vision calls these shortcuts "accelerator keys") is Ctrl-R.

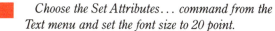

Now draw three rectangles that look like the ones shown here.

Now comes a fun part: creating the vertical text.

Choose the Set Attributes . . . command from the Text menu and set the font size to 20 point.

Choose text from the Draw menu or press Ctrl-T. Position the text pointer in the bottom rectangle, and put the insertion point there.

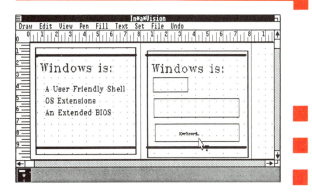

Type the first word to be aligned vertically:

Keyboard

It's easier to work with text this size if the drawing is larger.

Select the word Keyboard.

Choose View Actual Size from the View menu.

Choose Rotate Left from the Edit menu.

Automatically, the word *Keyboard* changes to the alignment you want.

Now position Keyboard *exactly where you want it.*

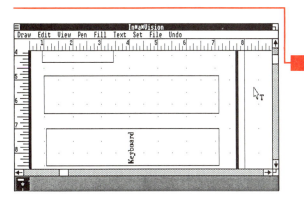

■ *Follow these same steps for the rest of the words on the first page:*

Mouse	Serial i/o
Timer	Cursor
Sound	Display

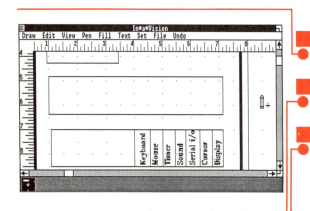

■ *Now use the Horz/Vert Line command from the Draw menu to draw lines that separate these words.*

■ *Separate the second rectangle into three parts with the Horz/Vert Line tool.*

■ *Now draw the connecting lines between the three rectangles, as shown here.*

The Horz/Vert tool makes drawing these lines easy. But if you make a mistake, don't forget the Undo menu. It works like a button. Just click it and it will undo your last step.

The last step is to add text for the larger boxes.

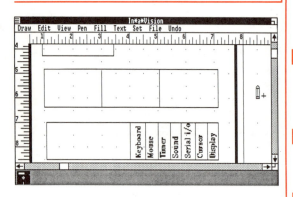

■ *Use the Set Attributes... command on the Text menu to set the Point Size.*

I used 48-point text for these boxes.

■ *In the top box, type:*

Shell

■ *In the first box in the second row, type:*

DOS

■ *In the second box, type:*

WIN

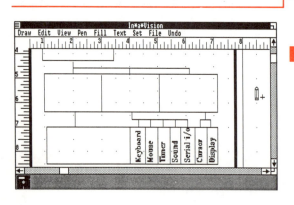

■ *In the third box, type:*

GDI

> GDI stands for Graphic Device
> Interface.

■ *In the first box in the third row, type:*

System BIOS

If you need to change the position of any of the
text, select it and move it where you want it.

■ *Change the view to Current Page and your screen
will look like the one shown here.*

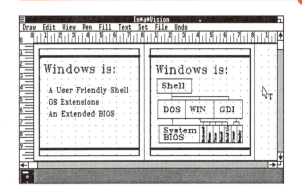

All you have left now is to print them using the
Print... command on the File menu, and run them
through your copying machine, using the plastic
transparencies instead of paper. And you've found a
really easy way to get professional-looking transparencies with minimal effort.

More sophisticated uses for In·a·Vision

You can, of course, use In·a·Vision for more sophisticated drawings than the simple transparencies
we just made. An example of a more sophisticated
drawing is the mouse shown here, one of the samples that come on the In·a·Vision disk.

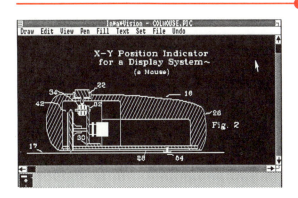

One of In·a·Vision's features that lets you create
sophisticated drawings more quickly is the template
feature. In·a·Vision lets you create and store templates of frequently used symbols. Then, when you
need a symbol in a drawing, instead of drawing it
again, you simply select it from the template library
and copy it into your drawing.

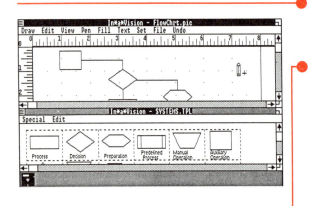

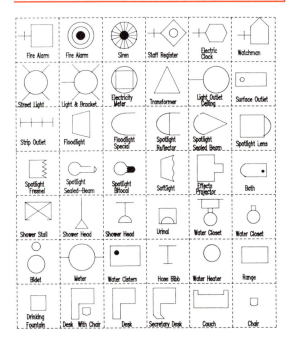

An In·a·Vision architectural template library (used with the permission of Micrografx, Inc.)

If I wanted to produce a flowchart, I would use the Load Template Window... command on the File menu to load the Systems template. Then, I would select the symbols I wanted and copy them into my drawing.

In·a·Vision comes with sample templates for architectural, electrical, and system drawings. A printout of an architectural template library is shown here. You can use the templates In·a·Vision provides or create and store your own.

You can see how In·a·Vision can be useful for creating these simple transparencies as well as for more sophisticated drawing tasks, such as the architectural drawing shown on the next page. And the Windows interface, which is the same from one application to the other, takes the pain out of learning new applications.

Now let's look at some other Windows applications in less detail.

CONTROL DATA'S MULTITASK/VE

MultiTask/VE is a combined spreadsheet and communications package. It is intended to work with a personal computer that connects to Control Data's Cyber/180. You use the PC to enter data and set up modeling for a spreadsheet as large as 1000 by 1000 cells and then you use the Cyber to do the calculations. The Cyber has greater precision (a word length of 64 bits, compared to the PC's 16 bits), speed, and tremendous data-storage capability. You can work with extremely large spreadsheets and never get an "out of memory" message.

And as its name suggests, MultiTask/VE is truly multitasking. While you're waiting for the host, the Cyber/180, to do its work, you can work on other tasks either on the current spreadsheet or on a different one.

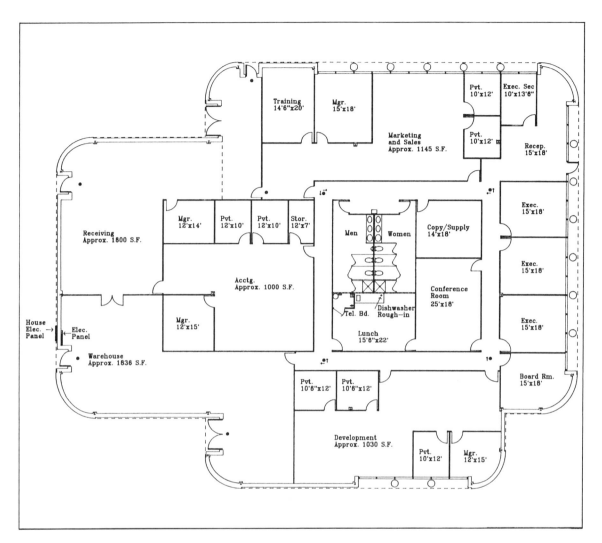

An architectural drawing that uses In-a-Vision template symbols (used with the permission of Micrografx, Inc.)

ABOUT...

Developer guidelines

Windows provides application developers with a tool kit and a set of guidelines for how Windows applications should look and behave. These are guidelines, not laws, so there is some variation in how application programmers have interpreted them. Some of the applications, such as In·a·Vision, adhere quite strictly to the guidelines; others, such as Palantir, incorporate non-Windows features, such as full-screen menus, in addition to the drop-down menus.

ALDUS CORPORATION'S PAGEMAKER

PageMaker, a page-design program first introduced for the Macintosh, allows you to design and produce small publications such as newsletters, data sheets, price lists, training manuals, and presentation materials. PageMaker is like an electronic layout board. You can paste up and lay out text and graphics on the screen, edit and rearrange text, crop and place pictures, and the screen looks like the page will look when it is printed.

You create text for your publication using a word-processing program and graphics with a drawing program. (PageMaker supports popular word-processing programs such as WordStar, Microsoft Word, and MultiMate, and graphics programs such as Lotus 1-2-3, Microsoft Chart, and Microsoft Paint.) Then you copy these text and graphics elements into your PageMaker document. Inside Page-Maker, you can edit text, you can proportionally reduce or enlarge graphics, and you can crop graphics, much as you would cut a picture to size with scissors. But you cannot edit graphics; you must do this in the drawing program you used to create the graphic.

PageMaker will work with laser printers, such as the HP Plus and the Apple LaserWriter, to produce near typeset-quality originals. In addition, Page-Maker produces files that can be read by powerful typesetters, such as the Linotronic typesetters from Allied Linotype. So you can compose, design, edit, and paste up a newsletter or report in-house and then send it out for typesetting.

Aldus chose to use Windows for the IBM version of PageMaker because page layout must integrate information, both text and graphics, from many sources, and Windows makes it easy to transfer information. PageMaker needed a graphic user interface, and Windows' graphic user interface is easy to use. Aldus expects that people designing publications with PageMaker will want to begin this work right away—they won't want to learn about computers first.

PALANTIR'S FILER

Filer is a non-relational database program that's designed to run with Windows. To use it, you first design a form for your data and then enter data in records, organized by fields, within a data file. A field can be a computed field (that is, it can perform a calculation), and you can index a field for faster searching. Using Filer, you can generate reports and merge data files with Palantir's or other word processors to create personalized form letters. A sample datafile looks like the one shown here.

You can, of course, select any portion of the information on the screen and use Windows' Clipboard to copy this information to another Filer record or to another Windows application.

Filer has a map function that shows you how the records for the particular file you're working with were set up. It lists the fields in the order you assigned them, their maximum length, and any attributes associated with the fields.

Filer also has an overlay function, which allows you to view up to five of the records you've previously edited, and you can display each record in a different window. This could be useful when making similar changes to several records in the file.

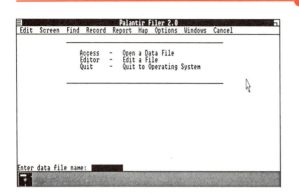

Filer does not have a File menu with the commands you use on File menus in other Windows applications for opening, closing, and naming files. Instead, Filer opens with a full-screen menu from which you can choose the task you want to work on and name the file you'll use.

The Filer program uses standard Windows features, such as drop-down menus and dialog boxes. However, one deviation from Windows' conventions is the Cancel menu, which operates more like a button than a menu. Clicking Cancel brings you back to the main menu.

Palantir has two additional Windows applications: a spelling checker that works with Microsoft Write and a communications package that's similar to their inTouch program for the Apple Macintosh. Because this communications program is a Windows application and is fully graphic, you can download images such as aviation weather maps from CompuServe.

INTUITION SYSTEMS' WORDSETTER

WordSetter is a program that uses Microsoft Word and your PC to prepare files for typesetting either on a Linotron 101 or on a Linotron 100P and a Compugraphic 8400. You compose your document in Word, then you use WordSetter to set up the fonts and styles you'll use in the typeset document. WordSetter puts this information into a printer file that Word can read. Then you go back into Word and format the document using this printer file. You see page breaks exactly where they will be in your typeset output. When you finish formatting, Word-Setter translates this file into one that can be read by your typesetting machine.

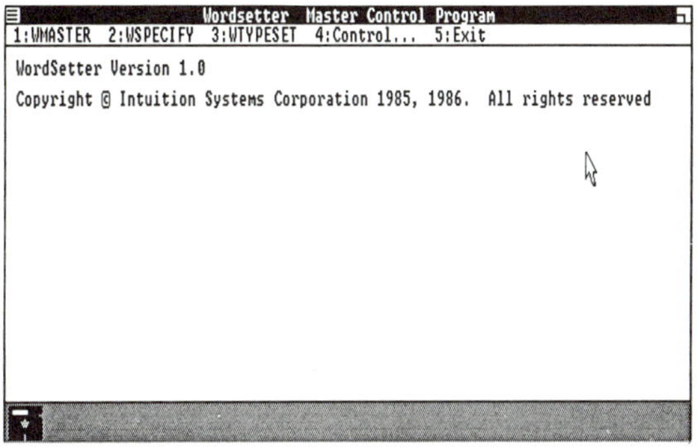
Wordsetter Master Control Program
1:WMASTER 2:WSPECIFY 3:WTYPESET 4:Control... 5:Exit
WordSetter Version 1.0
Copyright © Intuition Systems Corporation 1985, 1986. All rights reserved

WordSetter is ideal for text-intensive applications such as long, complex technical manuals and books, although WordSetter (and most typesetting equipment) isn't currently capable of producing graphics.

The WordSetter program has five menus, each with only one choice.

The 1: WMASTER menu is the place you specify the fonts available on your typesetting machine and set the necessary parameters, such as baud rate and communication port.

The 2: WSPECIFY menu is the place you specify the available fonts and font sizes you'll be using for the particular document you're formatting. WordSetter converts this information into a Word printer file.

The 3: WTYPESET menu takes the Word document you've formatted and converts it into a file the typesetting equipment can read.

The 4: Control... menu is the Windows Control Panel. This is included as part of WordSetter for quick accessibility and so people who just have WordSetter and not the entire Windows package can use Control Panel to set screen colors and add or change printers.

The 5: Exit menu allows you to leave the WordSetter program.

WordSetter's drop-down menus conform to the Windows interface in most respects. But each menu is numbered, which allows you to select it either with the mouse or by typing its number. The advantage of WordSetter as a Windows application is that you can run both Word and WordSetter at the same time and quickly switch between them.

ABOUT...

Using tiling

If you're running several Windows applications, you may wish to tile the screen with all of the Windows applications you'll be using. Then, when you want to give one application the entire screen, simply zoom that application. You'll find that zooming an application is faster than having all the applications as icons and dragging them into the work area as you need them. Memory isn't a concern with the tiling method, since neither an inactive window nor an icon takes up much memory.

Even if you don't have direct access to a typesetting machine, you can use WordSetter. You can send WordSetter documents on disk to a print shop that has the appropriate typesetting equipment and personal computer. If you don't know of a print shop with this setup, Intuition Systems will provide you with the names of people in your area who are using WordSetter.

INDEX TECHNOLOGY'S EXCELERATOR

Excelerator is a tool that systems analysts can use to automate the analysis, design, and documentation of large information systems. Systems analysts traditionally have automated the jobs of other people, while using pencil, paper, and plastic templates for their own work. Excelerator gives them computer-aided design tools to develop systems specifications.

Excelerator includes graphics, screen and report design, graph and dictionary analysis tools, document production, data sharing, a link to word processing, and a data dictionary that integrates all of these functions. It also provides cross-referencing and "where-used" analysis.

Making design changes to respond to new requirements or end-user's requests is easy. If a client requests a change in the flow chart or input screen, the analyst can make the change and it will be reflected on the chart or screen almost instantly—the client won't need to wait for an entire chart or screen to be manually redrawn.

Index Technology selected the Windows environment because of Windows' graphics capability, device independence, and memory management features. Device independence is important when using graphics on a variety of systems. Generally, each system has a slightly different aspect ratio and the program needs to be modified slightly for each system. Windows takes care of these modifications so the program does not have to change from system to system. Excelerator is a large program—nearly three megabytes—and Windows' memory management takes care of swapping in just the parts that are needed so it can run on a system with much less than three megabytes of memory.

SUMMATION INC.'S SIGMASERIES TEST SYSTEM

SigmaSeries Test System is not the kind of program most of us would use in our businesses or homes. It is an automated final-test system for companies that manufacture products with electronic components—from dishwashers to printers. The final test of these products is the last obstacle before shipping the product and, because most of a company's energy is put into development and design, often an inadequate amount of time is set aside for the final test. SigmaSeries Test System was designed to provide manufacturers with a method of performing quality final testing in a short period of time. It uses Windows on an AT to emulate the front panel of a test instrument.

HAS10/01 - High Accuracy Switch - S
Display Mode SRQ debug
Channel: -1- -2- -3- -4- -5- -6- -7- -8-
Pin: A D C B E H F K L M J N P T S R
☐ Enable
☐ Reset
☐ Actuate

HA.BUS
1
2

Break Before Make

appbio : initModules
Program Context Edit Instruments
Breakpoint   Import From Instrument
initModules   Export To Instrument
! init DMM
OUTPUT "DMM10/01" : "FUNCTI
ON DC.VOLTS;INPUT HA.BUS;R
ANGE 200.;DELTA 0.;MODE CO
NT;SAMPLE.RATE 12.5;LIMIT.
TRIGGER CT.BUS,0;HI.LIMIT
1.0E+10;LO.LIMIT -1.0E+10;
SRQ.ON;TRIGGER.INPUT CT.BU
S,0;EXECUTE"

DMM10/01 - Digital Multimeter - Slo
Display Input Measure
Trigger debug
☐ Enable   Max: 0 Vdc
☐ Reset
☐ Halt   0 Vdc
☐ Execute   Min: 0 Vdc
☐ Set Delta
0.

IO TFR DOL
10 10

DMM10/01 - Settings
Input
FUNCTION DC.VOLTS
INPUT BACKPANEL
RANGE AUTO
DELTA 0

Measure
MODE SINGLE
SAMPLE.RATE 2.5

Output
LIMIT.TRIGGER CT.BUS,0
HI.LIMIT 1.0E+10
LO.LIMIT -1.0E+10

SRQ
SRQ.ON

Trigger
TRIGGER.INPUT CT.BUS,0

ABOUT...

Raster vs graphic fonts

Before Windows, you would have been hard pressed to find any fonts available on a PC that weren't raster fonts (fonts that use a pattern of pixels for each character). With raster fonts, if you want a font in different sizes, you need to define each character in each size that you want. Windows has added a new type of font: vector, or stroke, fonts. (In·a·Vision calls raster fonts standard fonts and vector fonts graphic fonts.) Vector fonts define the lines that make up the characters. Consequently, you only need one set of characters for each font and Windows can redraw these characters in different sizes by varying the length of the lines, much like a connect-the-dots drawing. With vector fonts, you can easily rotate and scale text, especially in large font sizes.

Before the SigmaSeries Test System was developed, most manufacturers had stacked-up boxes of test equipment, called "rack and stack" systems, one box for each type of test to be performed and all boxes stacked up in a large rack. SigmaSeries replaced this system with a Motorola 68000-based TestStation box. Inside this box, the test for each component fits on a printed circuit board, and several boards fit inside one TestStation.

SigmaSeries Test System has an Import-Export program that automatically converts selections you make on the instrument panel window to IEEE (Institute of Electrical and Electronics Engineers) standard program commands. Because of the ease of using the Windows graphic user interface and the Import-Export program, you don't have to learn different programming commands for each part of the test you're performing, and you can reconfigure the same system to test new products. With Import-Export, it's easy to reprogram.

RUNNING STANDARD APPLICATIONS UNDER WINDOWS

When some standard applications run under Windows, they run in a window; when others run under Windows, they take over the entire screen. In this chapter, we'll first look at standard applications that run in a window, and then at standard applications that take over the entire screen. (Chapters 9 and 10 contain additional details about these two types of applications.) After that, we'll look at how to determine whether or not the standard applications you use will run in a window, and how to set up the applications you use to run with Windows. Then we'll look at some strategies for working with Windows and standard applications.

STANDARD APPLICATIONS THAT RUN IN A WINDOW

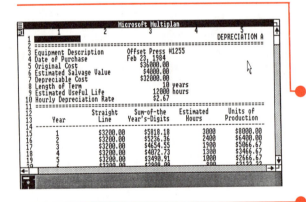

When a standard application runs in a window, the screen looks much the same as it does when it runs under DOS. The only difference is that the work area, the part of the screen that displays the standard application, is smaller. The application has to give up some of the screen to the title bar on the top, scroll bars on the right and bottom of the work area, and the icon area beneath the scroll bars.

The title bar at the top of the window displays the name of the application.

In the upper left corner is a System menu box. The System menu has nine commands Windows needs to manage the window in which the application will run—to size it, move it, shrink it to an icon, zoom it, close it, and edit it.

The first five commands—Size, Move, Icon, Zoom, and Close—are the same System menu commands that appear in all Windows applications and they work the same as they do in other Windows applications, such as the desktop applications, Microsoft Write, and Microsoft Paint. As you recall, you can use the Size command to change the sizes

of windows from Windows' default sizes when you
have more than one window open. You use the
Move command to move an icon up from the icon
area to start it. The Icon command turns an application currently running in a window into an icon,
freeing screen space for another application. The
Zoom command expands the work area of the application so the window takes up the entire screen and
covers the icon area. Choosing Zoom a second time
returns the window to its previous size. The Close
command closes the window for the standard application after you've quit the application the usual way
if you did not check the Close Window On Exit box
of the application's PIF.

The next four commands—Scroll, Mark, Copy,
and Paste—are commands Windows adds to the
System menu when it runs standard applications
in a window.

The Scroll command lets you scroll horizontally
or vertically so you can see parts of the application's
display that won't fit in the window. The Scroll command is independent of commands your application
may have for scrolling. Choose the Scroll command,
then use the PgUp, PgDn, Home, End, and direction keys to scroll in the desired direction. When
you're finished scrolling, you press Esc or Enter to
return to the application. If you have a mouse, you
can use either the Scroll command and the keyboard or the mouse and the scroll bars to scroll
information in a window.

Windows adds the next three commands—Mark,
Copy, and Paste—so you can select information
(text or a graphic) and transfer it from one standard
application to another place in that application, to
another standard application, or to a Windows application. First, you choose the Mark command. Windows puts a small rectangular cursor at the upper
left corner of the window. You use the direction
keys to move the cursor to the beginning of the information you want to transfer. Then hold down the
Shift key and use the direction keys to mark that information, or hold down the mouse button and drag
over the information to mark it. Next, choose the

Chapter 8: Running Standard Applications Under Windows

ABOUT...

Using About...

The About... command from the MS-DOS Executive System menu displays the amount of memory available on your system. Using the command, however, also reclaims and re-organizes unused memory (you might think of this as trash collection). Consequently, it's a good idea to use About... when you quit a standard application such as Microsoft Word. If you don't use the About... command when you quit, Windows may have some difficulty using memory in the best way possible be-cause the memory is set up for large program segments. This can mean excessive swapping and slowness.

Copy command to copy the marked text to the Clip-board. (Copy also removes the highlighting so the text is no longer marked.) Now move to the place where you want to insert the information and choose the Paste command (if your destination is a Windows application, remember that you'll most likely find Paste on the Edit menu). Text from the Clipboard is pasted in just as if you'd typed it in from the keyboard. There is one limitation when transferring information from standard applications: The Clipboard holds one screenful of information (25 lines) of either text or graphics. If you have more than one screenful of information to transfer, you'll have to make more than one trip.

You can transfer text from one standard applica-tion to another or to a Windows application. But you can only transfer graphics from a standard applica-tion to a Windows application. If you want to com-bine text and graphics from standard applications (for example, a chart from Lotus 1-2-3 with text from Microsoft Word), you can first use the Clip-board to copy the text into a Windows application, such as Microsoft Write, and then use the Clipboard a second time to copy the graphics.

You start standard applications from the MS-DOS Executive, just as you start the desktop applications and Windows applications such as Microsoft Write and Microsoft Paint. You switch between standard applications that run in a window just as you do with Windows applications: You drag the icon of the application you wish to run above the icon area. Windows uses rectangular icons for standard appli-cations and identifies them with two or three char-acters (for example, MP for Microsoft Multiplan or WOR for Microsoft Word). If you place the icon in the work area of another window, the new applica-tion will replace the current application and the cur-rent application will become an icon; if you place the icon on the border of the active window, Windows will split that window and give half of its work area to the new application. When you leave Windows, Windows applications will be closed for you, but you must close a standard application using the application's Quit or End command before leaving Windows.

STANDARD APPLICATIONS
THAT TAKE OVER THE SCREEN

Some standard applications require exclusive use of the screen, and cannot be run in a window. When you start a standard application that takes over the screen, it looks and works exactly as it did when you ran it under DOS before Windows, but you now have some useful advantages.

One is that if you have a hard disk or extended memory, you can run more standard applications than will fit in memory at the same time and move quickly from one to the other. You can do this without first saving and quitting the first application, and then starting the second one. You could, for example, switch directly from an open spreadsheet to an open database to an open word-processor file. Another advantage is that you can copy a snapshot of the screen of any standard application into the Clipboard and use this information in any Windows application. Copying an image of the screen lets you use information from several different standard applications in one Windows application, and Windows takes care of the necessary translation. These advantages cost very little in terms of the speed at which the application runs—standard applications that take over the screen run exactly as fast with Windows as they do under DOS without Windows.

You start standard applications that take over the screen the same way you start any application—from the MS-DOS Executive. But if you plan to run several standard applications and switch between them, you'll need to start the application that requires the most memory first. If you start the largest first, there will always be enough memory: When you start the second application (the smaller of the two), Windows will swap out the first (the one that takes the most memory) and give its memory to the second one. You can determine which is the largest of the standard applications you wish to run by looking at the system requirements in the documentation for each application. Multiplan, for example, requires 128K, while Lotus 1-2-3 requires 170K and Word requires 192K.

When you're running a standard application that takes over the screen (say, Lotus 1-2-3) and you want to switch to another application, press Alt-Tab. This takes you directly back to Windows and changes the application you were running before you pressed Alt-Tab (for example, Lotus 1-2-3) into an icon. Now you can start another application from the MS-DOS Executive, or, if the application you want was started previously and is an icon, simply move it above the icon area. Operation of the previous application (in this case, Lotus 1-2-3) is suspended until you go back to it by moving its icon into the work area. When you do, it will again reclaim the entire screen and start exactly where you left off when you pressed Alt-Tab.

Because these standard applications take over the entire screen, they do not have a System menu like the standard applications that run in a window. So, there is no way to mark text and copy it to the Clipboard. But you can copy a snapshot of the screen into the Clipboard and use this information in a Windows application. You could, for example, use text information from Lotus 1-2-3 in Notepad, a graphics chart in Paint, or both text and graphics in Microsoft Write. When you have information on the screen you'd like to copy, simply press Alt-PrtSc and Windows will copy everything on the screen (text and graphics) into the Clipboard. Then start a Windows application, move the insertion point to where you want the information to be pasted, and choose the Paste command from the Edit menu of the Windows application. Windows will paste in the contents of the Clipboard, starting at the insertion point. Text is stored in its character (ASCII—American Standard Code for Information Exchange) representation, so if you paste a text screen into a word-processing application, such as Microsoft Write, you can edit it and make it look just the way you'd like it. If you want to edit graphics screens, you can paste them into Paint and edit them there. This method can be used with any standard application, even those that run in a window.

ABOUT...

Windows applications

Don't bother looking for a PIF for Windows applications such as Microsoft Write or Control Panel in the PIF directory. A PIF tells Windows how a particular application is configured. But since Windows already knows how Windows applications are configured, it doesn't need to see a PIF.

WILL IT RUN IN A WINDOW?

One of the factors that determines how an application runs with Windows is the amount of memory the application requires. If you add the memory the application requires and the memory Windows requires (about 128K–175K for Windows, plus 15K for old application support, plus 32K so it can work quickly), and this total is greater than the amount of memory on your system, the application cannot be run in a window. Instead, when you start the application, Windows temporarily exits, giving all the available memory to the application, and allowing the application to take over the entire screen and all the system resources. Then, when you leave that application, Windows returns.

Another factor that determines whether or not an application will run in a window is the way the program uses system resources. If, for example, an application is written so it writes directly to the screen memory, the application will not run in a window, but will take over the entire screen. Many applications are written to bypass the MS-DOS conventions for putting characters on the screen and instead write directly to the screen memory. Because this bypasses the middleman (MS-DOS), it is a much faster way of putting characters on the screen. But if an application writes directly to the screen memory, it will not run in a window because Windows has no way of knowing what is written on the screen. (For example, if an additional window were opened, it could not manage changes.) Applications that display graphics also will not run in a window. Examples of standard applications in this category are Lotus 1-2-3 and Microsoft Word.

Another factor that determines whether or not a standard application will run in a window is the way the program is configured. Programs that have an option to run in a Topview window, such as the IBM Assistant series, will run in a window because Windows supports Topview's protocols. (Topview is IBM's non-graphic windowing program.) Programs that you can install to run with an ANSI-device driver (ANSI.SYS) will also run in a window. (An ANSI-device driver is one that uses standardized terminal commands established by the American National Standards Institute.) Microsoft Multiplan is an example of a program that can be installed using ANSI.SYS and will run in a window.

PIFS

When Windows runs a standard application, it looks for a PIF (program information file) for that application. The PIF tells Windows whether or not the application will run in a window. You set up or change a PIF in the PIF editor, which appears when you start PIFEDIT.EXE from the PIF directory.

This is what the PIF editor looks like when it's displaying the information required for Lotus 1-2-3 (the 123.PIF listing in your PIF directory).

The first four lines (Program Name, Program Title, Program Parameters, and Initial Directory) give Windows information about the program. Program Name is the place you specify the pathname and file name (including the extension) that runs the application. Program Title is the descriptive name that will appear in the title bar if the program runs in a window. The program title also appears when you select the program's icon. Program Parameters allows you to specify additional information about the way the program runs. (For example, Microsoft Word automatically runs in graphic mode if you have a graphics adapter. To run it in text mode, type /C.) Type ? if you want Windows to prompt you for parameters when you run an application. Initial Directory is where you specify the default drive and directory, the place Windows will find the program files for the application.

You use the next line of the PIF editor to specify memory requirements for your application. In the first box (KB Required—Windows uses the designation KB instead of K for kilobytes), type the minimum amount of memory required by your

ABOUT...

PIFEDIT help

You can display a considerable amount of information about the characteristics and use of program information files by choosing the About... command from the System menu of the PIF editor (PIFEDIT.EXE). When this command is chosen, a dialog box containing a list of topics appears. Topics include: About PIF Files, Default Settings, Determining How Your Application Will Be Displayed, Giving Applications More Memory, and options for each section of the PIF editor. When you choose a topic, a new dialog box appears, displaying information about that topic.

application. You can find this information in the system-requirements documentation for the application. Windows' default for required memory is 52K. If the amount of memory you specify here is too small, Windows will have difficulty running the application and may give the error message, "Not enough memory to run." If this happens, you may need to increase the number in the KB Required box. The KB Desired box is the place you type the maximum amount of memory your program can use. Some programs run more efficiently if they can get more than the minimum amount of memory. If you leave Memory Desired blank, Windows will give the application all the available memory.

In the Directly Modifies section, you specify the resources your program uses that can't be shared with other programs.

If you put an X in the Screen box, it means that your application requires exclusive use of the screen, it won't run in a window, and when it runs, it will take over the entire screen. You will need to put an X in the Screen box for graphics applications or for applications that write directly to the screen memory.

Choose the Keyboard box in the Directly Modifies section if the application you're working with modifies the keyboard buffer, the place keystrokes are stored until they are processed. Programs such as ProKey and SmartKey use the keyboard buffer. If you put an X in the Keyboard box, your program will not run in a window and you cannot switch back to Windows using Alt-Tab.

The next two boxes (COM1 and COM2) are the place to indicate whether the application you're working with uses either of the system's serial communications ports (COM1 or COM2). If you put an X in either of these boxes, Windows gives the application exclusive use of that port. It does this by refusing to run any application that uses COM1 or COM2 until you quit the first application. Generally, you will only choose COM1 or COM2 if you're running a communications application. Choosing COM1 or COM2 also prevents the application from being swapped to disk.

The last box in the Directly Modifies section (Memory) is the box to choose for terminate and stay-resident programs such as Sidekick, Spotlight, or Bellsoft Pop-Up. These are programs that stay in memory once you load them (say, before you start Windows), and can be activated during a Windows session by pressing a combination of keys. You can also choose Memory if you don't have enough memory for both Windows and the application. With the Memory option selected, Windows temporarily exits, gives its memory to the current application, and returns only after you exit the application.

The next section (Program Switch) determines whether or not you can use Alt-Tab to switch back to Windows from an application that requires exclusive use of the screen. You can select only one Program Switch option. If you choose Prevent, you won't be able to switch back to Windows and other applications and you'll conserve the amount of memory normally required to save the screen during a switch (saving the screen requires 4K for text applications and 16K to 36K for graphics applications). Choose Text if you have a text application or only want to switch back to Windows when your application is in text mode. Choose Graphics/Multiple Text if your application works in graphics mode and you want to use Alt-Tab to switch back to Windows. Microsoft Word is a standard application that runs in either text or graphics mode. When I run Word with Windows, I run it in text mode (/C) and specify the Text option of Program Switch in order to conserve memory.

The Screen Exchange line is the place you specify the kind of information you want copied to the Clipboard when you press Alt-PrtSc in a standard application that takes over the screen. As in Program Switch, you can choose only one Screen Exchange option. Select None if you won't be transferring information between applications using Alt-PrtSc and the Clipboard. This will conserve memory. Choose Text to take snapshots of text screens. This option requires about 2K of memory. Choose the Graphics/ Text option to take snapshots of text and graphics screens. This can require up to 32K of memory.

The last option (Close Window On Exit) should be selected unless your application displays information on the screen that you need to see as it exits. If you select Close Window On Exit, when you quit or end the application, the window will automatically close, saving you the extra step of closing it with the System menu's Close command.

Making a PIF

Windows comes with PIFs for most standard applications. You can use these built-in PIFs "as is" or modify them by using the PIF editor. When you install Windows, it puts PIFEDIT.EXE and all the PIFs it provides in a directory named, not surprisingly, PIF, which is a subdirectory of the default WINDOWS directory.

To see how the PIF editor works, let's use the PIF for Microsoft Word.

Use the MS-DOS Executive to display the PIF subdirectory.

Start PIFEDIT.EXE.

Your screen will look like the one shown here.

These are Windows' default PIF settings.

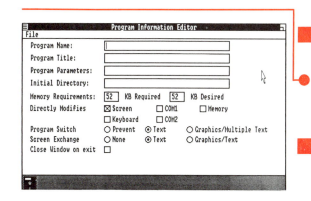

Choose the Open... command from the File menu (the PIF editor's only menu).

A dialog box with names of all the available PIFs in the PIF directory appears.

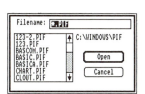

Select the PIF for Microsoft Word by selecting WORD.PIF from the list and pressing Enter or clicking the Open button.

You cannot start the PIF editor and open a PIF at the same time by double-clicking on a PIF name (WORD.PIF, for example). Double-clicking on WORD.PIF will use that PIF to start the application Microsoft Word rather than loading it into the PIF editor.

When you open WORD.PIF in the PIF editor, you'll see the information Windows will use when you run Microsoft Word.

Program Name displays the name WORD.COM, the name of the file used to start Word. Program Title displays the title *Microsoft Word,* which differentiates it from other applications that could start with a file named WORD.COM. The Program Parameters entry /X tells Word not to reserve any memory for Spell, a spelling-checker program that comes with Word. (When you run Spell, it has its own PIF and will claim its own memory.) I add a second Program Parameters entry (/C) to start Word in text mode. There is no initial directory specified, but you can enter information here if you wish. I add C:\WORD to specify the \WORD directory of my hard disk (C:) for my Word program files.

Word requires exclusive access to the screen (it writes directly to screen memory), so Screen in the Directly Modifies section is selected. This also tells us that Word will not run in a window.

I have set Program Switch to Text so I can use Alt-Tab to switch from Word in text mode to Windows (this requires only 4K of memory). I have also set Screen Exchange to Text, so Windows allows me to use Alt-PrtSc to take snapshots of text screens to use in other applications. (Remember: Windows will reserve 2K of memory for this.)

Close Window On Exit really doesn't matter for applications such as Microsoft Word, which do not run in a window. But if you were setting up a PIF for an application that runs in a window, you would select Close Window On Exit if you wanted the window closed after you'd used the application's Quit or End command.

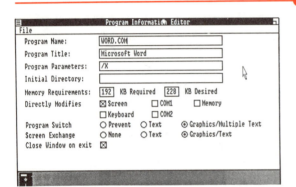

You can use PIFEDIT in this way to prepare PIFs for all of the standard applications you use. It allows you to enter information about the way your standard application will run with Windows.

If you want to use a standard application that does not have a PIF provided, you can create one for it. Start the PIF editor (by selecting PIFEDIT.EXE) and complete the necessary information. If you're not sure what to put in the Directly Modifies section, selecting Screen is the safest choice. That way, the application won't run in a window, but will run properly whether or not it writes directly to the screen. If you think an application may run in a window and want to try, leave Directly Modifies Screen blank and try starting the application with this PIF. The worst thing that can happen is that your system will lock up. Don't be alarmed if it does; it won't damage your hardware or software. Just reboot and then edit the PIF for that application so that Screen is selected in Directly Modifies.

Select whichever type of program switch you want: Text, Graphics/Multiple Text, or none (Prevent). If you select Text or Graphics/Multiple Text and later find that you don't have enough memory or switching does not work properly with your application, you can edit the PIF and change to Prevent. Do the same with Screen Exchange. When you finish, use the Save... command and name the PIF with the name of the program. Windows adds the .PIF extension.

If you try to run a standard application and Windows can't find its PIF, Windows will simply use the default settings.

STRATEGIES FOR USING STANDARD APPLICATIONS AND WINDOWS

Running standard applications with Windows adds the Windows advantages, but it may take a little time getting used to using your old favorites with Windows. Following are some strategies that will help you make the transition.

Two PIFs

The following are some popular standard applications that run in a window:

IBM Writing Assistant
IBM Filing Assistant
IBM Planning Assistant
IBM Reporting Assistant
dBASE II
R:base 4000
R:base 5000
DisplayWrite 3
DOS Utilities
BASIC (BASIC.COM)
Microsoft Multiplan

These applications can be run in a window but, because they were not specifically designed for Windows, they will run more slowly in a window than they would if they took over the entire screen. So, the best way to use an application that runs both ways is to have it take over the screen when you're working with that one application. That way, it will run at closer to its usual speed. Then, when you want to share information from it with another application that runs in a window or with a Windows application, simply run it in a window. That way, you can mark just what you want to transfer, copy it to the Clipboard, and paste it exactly where you want it in the second application.

To be able to run a standard application both in a window and in the take-over-the-screen mode, you need two PIFs: one for each method of running the application. Windows lets you start an application either by selecting its file name (for example, MP.COM for Multiplan), or by selecting the PIF for the application (MP.PIF).

Here's how to make two PIFs for Multiplan, one that will run Multiplan in a window and one that will run it by having it take over the screen. You can follow this example for any application that can be run both ways.

■ *Move to the PIF directory, start PIFEDIT.EXE, and open the file named MP.PIF.*

This is the PIF for Multiplan that comes with Windows and is set up to run Multiplan so that it takes over the screen. You can tell this by the X in front of the Directly Modifies Screen. We'll change this to a PIF that will let Multiplan run in a window.

M *Click on the Directly Modifies Screen box to remove the X.*

K *Press the Tab key to move to the Directly Modifies Screen box and press the Spacebar to remove the X.*

■ *Choose the Save… command and save this file as MP_W.PIF.*

The _W identifies this as the PIF that will run Multiplan in a window. Now you'll have two Multiplan PIFs: the original MP.PIF, which runs Multiplan so that it takes over the screen, and a second PIF, MP_W.PIF, which runs Multiplan in a window.

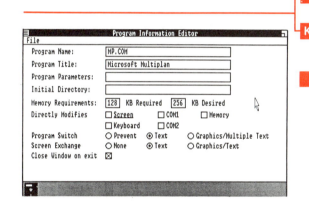

Start the application from the PIF

Now you have two PIFs. When you want to start Multiplan and use it in the take-over-the-screen mode, start it by selecting MP.PIF. When you want to use some information from Multiplan in a Windows application (say, to copy some figures from Multiplan into a Write memo), start Multiplan by selecting MP_W.PIF, the PIF that starts Multiplan in a window.

If you have two PIFs for each application that runs in a window, you can run the application in the way that best suits the job you have to do.

Copy the PIF to the \WINDOWS directory

Once you've made PIFs for the standard applications you use, the Windows manual says it's a good idea to copy them to the same directory as the application for which they provide information. But I prefer keeping the PIFs for the four or five standard applications I use regularly in the \WINDOWS directory. That way, I can start them right there, without first changing directories.

To start an application from the Windows directory (or from a directory other than the one that has the program files), you need to copy the PIF for that application to the Windows directory and designate the path to the directory where the program files are located. You do this by completing the Initial Directory box. For example, to start Word from the Windows directory, my PIF looks like the one shown here.

If you're using floppy disks, copy the PIF or PIFs to the startup disk for the application. This way, the PIF to start the application will be in the same place as the application startup file.

Loading standard applications

If you're working with more than one standard application (if, for example, you're using your spreadsheet, and you need to check some information in your database, then perhaps write a memo with your word processor), you can start all the standard applications as icons at the beginning of your session. Then as you need each one, just drag the icon

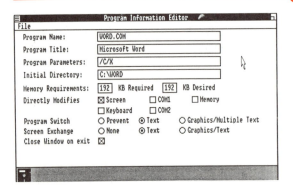

for the application of your choice into the work area and begin work, switching between the applications as needed.

To do this, you'll need to load the largest standard application (the one that takes the most memory) first. That way, as mentioned earlier in this chapter, Windows sets aside a block of memory large enough for this application. When you switch to a second application, Windows discards most of the first one and puts the second one into this block. If you load the largest application first, you'll have enough memory to switch to any other standard application.

Running pop-up applications

If you want to run pop-up applications (such as Sidekick, Spotlight, and Bellsoft Pop-ups) that you can call up with a keystroke or two when using another application, load them before you start Windows. That way, Windows won't interfere with the memory assigned to these applications.

But memory is a limited resource, and it's important to use it wisely. If the pop-ups you usually use perform the same functions as the desktop applications, you may find it preferable to use the desktop applications and give the memory the pop-ups would take to Windows and the standard applications you use.

Customizing WIN.INI

WIN.INI is a special file containing settings for many Windows features and applications. Windows checks WIN.INI each time you start.

If you find that you generally use the same group of applications (for example, a spreadsheet, a database, and a word processing program), you can customize the WIN.INI file so that these applications are automatically started as icons each time you start Windows. You do this by adding the file names of the applications you wish to start (as icons) to the "load" line in the WIN.INI file. Here's how:

Start the file named WIN.INI.

WIN.INI appears in a Notepad window.

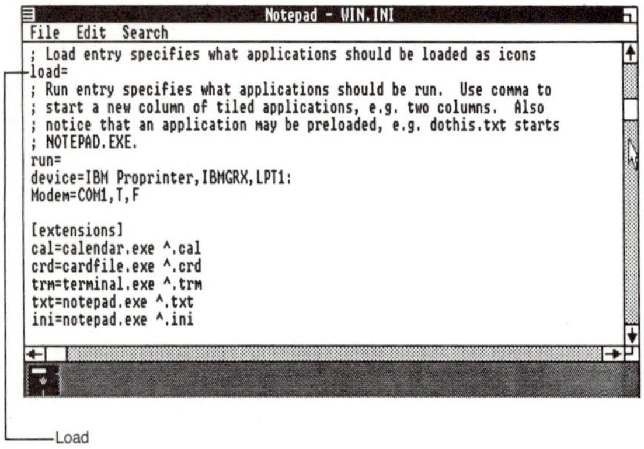
Notepad - WIN.INI
File Edit Search
; Load entry specifies what applications should be loaded as icons
load=
; Run entry specifies what applications should be run. Use comma to
; start a new column of tiled applications, e.g. two columns. Also
; notice that an application may be preloaded, e.g. dothis.txt starts
; NOTEPAD.EXE.
run=
device=IBM Proprinter,IBMGRX,LPT1:
Modem=COM1,T,F
[extensions]
cal=calendar.exe ^.cal
crd=cardfile.exe ^.crd
trm=terminal.exe ^.trm
txt=notepad.exe ^.txt
ini=notepad.exe ^.ini
Load

Look for the line that says load=.

This is the place you put the names of applications or files you want started as icons each time you start Windows.

Type the names of the files, separated by spaces. If they're not in the current directory, include the path. For instance, you could add a line like this:

load=RBASE WORD MP

Start with the standard application that requires the most memory.

If you want to open a specific file each time you start an application, you can specify the name of the file and the extension that indicates the type of application (.DOC for Write files). Windows will start the application and open the file you've specified.

Save the WIN.INI file and then close the WIN.INI window.

Now quit and restart Windows.

Now when Windows starts, the applications you specified after the *load=* line will automatically start as icons.

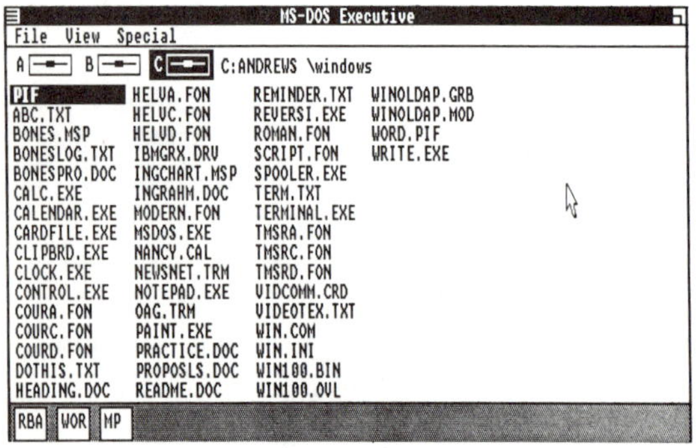
MS-DOS Executive
File View Special
A B C C:ANDREWS \windows
PIF
ABC.TXT
BONES.MSP
BONESLOG.TXT
BONESPRO.DOC
CALC.EXE
CALENDAR.EXE
CARDFILE.EXE
CLIPBRD.EXE
CLOCK.EXE
CONTROL.EXE
COURA.FON
COURC.FON
COURD.FON
DOTHIS.TXT
HEADING.DOC
HELVA.FON
HELVC.FON
HELVD.FON
IBMGRX.DRV
INGCHART.MSP
INGRAHM.DOC
MODERN.FON
MSDOS.EXE
NANCY.CAL
NEWSNET.TRM
NOTEPAD.EXE
OAG.TRM
PAINT.EXE
PRACTICE.DOC
PROPOSLS.DOC
README.DOC
REMINDER.TXT
REVERSI.EXE
ROMAN.FON
SCRIPT.FON
SPOOLER.EXE
TERM.TXT
TERMINAL.EXE
TMSRA.FON
TMSRC.FON
TMSRD.FON
VIDCOMM.CRD
VIDEOTEX.TXT
WIN.COM
WIN.INI
WIN100.BIN
WIN100.OVL
WINOLDAP.GRB
WINOLDAP.MOD
WORD.PIF
WRITE.EXE
RBA
WOR
MP

9

STANDARD APPLICATIONS THAT RUN IN A WINDOW

Chapter 8 gave you information about standard applications, and now you're ready for some hands-on experience. That's what this chapter does—it gives you specific examples of three standard applications that run in a window: R:base 5000, Microsoft Multiplan, and Microsoft Project. It shows how to set up PIFs to run each of these applications, describes the most efficient ways to use the applications with Windows, and shows how to transfer information from these applications to a Windows application (we'll use Microsoft Write).

For the example we'll use, imagine that you're the quality-assurance manager for a medium-sized company called B.C., Inc. that designs, manufactures, and markets bar-code readers, printers, and supplies for the industrial market.

Your products are used largely in production environments to track materials, to control inventory, and to record time and attendance. Companies use your products because entering data by scanning a bar code is faster and more reliable than typing in information from a keyboard.

You've been asked to design a new manufacturing quality-assurance plan. You've spent several weeks gathering data and putting together information for this plan. You plan to use B.C., Inc.'s bar-code readers to collect quality-assurance information and bring this data into R:base 5000. You'll analyze the data using two R:base reports. You'll use Multiplan to analyze the cost savings this system will provide the company, and Microsoft Project to detail an implementation schedule for your plan. You have all the information you need, and your task is to put together a report detailing your plan. You need this report by the end of the week, when you'll present it to top management.

This is a simpler task with Windows than it would be without. With Windows, you can take information from each of the different applications and combine it in your report. You won't have to copy information by hand from your applications into your

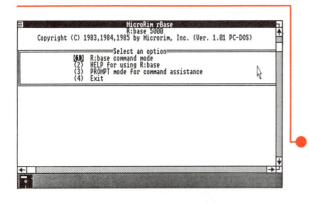

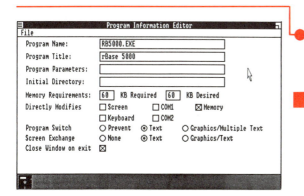

report or distribute separate pages with charts from Multiplan and reports from R:base. With Windows, you can put all this together in one nicely formatted report, shown on the next two pages, with the text created in Write.

SETTING UP THE STANDARD APPLICATIONS

Windows comes with PIFs for each of the standard applications we'll use that will run these applications in a window. Running in a window, R:base 5000 looks as shown here.

Although these standard applications run in a window, they also can be run under Windows in the take-over-the-screen mode. In the take-over-the-screen mode, R:base 5000 looks as shown here when you run it under Windows.

In this mode, applications look just as they do running under DOS and run almost as quickly as under DOS.

As explained in Chapter 8, the advantage of being able to run these applications both ways is this: When you run a standard application in a window, you can transfer information easily from one application to another. But, in most cases, the application will run more slowly in a window than in the take-over-the-screen mode because all Windows applications must run in graphics mode. In the take-over-the-screen mode, it will run at nearly the same speed as it does under DOS without Windows.

Making PIFs for R:base 5000

The PIF that Windows provides for the database package R:base 5000 looks as shown here.

If you have 640K of memory, you can use this PIF to run R:base in a window. Here's what to do:

Select the file named RB5000.PIF. Use Rename... on the File menu to rename it RB5000_W.PIF.

RB5000EXE is already set up to run in a window; the _W after RB5000 is just a visual reminder of this.

THE QA PLAN

Quality Assurance has developed a Data Collection and
Analysis system that will reduce the costs of producing our
printers, cables, and readers, and will enable us to better
understand and maintain control of the manufacturing
process.

The QA Data Collection and Analysis System will collect two
types of data: Work in Process (WIP) data and Configuration
(Config) data. The WIP data will allow us to better
understand and manage the assembly process. The Config data
will enable us to better track the configuration of units in
the field and units returned for repair. We can track which
products with which components have the most breakdowns and
use this information to more quickly repair returned
products and perhaps make changes in the way components are
used together in future products.

We'll accomplish this data collection using our own bar
codes and the 9420/1600 laser reader. This will simplify
the data collection and significantly reduce the probability
of input errors. Quality assurance reports will be easy to
produce. Reports can be run on demand giving immediate
feedback on manufactured quality. We have our own in-house
experts to program the readers. And because all employees
are familiar with using the bar codes and readers in our
Time Tracking System, training for the QA system should be
relatively simple.

COST SAVINGS

The following table details our current production costs and
then shows our projections for the amount the new QA Data
Collection and Analysis System will reduce these costs.

	Current Costs	Reduced Costs	Savings
impact printers	$1040000.00	$832000.00	$208000.00
thermal printers	$560000.00	$448000.00	$112000.00
TOTAL Printers	$1600000.00	$1280000.00	$320000.00
wedge readers	$240000.00	$192000.00	$48000.00
portable readers	$320000.00	$256000.00	$64000.00
display readers	$600000.00	$480000.00	$120000.00
on-line readers	$840000.00	$672000.00	$168000.00
TOTAL Readers	$2000000.00	$1600000.00	$400000.00
printer	$200000.00	$160000.00	$40000.00
on-line reader	$168000.00	$134400.00	$33600.00
utility	$32000.00	$25600.00	$6400.00
TOTAL Cables	$400000.00	$320000.00	$80000.00
TOTALS	$4000000.00	$3200000.00	$800000.00

These are annual costs and savings which will only be
achieved after the system for each of our products has been
implemented. The next table shows the cost savings
implementation. If the QA Data Collection and Analysis
System were implemented so that the Printer System was in
place at the beginning of the second quarter, the Cable
System in place at the beginning of the third quarter, and
the Reader System in place at the beginning of the fourth
quarter, the following savings would be achieved in 1986.

1986
Cost Savings Implementation

	Quarter 1	Quarter 2	Quarter 3	Quarter 4
Printers	$0.00	$80000.00	$80000.00	$80000.00
Cables	$0.00	$0.00	$20000.00	$20000.00
Readers	$0.00	$0.00	$0.00	$100000.00
TOTAL Savings	$0.00	$80000.00	$100000.00	$200000.00

TOTAL 1986 Savings	$380000.00

DATA ANALYSIS

The relational database program, R:base 5000, will be used
to analyze the data collected by the readers. We'll use the
communications program V_Term to take the raw Work-in-
Process data from the readers, analyze it in R:base, and
produce reports like this:

THERMAL PRINTER WORK IN PROCESS REPORT
DATE: 12/28/85

Number of Units Produced:	20
Total Number of Errors :	10
% Units Free of Error :	50

Number of Technical Errors	:	1	Accounting for	10%
Number of Parts Errors	:	3	Accounting for	30%
Number of Workmanship Errors	:	4	Accounting for	40%
Number of Documentation Errors	:	2	Accounting for	20%

PRODID	SERIAL#	BADGE	FAILURE	RESP
2926A	006262	ACE45	take-up reel defect	Part
2927	006321	MMS11	prt wheel rough	Part
2946	011921	TTY22	finish/cleanliness	Work
2959	011890	ACE45	wrong prog rev	Doc
2962	011754	ACE45	poor tooling	Tech
2975	011918	LLA33	PCB defective	Part
2982	011760	AAL00	loose connection	Work
2981	011841	AAL00	assm inst incrtly	Work
2077	012738	AAL00	loose/missing hrdwr	Work
2976	011813	TTY22	incrt paperwork	Doc
2983	015928	VVD69	No Failure	-0-
2989	011867	AMD98	No Failure	-0-
2990	011840	AMD55	No Failure	-0-
3058	011825	ACE33	No Failure	-0-
3060	011826	ACE33	No Failure	-0-
3061	011827	ACE33	No Failure	-0-
3065	011828	ACE33	No Failure	-0-
3069	011833	ACE33	No Failure	-0-
3071	011834	ACE33	No Failure	-0-
3072	011841	ACE33	No Failure	-0-

NOTE: Since this system has not yet been implemented, data
in this report is fictitious.

You can see how useful a report such as this could be. You
can quickly see the types of errors and the causes of these
errors, so correcting them will be direct and straightforward. Because the data is available, we'll be able to
focus on correcting the errors that account for the greatest
percentage of total errors, rather than working at solving
problems one by one without having the data to determine how
frequently each occurs.

We'll also be able to produce Config reports like these:

PRODID	SERIAL#	DATE	P/N-REV	#BURNS	#STEPS
2926A	006262	02/21/86	45075E	159523	52701
2927	006321	02/21/86	45075E	161406	52249
2946	011921	02/21/86	45075E	289301	86124
2959	011890	02/21/86	45075E	74951	16329
2962	011754	02/21/86	45075E	326330	113793
2975	011918	02/21/86	45075E	260313	72674
2976	011813	02/21/86	45075E	205146	67801
2077	011738	02/21/86	45075E	197273	65237
2981	011841	02/21/86	45075E	187998	64107
2982	011760	02/21/86	45075E	530017	15591

Configuration data will be recorded as part of the
manufacturing process. We can use this information to see
which products have which components and consequently be
better to make repairs and adjust the marriage of components
in future product releases. (Data in this report is also
fictitious.)

*A report written in Write, containing information from
R:base 5000, Multiplan, and Microsoft Project*

IMPLEMENTATION

Implementing the QA Data Collection and Analysis System should be done on a product by product basis. We recommend beginning with our printers, then adding our cables, and finally adding the readers. We recommend that one product line be added each quarter. Printer implementation could begin in the first quarter of 1986 with printer QA on-line at the beginning of the second quarter. Maintenance of the printer QA and implementation of the cable QA could take place second quarter with cables on-line at the beginning of the third quarter. Maintenance of printer and cable QA and implementation of reader QA could take place during the third quarter with readers on-line at the beginning of the fourth quarter.

Steps for the implementation of each product are detailed below:

```
                    January 1986        February 1986
                    6    13   20   27   3    10
                    +----+----+----+----+----+------
Det equip needs ****)
Procure equip            )).. ....)
Program readers          )**** ****)
Write doc                          )***)
Program VTerm                      )).. ....)
Install system                     )***)
Train users                             )***)
All systems go                             *
```

CONCLUSION

The QA Data Collection and Analysis System will reduce direct costs by 20 percent. It should also have indirect benefits of increased sales and lower required parts inventories.

The Qa Data Collection and Analysis System will give the QA department the data we need to see that our products exceed our already high quality standards. With this system we can get immediate feedback on manufactured quality and report the "as shipped" configuration as part of the manufacturing process. In addition, this system will provide a model for potential clients of an additional way to use B.C., Inc.'s equipment in yet another phase of the manufacturing process.

If you, like me, have 512K of memory, you'll need a different PIF from the one that comes with Windows, since 512K is not enough memory to run the entire R:base 5000 in a window. But, as you know if you use R:base, the RB5000.EXE file is a menu program that runs the six separate R:base applications: RBASE.EXE, EXPRESS.EXE, RBEDIT.EXE, GATEWAY.EXE, CLOUT2.EXE, and RCOMPILE.EXE. You do have enough memory to run each of these applications individually in a window, but each application must have its own PIF. The application you'll probably want to run in a window most of the time is RBASE.EXE. It's the one you use to run reports, add data, or make inquiries about data, so we'll make a PIF for RBASE.EXE to run it in a window and name it RBASE_W.EXE. It will be the one you'll use for the data to include in the B.C., Inc. report. If you need a PIF for any of the other modules, you can follow this model.

Choose the Open... command from the File menu of the PIF editor, and open the file named RBASE.PIF.

The parameters you'll need to run the RBASE module of R:base 5000 in a window are the default settings. In addition, you may wish to add -R in the Program Parameters box. This tells Windows to start RBASE without displaying the MicroRim logo. It's not a bad logo, but drawing it one asterisk at a time really does increase the amount of time it takes to start RBASE.

Choose the Save... command from the File menu. Change the name of this file to RBASE_W.PIF so you'll know this is the file to use when you want to run the RBASE module of R:base 5000 in a window.

Now we still need a PIF to run R:base 5000 in the take-over-the-screen mode.

■ *In the Program Name box, type:*

RB5000.EXE

With the fields I'm about to specify, you can run all the modules of R:base 5000 in the take-over-the-screen mode with 512K of memory.

The information in the Program Title box (in this case, *MicroRim rBase*) is what will appear in the title bar when an application runs in a window.

■ *If you wish, put -R in the Program Parameters box to run R:base without the initial logo.*

If you wish to start R:base from a directory other than the directory that has your R:base program files, specify the directory where your R:base program files are located in the Initial Directory box. I start R:base from the WINDOWS directory and keep my R:base files on my hard disk in a directory called R5K, so I specify C:\R5K in the Initial Directory box.

■ *In the KB Required box, type:*

256

■ *In the KB Desired box, type:*

320

■ *In the Directly Modifies section, put an X in front of Screen and one in front of Memory.*

This setting tells Windows that this application can't run in a window.

If you accept the default options for Program Parameters and directory paths, your completed PIF should look like the one shown here.

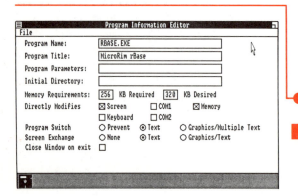

■ *Choose the Save... command from the File menu, and name this file RB5000.PIF instead of keeping the default name (RBASE.EXE).*

Now you have two PIFs for R:base 5000: one for running it in a window (either RB5000_W.PIF, if you have 640K of memory, or RBASE_W.PIF, if you want to run only the RBASE.EXE application) and one for running it when you want it to take over the screen (RB5000.PIF).

■ *Copy these files to the directory that has your R:base program files, to your R:base startup disk, or, if you prefer, to your Windows directory.*

When you start R:base, instead of starting the program file, start the R:base PIF of your choice.

Making PIFs for Multiplan

Chapter 8 gives directions for making two PIFs for Multiplan: MP_W.PIF for running Multiplan in a window and MP.PIF for having it take over the screen.

If you haven't already done so, when you install Multiplan to run on your computer, select the option that allows it to run with Microsoft Windows.

Making PIFs for Microsoft Project

We'll make PIFs for Microsoft Project the same way we did for Multiplan and R:base. The PIF that comes with Windows can run Microsoft Project (Version 2.0) in a window.

■ *From the PIF editor, open the file named PROJ.PIF.*

■ *Check the memory requirements. They should be 128 in KB Required and 256 in KB Desired. If they are different from these, change them.*

■ *Take the X out of the Directly Modifies Screen box so Microsoft Project can run in a window.*

■ *Choose the Save... command from the File menu, and name this file PROJ_W.PIF.*

Now you have two PIFs for Microsoft Project.

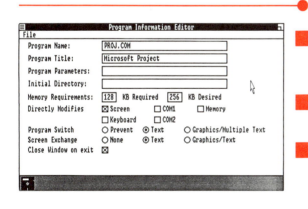

Copy PROJ_W.PIF and PROJ.PIF to the directory with your Microsoft Project program files, to your Microsoft Project startup disk, or to your Windows directory.

When you start Microsoft Project, you should start it with the PIF of your choice rather than with the program file.

That's all there is to setting up two PIFs for each of the standard applications we'll be using. You can use these same procedures to make two PIFs for any other standard application you'll be using that will run either in a window or in the take-over-the-screen mode. The appendix of this book gives PIF information for many standard applications.

WRITING THE REPORT

Let's start by writing the text part of the report with Microsoft Write. You want to use this word processor because it's the place you can combine both text and graphics from other applications. Windows will take care of translating the different file formats so Write can read them.

The QA Data Collection and Analysis System report will have these parts:

1. The QA Plan

    This section introduces the system.

2. Cost Savings

    This section details cost savings by bringing in information from Multiplan.

3. Data Analysis

    This section shows samples from R:base of the types of data collection and analysis this system proposes to use.

4. Implementation

This section details exactly how the plan will be implemented. It shows this graphically with a chart from Microsoft Project.

5. Conclusion

This section restates the benefits of the QA Data Collection and Analysis System.

■ *Start Write.*

We will write this report in the Courier font. Courier is the only standard font that is not proportionally spaced, but is monospaced—that is, each character takes up the same amount of space on the screen. If we use Courier, we won't have to change fonts when we copy in numbers from the standard applications; our columns will line up precisely.

■ *Choose the Courier font from the Character menu.*

Now Write will display and print in the Courier font everything you type or paste in.

■ *Type the three paragraphs in the first section of your report, using Write as you usually do. Here is the text for this section:*

THE QA PLAN[Enter][Enter]
Quality Assurance has developed a Data Collection and Analysis system that will reduce the costs of producing our printers, cables, and readers, and will enable us to better understand and maintain control of the manufacturing process.[Enter][Enter]

The QA Data Collection and Analysis System will collect two types of data: Work in Process (WIP) data and Configuration (Config) data. The WIP data will allow us to better understand and manage the assembly process. The Config data will enable us to better track the configuration of units in the field and units returned for repair. We can track which products with which components have the most breakdowns and use this information to more quickly repair returned products and perhaps make changes in the way components are used together in future products.[Enter][Enter]

We'll accomplish this data collection using our own bar codes and the 9420/1600 laser reader. This will simplify the data collection and significantly reduce the probability of input errors. Quality assurance reports will be easy to produce. Reports can be run on demand giving immediate feedback on manufactured quality. We have our own in-house experts to program the readers. And because all employees are familiar with using the bar codes and readers in our Time-Tracking System, training for the QA system should be relatively simple.[Enter][Enter]

Now type the two paragraphs for the second section (Cost Savings):

COST SAVINGS[Enter][Enter]
The following table details our current production costs and then shows our projections for the amount the new QA Data Collection and Analysis System will reduce these costs.[Enter][Enter]
**********paste MP cost-savings worksheet here[Enter][Enter]
These are annual costs and savings which will only be achieved after the system for each of our products has been implemented. The next table shows the cost savings implementation. If the QA Data Collection and Analysis System were implemented so that the

Chapter 9: Standard Applications That Run in a Window

Printer System was in place at the beginning of the second quarter, the Cable System in place at the beginning of the third quarter, and the Reader System in place at the beginning of the fourth quarter, the following savings would be achieved in 1986.[Enter][Enter]
***********paste MP cost-savings implementation worksheet here[Enter]*

The lines beginning with asterisks are markers where the Multiplan worksheets will be pasted.

Press Ctrl-Enter to insert a page break and begin the next section (Data Analysis) on page 3. Type the following text for the third section:

DATA ANALYSIS[Enter][Enter]
The relational database program, R:base 5000, will be used to analyze the data collected by the readers. We'll use the communications program V_Term to take the raw Work-in-Process data from the readers, analyze it in R:base, and produce reports like this:[Enter][Enter]
*********paste WIP report here[Enter][Enter]*
NOTE: Since this system has not yet been implemented, data in this report is fictitious.[Enter][Enter]
You can see how useful a report such as this could be. You can quickly see the types of errors and the causes of these errors, so correcting them will be direct and straightforward. Because the data is available, we'll be able to focus on correcting the errors that account for the greatest percentage of total errors, rather than working at solving problems one by one without having the data to determine how frequently each occurs.[Enter][Enter]
We'll also be able to produce Config reports like these:[Enter][Enter]
*****paste config table here[Enter][Enter]*
Configuration data will be recorded as part of the manufacturing process. We can use this

information to see which products have which components, and consequently be better able to make repairs and adjust the marriage of components in future product releases. (Data in this report is also fictitious.)[Enter]

■ *Start the fourth section (Implementation) on a new page and type this text:*

IMPLEMENTATION[Enter][Enter]
Implementing the QA Data Collection and Analysis System should be done on a product by product basis. We recommend beginning with our printers, then adding our cables, and finally adding the readers. We recommend that one product line be added each quarter. Printer implementation could begin in the first quarter of 1986 with printer QA on line at the beginning of the second quarter. Maintenance of the printer QA and implementation of the cable QA could take place in the second quarter, with cables on line at the beginning of the third quarter. Maintenance of printer and cable QA and implementation of reader QA could take place during the third quarter, with readers on line at the beginning of the fourth quarter.[Enter][Enter]
Steps for the implementation of each product are detailed below:[Enter][Enter]
*****paste in Microsoft Project chart here[Enter]

■ *Start the last section (Conclusion) on a new page, and type this two-paragraph conclusion:*

CONCLUSION[Enter][Enter]
The QA Data Collection and Analysis System will reduce direct costs by 20 percent. It should also have indirect benefits of increased sales and lower required parts inventories.
[Enter][Enter]
The QA Data Collection and Analysis System will give the QA department the data we need to see that our products exceed our already

high quality standards. With this system we can get immediate feedback on manufactured quality and report the "as shipped" configuration as part of the manufacturing process. In addition, this system will provide a model for potential clients of an additional way to use B.C., Inc.'s equipment in yet another phase of the manufacturing process.[Enter]

Now you've finished the text for your report. Save it in a file called QAPLAN and quit Write so enough memory is free to start the standard applications.

ASSEMBLING THE PARTS OF THE REPORT

If you have 640K of memory and you are going to be working with several standard applications, it's a good idea to start them all first. As explained in Chapter 8, Windows works best if you start the standard application that requires the most memory first (in this example, that's R:base).

If you have 512K of memory or less, running fairly large standard applications and Microsoft Write is possible, but not very practical. Here's what happens:

The standard application and Windows take up most of the memory, but Write will still run in the very limited amount of memory that is left because Windows swaps in only the parts of the program it needs. However, because it's running in an extremely tight memory space, it runs VERY slowly, really too slowly to use it for useful work.

It really is much more efficient to run one standard application (such as Multiplan, R:base, or Microsoft Project) at a time, copy the information you need to the Clipboard, then quit the standard application, load the Write document you want the information in, and paste it in from the Clipboard. I'll give instructions for doing this project on a 512K XT, running one standard application at a time, then closing it and starting Write.

You'll be running each of the standard applications in a window. That way, you can mark and transfer just the parts you want to use in the report. It's a good idea to run standard applications in the take-over-the-screen mode when you're doing work with them one by one—building the worksheets, data-files, and charts—and only run them in a window when you're combining information from several applications. They will run more slowly in a window, but not so slowly as not to be useful.

Copying from Multiplan

You'll start with Multiplan and load the worksheet that has the projected annual cost savings for each B.C., Inc. product.

Start Multiplan with the file named MP__W.PIF.

Recall from Chapter 8 that when standard applications run in a window, they have a System menu in the upper left corner and a size box in the upper right corner. If you zoom the window by using either the size box or the Zoom command from the System menu, it will expand over the icon area and you will be able to see three additional lines without scrolling.

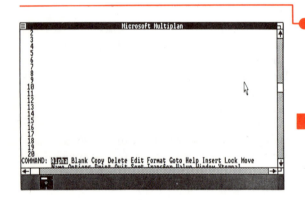

Zoom the Multiplan window so it expands over the icon area.

To return to a standard-size window so you can use the icons to start other applications, double-click the size box or choose the Zoom command from the System menu a second time.

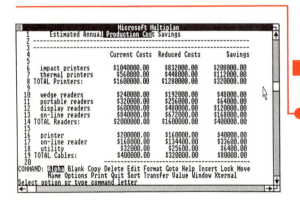

Use Multiplan to create a Cost Savings worksheet that looks like the worksheet shown here, or load an existing worksheet of your own that you'd like to copy into the report.

The first column of figures (labeled *Current Costs*) details current production costs for each of B.C., Inc.'s three product lines: printers, readers, and cables. The second column (*Reduced Costs*) shows how production costs for each of these lines would be reduced with the implementation of the new QA system. Note that costs are reduced by 20 percent with the new system. The third column (Savings) shows dollars saved for each product.

First, select the information you want to transfer to your report and then choose the Copy command from the system menu to put this information in the Clipboard.

M *Move the mouse pointer to the upper left corner of the section you want to mark. Hold down the mouse button and drag down and right until the section you want to copy to the Clipboard is highlighted.*

K *Choose the Mark command from the System menu. This puts a rectangular cursor in the upper left corner of the window. Use the direction keys to move the cursor to the upper left corner of the area you wish to mark. Hold down the Shift key and press the down and right direction keys to mark the section you want to copy to the Clipboard.*

In the example, you need to mark the section of the Multiplan worksheet shown here.

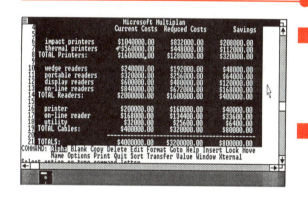

Choose the Copy command from the System menu.

Windows copies the marked text to the Clipboard and then removes the selection marking.

Quit Multiplan.

Because you selected the Close Window On Exit option for Multiplan in the PIF editor, when you quit, the Multiplan window disappears from the screen and the MS-DOS Executive takes over.

Now you run Write and paste in the Multiplan information.

M *Start Write by double-clicking on the name of the report file (QAPLAN.DOC).*

K *Start Write by selecting the name of the report file (QAPLAN.DOC) and pressing Enter.*

This starts Write and opens QAPLAN in one step.

Use the Find... command on the Search menu to locate the asterisks marking the place for the first Multiplan worksheet.

Position the cursor at the left margin just below this marker.

If you choose the Reduce Font command before you paste in this chart, all the columns from the Multiplan worksheet will line up properly and fit inside Write's margins. The Multiplan data will be a slightly different size so you can see it clearly when you view the entire completed QA Plan document. You may size the worksheets differently if you wish with the Size Picture command.

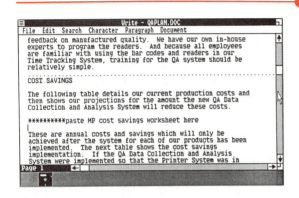

Choose the Reduce Font command from the Character menu. Now choose the Paste command from the Edit menu.

You can use Write's keyboard short-cut for the Paste command, the Ins key. Using the keyboard shortcuts for selecting these commands is faster because you don't have to wait for the menu to be displayed.

Windows pastes in the text you marked, starting at the cursor position.

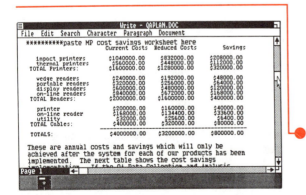

■ *Now you can delete the marker for this worksheet (the line that reads:* ***********paste MP cost savings worksheet here).*

That's all there is to copying from one standard application to a Windows application. Whenever you run a standard application that runs in a window, it will have the same System menu with the same commands and will work the same way.

■ *Quit Write.*

You don't need to save first. Before closing, Windows prompts you to save changes.

Now let's copy in the second Multiplan worksheet.

■ *Start Multiplan the same way as before, with the PIF named MP_W.PIF.*

■ *Zoom this window, just as before, so the window is as large as possible.*

■ *Use Multiplan's Transfer Load command to load your second Multiplan worksheet, or create the 1986 Cost Savings Implementation worksheet shown here.*

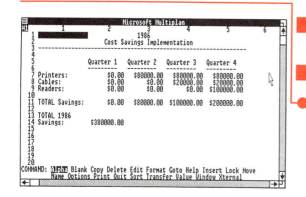

This worksheet details the order in which cost savings will occur as the QA plan is implemented quarter by quarter. The printer QA system will be in place in the second quarter, resulting in production cost savings of $80,000. Cables will be added in the third quarter for additional production cost savings of $20,000, and readers will be added in the fourth quarter for additional savings of $100,000, making the total production cost savings each quarter $200,000, once all systems are implemented, and the total 1986 savings $380,000.

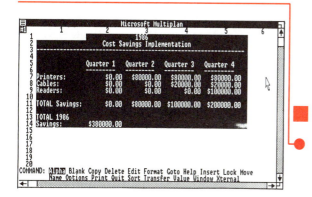

■ *Use the Mark command from the System menu to mark this worksheet, just as you did with the previous worksheet.*

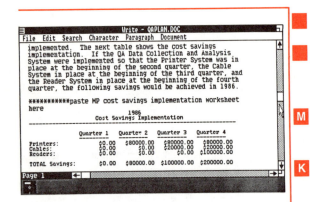

```
THERMAL PRINTER WORK IN PROCESS REPORT
                    DATE: 01/02/80
Number of Units Produced:    20
Total Number of Errors   :   10
% Units Free of Error    :   50

Number of Technical Errors    :  1   Accounting for   10%
Number of Parts Errors        :  3   Accounting for   30%
Number of Workmanship Errors  :  4   Accounting for   40%
Number of Documentation Errors:  2   Accounting for   20%

PRODID    SERIAL#   BADGE    FAILURE                RESP
2926A     006262    ACE45    take-up reel defect    Part
2927      006321    NNS11    prt wheel rough        Part
2946      011921    TTY22    finish/cleanliness     Work
2959      011890    ACE45    wrong prog rev         Doc
2962      011754    ACE45    poor tooling           Tech
2975      011918    LLA33    PCB defective          Part
2982      011760    AAL00    loose connection       Work
2981      011841    AAL00    assm inst incrtly      Work
2077      012738    AAL00    loose/missing hrdwr    Work
2976      011813    TTY22    incrt paperwork        Doc
2983      015928    VVD59    No Failure             -0-
2989      011867    AND98    No Failure             -0-
2990      011840    AND55    No Failure             -0-
3058      011825    ACE33    No Failure             -0-
3060      011826    ACE33    No Failure             -0-
3061      011827    ACE33    No Failure             -0-
3065      011828    ACE33    No Failure             -0-
3069      011833    ACE33    No Failure             -0-
3071      011834    ACE33    No Failure             -0-
3072      011841    ACE33    No Failure             -0-
```

■ Choose the Copy command from the System menu to copy the marked information to the Clipboard.

■ Quit Multiplan.

The Multiplan window closes and the MS-DOS Executive returns.

■ Start your Write document named QAPLAN.DOC.

■ Use the Find command to locate your second marker **********paste mp cost savings implementation here.

M Click to put an insertion point just below this marker, choose Reduce Font from the Character menu, and then choose Paste from the Edit menu.

K Use the direction keys to position the insertion point just below this marker, press F9, the keyboard shortcut for Reduce Font, and then press Ins, the keyboard shortcut for the Paste command.

Windows pastes in the information from the Clipboard, starting at the insertion point.

■ Delete the marker for this paste and you've again successfully copied information from one standard application (Multiplan) into Write.

■ Quit Write.

Copying from R:base

Next, you'll copy two kinds of information from R:base—a report and a table—into Write.

The R:base report you'll paste into Write would look like the report shown here if you printed it. It was generated from an R:base table containing the

```
 MicroRim rBase
R)select all from wip
PRODID   SERIAL#  BADGE   FAILURE              RESP
-------- -------- ------- -------------------- -------
2926A    006262   ACE45   take-up reel defect  Part
2927     006321   NNS11   prt wheel rough      Part
2946     011921   TTY22   finish/cleanliness   Work
2959     011890   ACE45   wrong prog rev       Doc
2962     011754   ACE45   poor tooling         Tech
2975     011918   LLA33   PCB defective        Part
2982     011760   AAL00   loose connection     Work
2981     011841   AAL00   assm inst incrtly    Work
2077     012738   AAL00   loose/missing hrdwr  Work
2976     011813   TTY22   incrt paperwork      Doc
2983     015928   UVD59   No Failure           -0-
2989     011867   AND98   No Failure           -0-
2990     011840   AND55   No Failure           -0-
3058     011825   ACE33   No Failure           -0-
3060     011826   ACE33   No Failure           -0-
3061     011827   ACE33   No Failure           -0-
3065     011828   ACE33   No Failure           -0-
3069     011833   ACE33   No Failure           -0-
3071     011834   ACE33   No Failure           -0-
3072     011835   ACE33   No Failure           -0-
```

information shown here. This is the information the manufacturing people will enter for each product as they assemble it. For the example, you'll need an existing R:base report, so create this one now.

■ *Create an R:base work-in-process datafile and save it as WIP.*

■ *Use the R:base report generator to create a report like the one shown on the previous page.*

You'll display this R:base report, mark it, and copy it exactly where you want it in your QA report. This is not quite as simple as copying the Multiplan worksheet. Because the Clipboard has a size limitation, Windows allows you to mark and copy only 25 lines at a time. So you need to set up the report to display (actually, print to the screen) 25 lines and then pause. You'll copy these lines to Write. Then you'll display the remaining lines of the report and copy these in.

■ *Start R:base from RBASE_W.PIF.*

■ *Zoom the R:base window so it expands over the icon area.*

First, use R:base's Reports command to set the page length for this report.

■ *Enter the R:base report generator by typing:*

reports

■ *Type a space and then the name of your report.*

■ *Select Set Number Of Lines Per Page from the Reports menu.*

You'll see a prompt that reads "Current number of lines per page is 66. New number:"

ABOUT...

File/application pairing

Many applications supply a file-name extension to data files you create with them. For example, Paint adds the extension .MSP to files created with Paint. Windows stores this information in the WIN.INI file, which makes it possible for you to specify the application that's opened when you open a file with a particular extension. For instance, if you want to open .DOC files with Word instead of with Write (Windows' default), you can change the line that reads *doc=write.exe ^.doc* to *doc =word.com ^.doc* in the WIN.INI file.

As the page length, enter:

12

You compute the page length basically by trial and error. This is what I did: I entered *12* rather than *25* because the heading in the R:base report is a total of 13 lines. This means I can print only 12 lines of rows from the table in the report and still keep the total page length at 25 lines. The summary information in the report heading is at least as important as the rows from the information in the table.

Now leave the report generator and return to the R> prompt, the prompt for the R:base command module.

Run the report using the R:base Print command and specifying the report name.

R:base will send the report to the screen.

After 25 lines, the display will pause and you'll see the message shown at the bottom of the screen.

Now is the time to use the Scroll, Mark, and Copy commands and copy the first 25 lines to the Clipboard. The first five lines of the report have scrolled off the screen. So, first you need to scroll back up to the top of the report so that you can mark the entire 25 lines to copy in to the Clipboard.

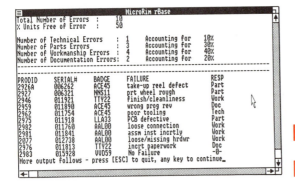

M   *Drag the right scroll bar's scroll box up to the top of the bar.*

K   *Choose the Scroll command from the System menu. Use the up direction key to scroll back up to the top of the report. Press Enter to terminate the Scroll command and return control to R:base.*

Position the mouse pointer at the top of the report. Hold down the mouse button and drag over the report. When you get to the bottom of the screen, continue to drag down and the report will scroll up to the 25-line maximum. Stop just above the "More output follows" message.

Choose the Mark command from the System menu. Hold down the Shift key and press the down direction key and then the right direction key to mark the report. When you reach the bottom of the window, continue pressing the down direction key. Windows will continue to mark and scroll the report up to the 25-line maximum. Stop just above the "More output follows" message.

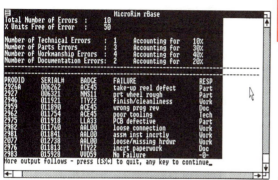

Choose Copy from the System menu and the marked information will be copied to the Clipboard.

Quit R:base and restart your Write report (QAPLAN.DOC) and move the insertion point to just below the first R:base (WIP) place marker.

You'll copy this report into Write in the reduced font so the columns line up.

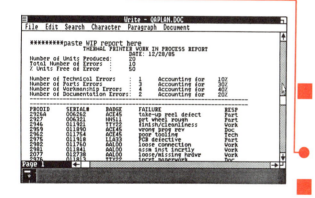

Choose Reduce Font from the Character menu, then Paste from the Edit menu.

The first part of the report is copied into Write.

Quit Write.

Start R:base the same as before. Open your database and run the report a second time. When you get the "Press a key to continue" message, press any key to display the second part of the report.

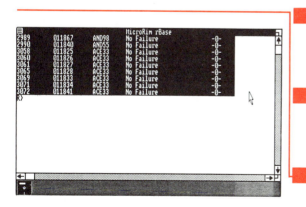

When the rest of the report is displayed and you see the R> prompt, scroll to the top of this section of the report using either the keyboard or mouse, just as you did before.

Select the last nine lines of the 33-line report.

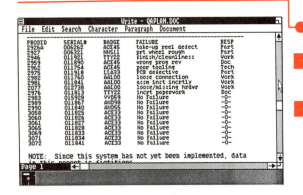

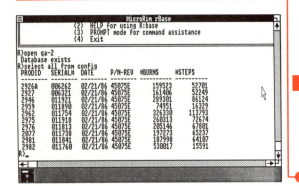

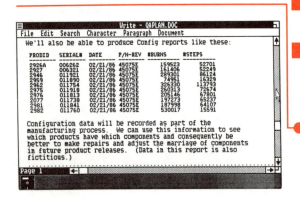

Now choose the Copy command and copy this to the Clipboard.

Quit R:base.

Start your Write report (QAPLAN.DOC), move the insertion point to the line just below the part of the R:base report you just copied in. Reduce the font and paste in the last part of the report.

Delete the place marker indicating the place to paste this report.

Quit Write.

Next you need to copy in the R:base configuration table, additional information in your R:base QA database you'd like in your report. This table contains information on the "as-shipped" configuration of printers manufactured by B.C., Inc. This will be easier than copying in the R:base report because the table is less than 25 lines long. All you need to do is display it on the screen, mark it, and then copy it in.

Start R:base again and open your database. After the R> prompt, use the Select command to display the information in the table.

I used the Select All From Config command. (Config is the name of the table with the configuration data.)

Select this information and choose the Copy command to copy it to the Clipboard.

Start your Write report (QAPLAN.DOC). Move the insertion point to the place marker for the configuration table. Press F9 to reduce the font size. Choose the Paste command from the Edit menu and Windows will copy the marked text in. Then delete the marker.

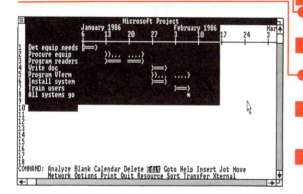

A Gantt chart created in Microsoft Project

■ *Quit Write.*

Now you've finished copying in both the Multiplan and the R:base information and all you have left to do to complete the report is to copy in the Microsoft Project chart.

Copying from Microsoft Project

In Microsoft Project, you need to create a Gantt chart detailing implementation steps. You'll copy this chart into your Write report.

M *Start Microsoft Project by double-clicking the PIF named PROJ_W.PIF.*

K *Start Microsoft Project by selecting the PIF named PROJ_W.PIF and pressing Enter.*

■ *Use Project to create a Gantt chart like the one shown here or use a chart of your own.*

■ *Select the parts of the screen you want to copy to your report with the mouse or the Mark command from the System menu.*

■ *Choose the Copy command and the chart will be copied to the Clipboard.*

■ *Start your Write report (QAPLAN.DOC) one last time and scroll to the place marker for the Project chart. Move the insertion point to just below this marker. Reduce the font and paste in the chart. Then delete your marker.*

Now your report is finished, complete with information from Multiplan, R:base, and Microsoft Project, compiled with appropriate text in Write. And Windows also takes care of letting you combine information with different formats into one Windows application.

Now that you've pasted in all the information, check the page breaks to be sure they fall in the right places.

■ *Choose Repaginate... from the File menu.*

Write displays a dialog box asking
you if you want to confirm page
breaks.

Repaginate Document   [Ok]

☐ Confirm Page Breaks   [Cancel]

■ *Select the Confirm Page Breaks option, then click
OK or press Enter.*

Now Write will go through the
document, display each page break,
and ask for confirmation or changes:
If the page break is one you've inserted with Ctrl-Enter, Write asks if
you want to keep or delete it. If it is
a page break that Write inserts, it
displays the dialog box shown here.
You can use the Up or Down button
to change the position of the break,
then the Confirm button to verify it.

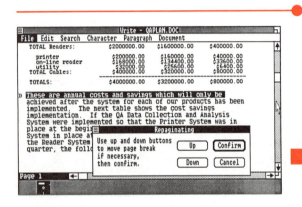

As you're repaginating the QAPLAN report, you'll
come to one page break that Write inserted in the
middle of the second R:base table.

■ *Use the Up button to move the page break to the
sentence just above this table, then click Confirm
or press Enter.*

One cosmetic change you may wish to make before printing is to add an additional line of white
space at the top and bottom of each of the charts
you pasted in. Adding white space will set them off
a bit more from the surrounding text.

■ *Choose Print... from the File menu.*

Your finished report now looks like
the report shown at the beginning of
this chapter.

If you have time before Friday (your presentation deadline), you could use Paint to make an attractive cover page to accompany the report, such as the one shown here.

You can print the cover from Paint or copy it to Write and have the entire report—graphics and text from five applications—in one place.

QA DATA COLLECTION & ANALYSIS SYSTEM

IMPLEMENTATION PLAN

BC, Incorporated
January 1986

10

STANDARD APPLICATIONS THAT DON'T RUN IN A WINDOW

In Chapter 9, you learned how to use standard applications that run in a window and how to run them either in a window or in the take-over-the-screen mode. You learned how to take information from any one of these standard applications and combine it with other information in a Windows application. This is easy when the standard application runs in a window, because Windows provides the tools to mark, copy, and paste the information you want to transfer.

With standard applications that won't run in a window, combining information from several applications is not quite as easy. There is no way for Windows to provide tools to mark the text or graphics you want to transfer. But Windows does provide the facility to take a snapshot of the screen of a standard application and copy this to the Clipboard. And you can paste this screen into a Windows application. So, you can transfer information from standard applications that don't run in a window to Windows applications. But you can't mark only the section you want to transfer; you must transfer information one screenful at a time.

In this chapter, we'll look at how this works. We'll combine information (both text and graphics) from three standard applications that don't run in a window—Microsoft Word, dBASE III, and Lotus 1-2-3—in Microsoft Write.

Here's what we'll do with these applications: Imagine that you are Celestial Smith, the vice president of corporate communications for Mythical Corporation, a diversified company with interests in life sciences, wizardry, astrology, and alchemy. It's annual report time once again, and your job is to coordinate the efforts to produce the report. You've had a preliminary meeting with the president, the chief financial officer, and the vice president of operations at which you presented a plan for this year's report and assigned responsibility for each section. The chief financial officer will do the financial reports for the back of the report, as usual. The vice president of operations will be responsible for the middle section, in which the executive from each group responds to questions about his or her area. And you, as usual, are responsible for writing the opening section, a letter to shareholders from Mythical's president, Dr. Charles B. Unicorn.

You've discussed the letter with Dr. Unicorn, and have an outline of points he wants covered. Because you have Windows, you decide you may be able to communicate more effectively if you lighten up on the amount of text in the letter and show as much as possible graphically. You want to use your familiar tools—Lotus 1-2-3, dBASE III, and Word—because you're comfortable with them and they have the information you need. Using Windows will allow you to combine information from these applications in Write to create your opening letter. Taking snapshots of the Lotus 1-2-3 and dBASE III information and pasting them into Write will make the report easier to edit because you'll be able to eliminate transmission errors that could occur if you had to enter figures by hand. Write and Word files are compatible, so you can prepare the letter in Word and just load it into Write when you're ready to paste in information from 1-2-3 and dBASE. The vice president of operations will give you his information in a Word file and the chief financial officer will give you 1-2-3 files. This way, you can add their information to the text you've already created in Write, make any editing changes you wish, print it, and you'll be finished.

USING WORD

First, you need to create the text of the president's letter. If Word is the word-processing program you're most comfortable with, use it for this part. As I just mentioned, Write is compatible with Word, so you won't need to go through any conversion programs or elaborate copying to move the letter from Word to Write. If you are not used to Word and you are becoming more comfortable with Write, you might as well draft your letter with Write. The key is to use the tools that do the job and that you are most comfortable and familiar with.

The PIF I use for Word is shown here.

As you may recall from Chapter 8, the /X parameter tells Word not to reserve space for Spell. Spell has its own PIF and can claim its own memory. The /C tells Word to run in the text mode; this uses less memory, and if you want to take a snapshot of a Word screen to use in another application, it will be a text screen, which also uses less memory. You may wish to save this PIF as WORD_TEX.PIF so you'll know it's the PIF that starts Word in text mode. If you keep your Word program files in one directory, you may wish to specify that directory in the Initial Directory box of the Word PIF.

Copy the file named WORD.PIF to your Word program directory, to your Word startup disk, or to your Windows directory.

Start Word (or Write) and use it to enter the text of Dr. Unicorn's letter:

To Mythical Shareholders:[Enter][Enter] 1984 was a year of significant change for Mythical, a year in which we completed our health-care programs in Xanadu and made a major commitment to domestic prepaid health care.[Enter][Enter]

```
≡              Program Information Editor            ⌐
 File
 Program Name:       WORD.COM
 Program Title:      Microsoft Word
 Program Parameters: /X/C
 Initial Directory:  C:\WORD
 Memory Requirements: 192  KB Required  228  KB Desired
 Directly Modifies   ⊠ Screen    □ COM1     □ Memory
                     □ Keyboard  □ COM2
 Program Switch      ○ Prevent  ⊙ Text     ○ Graphics/Multiple Text
 Screen Exchange     ○ None     ⊙ Text     ○ Graphics/Text
 Close Window on exit ⊠
```

First, I will review our 1984 operating results and outline our long-term strategy. In the next section, Mythical's group executives respond to questions about their areas asked by shareholders, customers, wizards, and financial analysts.[Enter][Enter]
The last section, beginning on page 28, contains the financial statements and notes. I invite your close attention to this detailed information on the company's performance and financial condition.[Enter][Enter][Enter]
1984 in Review[Enter][Enter]
The following table details Mythical's sales and profits (in thousands) for 1984 compared with 1983.[Enter][Enter]
******insert dbase table here[Enter][Enter]
Sales for the fiscal year ending October 31, 1984 were $1,437,026,000, down from $1,602,825,000 in 1983, while net income increased to $43,870,000, or $3.01 per share, from $37,609,000, or $2.55 per share, in 1983.[Enter][Enter][Enter]
Financial Condition[Enter][Enter]
Mythical ended fiscal 1984 in good financial condition with cash and equivalents of $67 million and working capital of $252 million.[Enter][Enter]
*******insert Lotus Sales chart[Enter]
*******insert Lotus assets chart[Enter]
*******insert Lotus net income chart[Enter]
*******insert Lotus earnings per share chart[Enter]
*******insert dBASE pricediv report[Enter]
Both long-term and short-term debt were down, shareholders' equity was up, and our debt-to-equity ratio stood at .44:1, compared with .68:1 at year end 1983.[Enter][Enter][Enter]
Long-term Strategy[Enter][Enter]
There are five things that we at Mythical strive for continuously:[Enter]
[Tab]customer satisfaction with Mythical as a supplier;[Enter]

[Tab]employee satisfaction with Mythical as an employer;[Enter]
[Tab]community satisfaction with Mythical as a neighbor;[Enter]
[Tab]shareholder satisfaction with Mythical as an investment;[Enter]
[Tab]deity satisfaction with Mythical as a supplicant.[Enter][Enter]
If we are to be deserving of shareholder support, I believe we must, over the long term:[Enter]
[Tab]achieve or exceed a 15 percent after-tax return on equity;[Enter]
[Tab]establish a minimum annual earnings growth rate of ten percent; and[Enter]
[Tab]pay out approximately one third of our earnings as dividends.[Enter][Enter]
Our strategy for achieving these objectives in the 1980s and beyond is to build on our strengths in the fields of elf care, gnome technology, specialty spells, and consulting with demigods—both internally and through acquisitions, specifically the purchase of rare Ecuadoran bat parts. While we are not abandoning our interests in our other businesses, we are changing the nature and extent of our involvement in them in order to concentrate more of our interests in these strategic growth areas.[Enter][Enter]
In looking forward to the challenges of 1985 and beyond, what encourages us most is the ability and character of the people and creatures in the Mythical organization. All of us at Mythical look forward to the continuing support of our shareholders as we enter an exciting and, we believe, rewarding period for Mythical Corporation.[Enter][Enter][Enter]
Charles B. Unicorn[Enter]
President[Enter]

As in the report in Chapter 9, the lines beginning with asterisks are place markers that will tell you where to paste the dBASE tables and Lotus charts.

Use Word's Transfer Save command (or Save As... if you're using Write) and name this file ANNREP. Word (and Write) adds the .DOC extension.

The .DOC extension identifies this file as one that can be read by either Word or Write.

USING WRITE

Now open ANNREP.DOC in Write.

Start Write and open the file named ANNREP.DOC if it's not already open.

When Write starts a Word file, unless you've changed the font in Word, it uses Courier, Word's default font.

First, change the font to Helv (or whichever font you prefer from the list available for your printer found in the Character menu).

To change the font for the entire report, you need to select the entire document first.

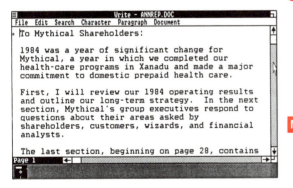

M *Move the mouse pointer to the selection bar (anywhere along the left edge of the text). You'll know you're there when the mouse pointer changes to an arrow that slants to the right. Hold down the Ctrl key and press the mouse button.*

K *Position the insertion point at the beginning of the document. Hold down the Shift key, press the GoTo key (5 on the keypad), and then the End key.*

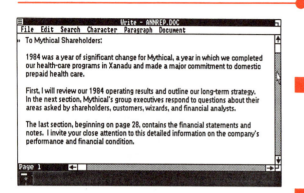

With the entire document selected, choose the Helv command from the Character menu.

The font for the document changes from Courier to Helv.

Now make the section titles larger and bold so they stand out.

One at a time, select these titles:

To Mythical Shareholders:
1984 in Review
Financial Condition
Long-term Strategy

Then press F6, the keyboard shortcut for the Bold command, and F10, the keyboard shortcut for Enlarge Font. Write will only enlarge the fonts if your printer has a larger font available. (The IBM Proprinter has a larger Helv font. The HP LaserJet with the 92286B font cartridge does not.)

As I've mentioned before, using keyboard shortcuts, when you can remember them, is faster than using the mouse because you don't have to wait for Write to display the menu.

That's all there is to loading a Word file into Write, changing fonts, and making the titles stand out.

You need to close Write now to give all the memory to dBASE. Closing without first saving is a shortcut. If you close and the document has not been saved or if you've made changes since the last time you saved, Write will display a dialog box asking you whether or not to save.

Simply choose Yes and you'll have closed and saved in one step.

COPYING INFORMATION FROM DBASE III

Now you're ready to copy information from dBASE into the annual report draft in Write.

Let's say you have a dBASE III file with detailed information about sales and operating profit for each of the Mythical industry segments. You'll use summary information from this database (summary sales and operating profit for each segment in 1983 and 1984), and display it on the screen so Windows can take a snapshot of it and copy it to the Clipboard. To do this, you need to clear the screen and have dBASE list just the fields from this database that you want in the report. (Your databases or summaries will most likely be longer than one screen, so you'll have to copy them one screenful at a time, as you did in Chapter 9.)

To start dBASE from Windows, you can use the dBASE III PIF that comes with Windows, which is shown here.

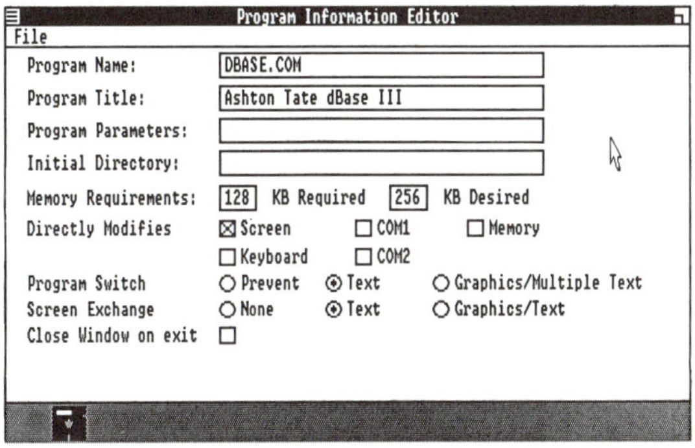

Notice the X in the Directly Modifies Screen box, signifying that dBASE III writes directly to the screen memory and thus cannot be run in a window. (But dBASE III Plus will run in a window if you remove the X.)

Copy the file named DBASE3.PIF from the PIF directory either to your dBASE III directory, to your dBASE III startup disk, or to your Windows directory.

Start dBASE III by using the file named DBASE3.PIF.

Next, open the datafile with the information you want and use the .clear command to clear the screen.

For this example, use the following command to display the information you want:

.list off segment, sales_84, profit_84, sales_83, profit_83

```
=                Program Information Editor
File
Program Name:        [DBASE.COM                        ]
Program Title:       [Ashton Tate dBase III            ]
Program Parameters:  [                                 ]
Initial Directory:   [                                 ]
Memory Requirements: [128] KB Required  [256] KB Desired
Directly Modifies    ⊠ Screen   □ COM1      □ Memory
                     □ Keyboard □ COM2
Program Switch       ○ Prevent  ⊙ Text   ○ Graphics/Multiple Text
Screen Exchange      ○ None     ⊙ Text   ○ Graphics/Text
Close Window on exit □
```

```
dBASE III  version 1.10 IBM/MSDOS ***

COPYRIGHT (c) ASHTON-TATE 1984
AS AN UNPUBLISHED LICENSED PROPRIETARY WORK.
ALL RIGHTS RESERVED.

Use of this software and the other materials contained in the software package
(the "Materials") has been provided under a Software License Agreement (please
read in full).  In summary, Ashton-Tate grants you a paid-up, non-transferrable,
personal license to use the Materials only on a single or subsequent (but not
additional) computer terminal for fifty years from the time the sealed disk
has been opened.  You receive the right to use the Materials, but you do not
become the owner of them.  You may not alter, decompile, or reverse-assemble the
software, and YOU MAY NOT COPY the Materials.  The Materials are protected by
copyright, trade secrets, and trademark law, the violation of which can result
in civil damages and criminal prosecution.

dBASE, dBASE III and ASHTON-TATE are trademarks of Ashton-Tate.

Press the F1 key for help
Type a command (or ASSIST) and press the return key (←┘).

. use b:segprof
. clear
```

The words *segment, sales_84, profit_84, sales_83,* and *profit_83* are the names of fields in this dBASE datafile. The word *off* tells dBASE not to include record numbers in the display.

With this command, dBASE displays the information shown here.

You also want dBASE to compute totals for sales and profit for each year and can get this with the sum command.

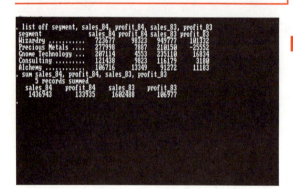

```
. list off segment, sales_84, profit_84, sales_83, profit_83
segment             sales_84 profit_84 sales_83 profit_83
Wizardry .........    723677     98323   949777    101332
Precious Metals ...   277998      7887   210150    -25552
Gnome Technology ..   207114      4553   235110     16834
Consulting ........   121438      9823   116179      3180
Alchemy ...........   106716     13349    91272     11183
```

Use the following command:

.sum sales_84, profit_84, sales_83, profit_83

Now dBASE displays the totals shown here.

This is exactly the information you want in the annual report.

To copy this screen to the Clipboard for use in Write, simply press Alt-PrtSc.

Windows takes a snapshot of the screen. You can tell that the snapshot is taken by the screen momentarily switching to inverse video (black characters on a white background).

When Windows is finished copying, the screen returns to normal. The snapshot is now safely in the Clipboard, and you may resume normal work in dBASE.

Quit dBASE with the .quit command.

M *Start Write by double-clicking on the file named ANNREP.DOC.*

K *Start Write by selecting the file named ANNREP.DOC and pressing Enter.*

Chapter 10: Standard Applications That Don't Run in a Window

This starts Write and opens the
annual report (ANNREP.DOC) in
one step.

You can use the Find... command to quickly
locate the place to paste this information.

■ *Use the Find... command on the Search menu.*
In the Find What box, type:

****

M *Click the Find Next button.*

K *Use the Tab key to move past Whole Word and*
Match Upper/Lower Case. When the blinking
underline is beneath Find Next, press the Spacebar.

Write scrolls to the text you
specified and highlights it.

■ *Choose the Close command from the Find*
window's System menu or press Esc to close the
Find window.

You won't be needing the Find...
command again for a while.

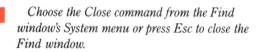
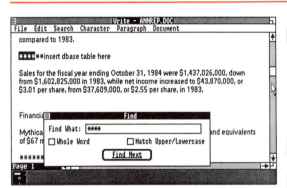

M *Click to get the insertion point at the end of*
this line.

K *Press the End key to move the insertion point to*
the end of the line.

■ *Press Enter for a blank line below the "insert*
dbase table" place marker.

This marks the place for the upper
left corner of the table.

Before you paste, you can choose the Courier
font. Courier is a monospaced font that works best
with columns of figures that should be aligned. You
can also reduce this font and use the smallest size
Courier so the lines won't wrap.

Choose the Courier font from the Character menu. Press F9 twice for the smallest font.

> As always, if you have a question about what sizes are available for your printer, choose the Fonts... command from the character menu. All the font sizes are displayed.

Now you're ready to paste.

Choose the Paste command from the Edit menu.

Press the Ins key, the keyboard shortcut for the Paste command on the Edit menu.

> Your dBASE screen is pasted in, starting at the insertion point.

Now use Write to add commas, dollar signs, and better headings; to position the totals underneath the columns they're totaling; to delete unwanted information; and to make other cosmetic changes so that the information is more readable. The reason you can edit the information copied in from dBASE is that Windows transfers information in its ASCII, or text, format and Write treats this information just like characters typed in from the keyboard.

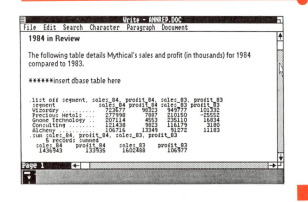

Use Write to make your dBASE information look like the information shown here.

Close Write and when Write prompts you to save ANNREP.DOC, select the Save option.

You have one more piece of information you want to bring into the report from dBASE. Let's assume that in dBASE you keep a table of Mythical's stock prices and dividends. Each quarter, you record the high and low price and the dividend. Because the annual report traditionally includes this information for the last two years, you have a dBASE report you can run for the last two years. You can display this report on the screen, copy it to the Clipboard, and paste it into the report.

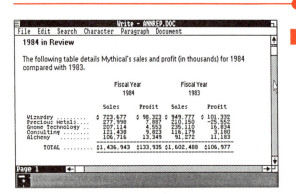

■ *Start dBASE III again by using DBASE3.PIF.*

■ *Open the datafile with the price-dividend information and use the .clear command to clear the screen.*

In this example, let's assume you have a report called PRICEDIV, which you'll run for the years 1983 and 1984.

■ *Type this command:*

.report form pricediv for year > '1982'

This command produces a report that looks like the report shown here.

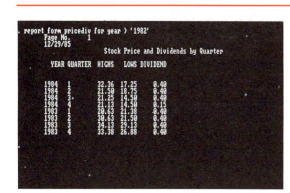

■ *Press Alt-PrtSc and the contents of the screen (in this case, the report information) are copied to the Clipboard.*

■ *Quit dBASE and restart Write with your annual report file (ANNREP.DOC).*

Use the Find... command on the Search menu as before to go directly to the marker.

■ *Choose the Find... command. In the Find What box, type:*

****

M *Click Find Next.*
K *Press Enter.*

■ *Continue clicking Find Next or pressing Enter until you reach the line that says: "********insert dbase pricediv report." Close the Find box.*

■ *Press the End key to move the insertion point to the end of the marker line and then press Enter for a blank line beneath the marker.*

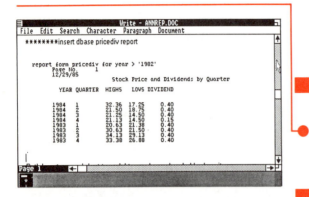

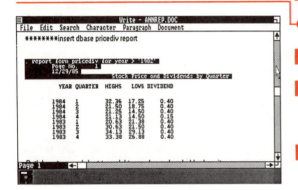

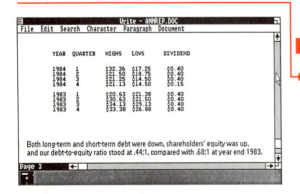

■ *Choose the Courier font from the Character menu so that the dBASE information will be copied into the report in a monospaced font.*

■ *Choose Reduce Font from the Character menu (or press F9) twice.*

This way, columns won't wrap and they will be aligned.

■ *Choose Paste from the Edit menu.*

The dBASE report from the Clipboard is copied in.

Now delete any information from the dBASE screen that you don't want in this report.

■ *Select the dBASE command (the line beginning with ".report") and the three lines just below it (the report header and title).*

■ *Delete these four lines.*

■ *Next, insert a blank line between the 1984 and the 1983 information. This will make it easier to locate information by year.*

■ *Add dollar signs.*

You're almost finished with this report, but first you may wish to align the column headings over the columns.

■ *Add spaces where necessary to align the headings so that they look as shown here and delete the marker.*

The only thing left to do to complete this section is to add a title.

■ *Move the insertion point to the line above the column headings. Type the title:*

Stock Price by Quarter

■ *Press Enter.*

Pressing Enter creates a blank line between the title and the headings.

■ *Select the title. If it's displayed in Courier, change it to Helv by using the Helv command from the Character menu. Then enlarge it and make it bold.*

● Your Stock Price by Quarter table is now complete and looks as shown here.

■ *Close Write and, at the same time, save the changes to your ANNREP.DOC file.*

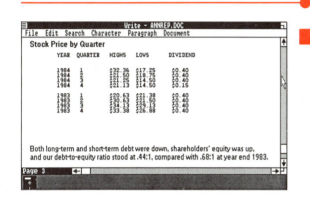

COPYING IN INFORMATION FROM LOTUS 1-2-3

Let's assume you have a 1-2-3 worksheet with information you want in the annual report.

Instead of copying this worksheet directly into the report, you can show it as a series of graphs. 1-2-3 has a graphing feature that will generate the graphs, which you can then copy one at a time to your annual report.

Windows provides four PIFs for Lotus. LOTUS.PIF and LOTUS2.PIF (Release 2) run all the Lotus modules. 123.PIF and 123-2.PIF (Release 2) contain the information to run only the 1-2-3 Worksheet/Graphics/Database program. 123.PIF has the information shown here.

Either PIF works to start Lotus under Windows on my 512K system. I use LOTUS.PIF if I'm planning to use more than 1-2-3; otherwise, I use 123.PIF.

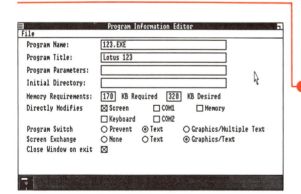

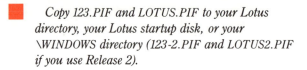 *Copy 123.PIF and LOTUS.PIF to your Lotus directory, your Lotus startup disk, or your \WINDOWS directory (123-2.PIF and LOTUS2.PIF if you use Release 2).*

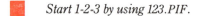 *Start 1-2-3 by using 123.PIF.*

For this example, you'll retrieve the worksheet with the information you want.

Next, turn each of the columns (Sales, Total Assets, Net Income, and Earnings per Share) into a graph that you can copy into the annual report.

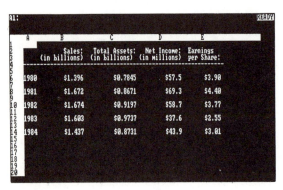

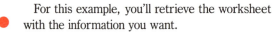 *Use the 1-2-3 /Graph command.*

You will want to use a bar chart.

Select the years 1980 to 1984 as the range of values for the X-axis and the Sales column for the range of values for the Y-axis.

Format the Y-axis values for currency by using the /Graph Options Scale Format command and selecting the Currency format with three decimal places. (For this example, sales in billions are displayed.)

Choose the /Graph View command and 1-2-3 will display a Sales graph.

Press Alt-PrtSc and Windows will copy this screen to the Clipboard.

Press any key to return from the graph display to the worksheet and use /Quit to leave Lotus.

You need to quit Lotus before starting Write so Write will have all the memory. When Write runs in tight memory, it can be very slow.

Start Write and the annual report with the file named ANNREP.DOC.

■ *Use the Find... command to find the place-marker line for the Lotus Sales chart.*

M *Click to put the insertion point at the end of the place-marker line.*

K *Press the End key to move the insertion point to the end of the place-marker line.*

■ *Press Enter for a blank line beneath the marker.*

■ *Choose Paste from the Edit menu.*

Windows pastes in the first chart starting at the insertion point.

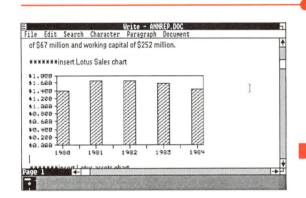

This is magic—one of the easiest ways I know to get a quality-looking graph inserted into a report. If the chart looks a bit squashed, it's because the chart has been adjusted for the printer you're using; you can size it with the Size Picture command on the Edit menu.

■ *Select the chart, choose the Centered command from the Paragraph menu, and the graph will be centered on the page.*

Now all that's left is to add a title.

■ *Move the insertion point to the line above the graph. Use the Spacebar to move the insertion point to just above the top left corner of the graph box.*

■ *Type this title:*

Sales in Billions of Dollars

■ *Select the title, enlarge the font, make it bold, and delete the marker.*

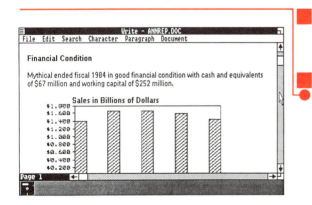

That's all there is to copying in a graph from Lotus 1-2-3.

Follow these steps to create, copy, and paste in charts for each of the remaining areas (Total Assets, Net Income, and Earnings per Share).

When you're finished, the Financial Condition section of your annual report will look like the printout shown here.

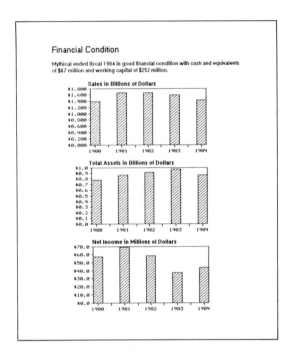

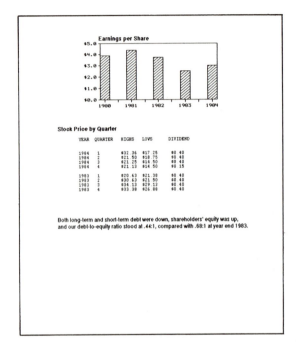

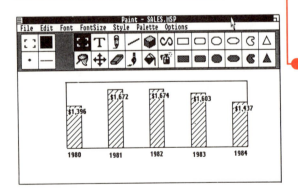

If you prefer making changes to the Lotus charts, you can copy them from Lotus to Paint, make changes in Paint, and then copy them from Paint to Write as I did to create the one shown here.

If you wish to make more sophisticated editing changes than Write's simple Size Picture command will allow for graphics, Paint is the place to make these changes.

FINAL TOUCHES

Now that you've compiled the parts for your section of the annual report, all you have to do is to add a footer with a label and page number, repaginate to be sure page breaks fall in acceptable places, and then print.

■ *Choose Footer... from the Document menu.*

■ *Type:*

Annual Report Draft - Page

■ *Press the Spacebar once after typing the footer text.*

■ *Choose Right from the Paragraph menu.*

> This aligns the footer at the right margin.

M *Click the Insert Page # button in the Page Footer dialog box.*

K *Press Alt-Tab to make the Page Footer dialog box active. Use the Tab key to move the blinking underline to Insert Page #. Press the Spacebar.*

> Write inserts *(page)* in the text of the footer, but replaces *(page)* with the current page number when it prints.

That's all there is to creating a footer.

■ *Select the Return To Document button.*

> Your footer is saved and the Footer window is closed.

Now check page breaks with the Repaginate... command.

■ *Choose Repaginate... from the File menu.*

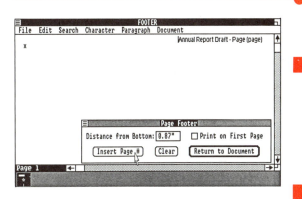

You'll see the dialog box shown.

Repaginate Document | Ok
☐ Confirm Page Breaks | Cancel

■ *Put an X in the Confirm Page Breaks box.*

M *Click Ok.*

K *Press Enter.*

Write begins repaginating the document, and pauses at the place the first page break will fall and displays a dialog box.

Repaginating
Use up and down buttons to move page break if necessary, then confirm. | Up | Confirm
| Down | Cancel

■ *Use the Up or Down buttons to adjust the page break so that it's in a reasonable place, and press Confirm.*

In the Annual Report document, you need the first page break just before the Financial Condition section, the second break before the Earnings per Share chart, and the third just before the Long-term Strategy section.

■ *Now print the report with the Print... command from the File menu.*

The printed report looks like the printout shown on the next page.

You've produced a pretty impressive beginning for Mythical's annual report with the help of Windows and your old favorites—the standard applications Microsoft Word, Lotus 1-2-3, and dBASE III. When you get the remaining parts of the report from Finance and Operations, you can add them to this file and edit the entire report for consistency. You can print drafts for each person who needs to approve the report and easily incorporate changes before sending it to the art department for final polish and then to typesetting. And you can see how using Windows to combine separate modules can add consistency and make the entire annual report process easier and more efficient.

To Mythical Shareholders:

1984 was a year of significant change for Mythical, a year in which we completed our health-care programs in Xanadu and made a major commitment to domestic prepaid health care.

First, I will review our 1984 operating results and outline our long-term strategy. In the next section, Mythical's group executives respond to questions about their areas asked by shareholders, customers, wizards, and financial analysts.

The last section, beginning on page 28, contains the financial statements and notes. I invite your close attention to this detailed information on the company's performance and financial condition.

1984 in Review

The following table details Mythical's sales and profit (in thousands) for 1984 compared with 1983.

	Fiscal Year 1984		Fiscal Year 1983	
	Sales	Profit	Sales	Profit
Vizardry	$ 723,677	$ 98,323	$ 949,777	$ 101,332
Precious Metals	277,998	7,887	210,150	-25,552
Gnome Technology	207,114	4,553	235,110	16,834
Consulting	121,438	9,823	116,179	3,180
Alchemy	106,716	13,349	91,272	11,183
TOTAL	$1,436,943	$133,935	$1,602,488	$106,977

Sales for the fiscal year ending October 31, 1984 were $1,437,026,000, down from $1,602,825,000 in 1983, while net income increased to $43,870,000, or $3.01 per share, from $37,609,000, or $2.55 per share, in 1983.

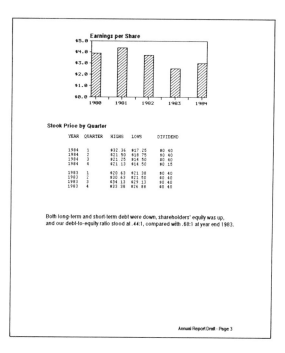

Earnings per Share

Stock Price by Quarter

YEAR	QUARTER	HIGHS	LOWS	DIVIDEND
1984	1	$32.36	$17.25	$0.40
1984	2	$21.50	$18.75	$0.40
1984	3	$21.25	$14.50	$0.40
1984	4	$21.13	$14.50	$0.15
1983	1	$20.63	$21.38	$0.40
1983	2	$30.63	$21.50	$0.40
1983	3	$34.13	$29.13	$0.40
1983	4	$33.38	$26.88	$0.40

Both long-term and short-term debt were down, shareholders' equity was up, and our debt-to-equity ratio stood at .44:1, compared with .68:1 at year end 1983.

Financial Condition

Mythical ended fiscal 1984 in good financial condition with cash and equivalents of $67 million and working capital of $252 million.

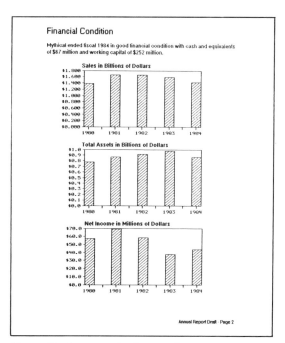

Sales in Billions of Dollars

Total Assets in Billions of Dollars

Net Income in Millions of Dollars

Long-term Strategy

There are five things that we at Mythical strive for continuously:

o   customer satisfaction with Mythical as a supplier;
o   employee satisfaction with Mythical as an employer;
o   community satisfaction with Mythical as a neighbor;
o   shareholder satisfaction with Mythical as an investment;
o   deity satisfaction with Mythical as a supplicant.

If we are to be deserving of shareholder support, I believe we must, over the long term:

o   achieve or exceed a 15 percent after-tax return on equity;
o   establish a minimum annual earnings growth rate of ten percent; and
o   pay out approximately one third of our earnings as dividends.

Our strategy for achieving these objectives in the 1980s and beyond is to build on our strengths in the fields of elf care, gnome technology, specialty spells, and consulting with demigods -- both internally and through acquisitions, specifically the purchase of rare Ecuadoran bat parts. While we are not abandoning our interests in our other businesses, we are changing the nature and extent of our involvement in them in order to concentrate more of our interests in these strategic growth areas.

In looking forward to the challenges of 1985 and beyond, what encourages us most is the ability and character of the people and creatures in the Mythical organization. All of us at Mythical look forward to the continuing support of our shareholders as we enter an exciting and, we believe, rewarding period for Mythical Corporation.

Charles B. Unicorn
President

The president's message for the annual report

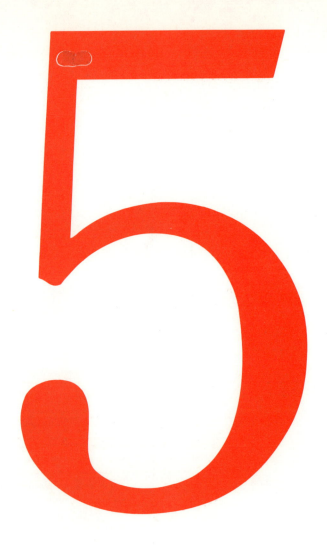

11

Windows running with the standard equipment—a PC, color graphics card, and monitor—is quite remarkable. Windows' graphic capability and the ability to integrate text and graphics from several applications into one document are well worth $99 (Windows' suggested retail price).

But now, with the addition of the EGA, you can set screen colors in Control Panel and get living color, not just shades of gray. Windows in color with the Enhanced Graphics Adapter (EGA) is truly remarkable.

VARIATIONS ON WINDOWS AND THE EGA

If you decide to run Windows with an EGA and use your standard color display, when you start Windows the Microsoft logo will have a bright blue background. This is an indication that something has changed. But when the MS-DOS Executive opens, it's still black and white, just as it was before you installed the EGA. That is because, as yet, you haven't specified screen colors.

You specify screen colors by starting Control Panel and choosing the Screen Colors... command from the Preferences menu. When you do, the Screen Colors dialog box appears. When you see the bars in the Screen Colors dialog box displaying colors instead of shades of gray, you can be certain your EGA is alive and well.

You can use the Color, Hue, and Brightness bars to set colors for various parts of the Windows display (such as the scroll bars, title bars, window background, and text). You use the Hue bar to set the actual color you want. You can choose from any of the eight colors available: black, blue, green, cyan (blue-green), red, magenta, yellow, and white. Then you can adjust the shade of that color with the Bright bar and the intensity with the Color bar. Moving the Bright bar to the right increases the white in the color. Moving the Color bar to the right gives a more vibrant, intense color.

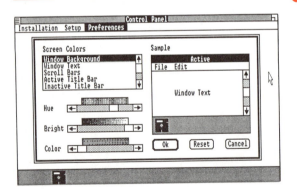

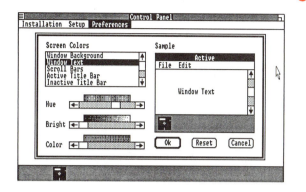

Choose the element of the screen for which you want to set colors from the Screen Colors box. If, for example, you wanted to change the color of the window text, you would select Window Text. Then you'd choose a color from the Hue bar and adjust the brightness and intensity.

Start by making the window background the color you want, then work on the text color, and then set colors for the other parts of the screen, choosing those that work well with the background and text. As you change the hue, brightness, or intensity of the color, your changes are reflected in the Sample window in the right half of the dialog box. When you get exactly what you want, click Ok or press Enter. Occasionally, you may find that you want to return to the colors you had before you started making changes. Windows gives you this option with the Reset button.

Now let's look at each of the equipment options.

Color with an EGA and a standard color display

The standard EGA card comes with 64K of video memory. IBM provides the option of adding more video memory to the EGA with a "daughter board" containing one to three additional 64K memory chips.

If you install the standard EGA and use it with a standard color display, you have relatively high resolution: a 640- by 200-pixel display, the same resolution you had in black and white without the EGA. (Graphics screens are divided into small dots called pixels. On a 640- by 200-pixel display, there are a total of 128,000 dots, or pixels.) And you have eight standard colors: black, blue, green, cyan, red, magenta, yellow, and white. But you can also have various shades of each color. Characters are made up of an 8 by 8 matrix of pixels. By turning on different pixels in different colors (what programmers call "dithering the dots"), you can get many shades of each of these colors. By varying the pixels in each 8 by 8 matrix, Windows actually gives you 64 shades for each of the eight colors.

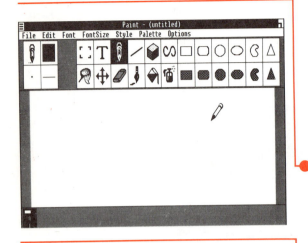

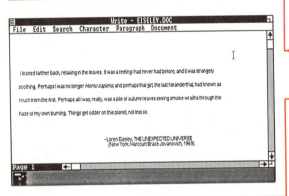

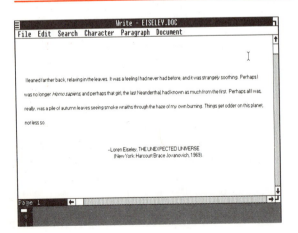

Black and white with an EGA and a standard color display

You may wonder why you'd add an EGA and then run Windows in black and white. Here's the reason:

With an EGA and a standard display, running in color, you get standard resolution—640 by 200 pixels. If, instead, you choose to run in black and white, you can get very high resolution: a 640- by 350-pixel display, close to twice the resolution you get if you run in color. So, in cases where resolution is more important than color, you may wish to run in black and white.

When you run Windows in very high resolution black and white, Paint looks as shown here. You can see that the screen is less grainy and the characters have more detail. In 640 by 350 resolution, characters are formed from an 8 by 14 matrix, so they can be formed more precisely.

If you're using Write and choose the Helv font in the 8-point size, with standard black and white 640- by 200-pixel resolution, your text will look like the text shown here.

If you run Windows and Write in very high resolution black and white, the same Helv font in 8 point looks as shown here.

Using smaller fonts allows you to see more lines of text on the screen at once, and using a small font size in very high resolution makes the text much more readable.

Windows starts with the parameters you specified when you ran the Setup program. If you specified an EGA and a standard color display, Windows will run in color (640 by 200). If you specified an EGA in black-and-white mode, Windows will run in very high resolution (640 by 350) black and white. There is no way, once you're inside Windows, to change from one resolution to another. But if you would like the option of running Windows in color for some of your work and using very high resolution black and white for other tasks, here's what to do:

You'll need to install Windows twice on your hard disk. Install it the first time in the \WINDOWS directory and specify this installation to run in color.

Complete the entire installation, including the desktop applications, Write, and Paint. Then run the Setup program a second time and specify Windows to be set up in a directory called something like \WINBW (for Windows black and white). Just copy the Windows programs here. You can stop Setup after you have finished with the third disk 3, the Utilities disk. You can run the desktop applications, Write, and Paint in very high resolution black and white from the \WINDOWS directory (Windows will remain in the mode you started it in). You can save disk space by not duplicating them in the \WINBW directory.) When you want color, start Windows from the \WINDOWS directory. When you'd rather work in very high resolution black and white, start Windows from the \WINBW directory.

An EGA and a monochrome monitor

If you install an EGA in your system and use a monochrome monitor, you naturally will not get color. But you will be amazed at what your monochrome monitor will do. Previously, if you've used the standard monochrome card, you've only seen it display text. With the EGA, you'll see graphics as well as text on your old monochrome monitor, displayed in very high (640 by 350) resolution.

An EGA with additional memory, and an enhanced color display

If you install an EGA with an additional 64K of memory (making a total of 128K on the EGA card) and add an Enhanced Color Display, you'll be able to get everything: Windows and very high resolution (just as you could in black and white without the additional memory and the enhanced monitor), plus colors!

This is the equipment to have if you want very high resolution color graphics and text.

Note: The EGA memory add-on card allows you to add an additional 192K of memory, for a total of 256K (64K comes with the standard EGA). But Windows only needs an additional 64K to display eight colors in very high resolution.

ABOUT...

Screen colors

The names of the three categories of color attributes listed in the Screen Colors dialog box of Control Panel—Hue, Brightness, and Color—may be misleading. Hue is what is more commonly thought of as color and color is more like intensity. Hue is the control you use to change the color. Color mixes gray pixels into the color (or Hue), changing the intensity of the color. Brightness mixes either white or black pixels into the color (or Hue).

BENEFITS OF THE EGA

The most obvious benefit of adding the EGA is color, and color is a real advantage in any visual display. Another benefit is the additional resolution either in black and white or, with additional EGA memory and the enhanced display, in color.

Windows takes advantage of the EGA, and so do some standard applications you use. Microsoft Word, for example, was one of the first standard applications to take advantage of the EGA, and now Lotus 1-2-3 (both Release 1A and Release 2) also takes advantage of the EGA's color and resolution.

In order for standard applications such as Lotus 1-2-3 and Word to take advantage of the EGA, the software needs to be modified. With Lotus 1A, for example, you need the new external library, programs supplied by Lotus that you can get from your dealer. With Windows applications, however, this is not the case. Windows takes care of translating its applications to run with the hardware on your system. So Write, Paint, and Micrografx's In·a·Vision will run with a standard color-graphics adapter and display, with an EGA and standard display, with an EGA card and enhanced display, or with an EGA with extra memory and enhanced display, taking advantage of the features of the equipment you add, with no change to Write, Paint, or In·a·Vision.

This was first proved true by members of the Windows development group with Micrografx's In·a·Vision. They first tried it on a machine with a standard graphics adapter and display and produced a map of the United States with the states shown in different patterns of black, gray, and white. They took the same In·a·Vision map to a second machine equipped with an EGA and enhanced monitor, inserted the same disk, and with no changes to the program, the states appeared in different colors!

LIMITATIONS OF THE EGA

But what, you might ask, do I have to pay, in addition to the cost of the hardware, for these advantages of color and better resolution? And that's a good question, because there is a cost.

One of the major penalties is speed. In 640 by 200 high-resolution black and white, writing or updating a screen requires processing 128,000 bits, or 16K of memory. A very high resolution, black-and-white screen requires processing 28K, and a high-resolution, color screen requires 32K. But with very high resolution color, writing or updating a screen requires 4 bits per pixel, or 112K—seven times more processing than a high-resolution, black-and-white screen. Although Windows has optimized this code, very high resolution color runs more slowly.

If you add a standard EGA to a PC and run Windows in high-resolution color or very high resolution black and white, it still runs acceptably fast. (I really didn't notice any obvious speed degradation when I ran this configuration on my system.) But if you run a PC with an EGA with additional memory in very high resolution color, you may find this speed penalty unacceptable. On an AT, because of its faster processor, the speed penalty even in very high resolution color is virtually unnoticeable.

Another limitation of the EGA is that you can't use Alt-Tab to go from a standard graphics application back to Windows. One of the reasons Windows doesn't support this feature for the EGA is because it requires 112K to save and restore a screen in a graphics application running in very high resolution. Another reason is that the EGA has write-only registers (rather than read-and-write registers). What this means is that Windows cannot tell exactly how the EGA was being used in the standard application when you Alt-tabbed out and, because of this hardware limitation, cannot guarantee that it can set up the screen exactly as it was before you left.

Microsoft Word is a standard application that takes advantage of the EGA, and if you run Word in text rather than graphics mode, you can still Alt-Tab out. But when you return to Word, the screen background color may not be the same as when you left.

Because of the write-only registers, Windows cannot determine this color and so merely guesses what background color to restore.

The third limitation is that you can't use Alt-PrtSc to take a snapshot of the screen with a standard application running in very high resolution graphics. This is, again, because of the extensive memory required and the inability of Windows to reproduce the screen accurately because of the EGA's lack of read-write registers.

Personally, I think the advantages of color and the increased resolution outweigh the speed penalties. I'm willing to live without Alt-Tab and Alt-PrtSc to gain color and very high resolution. But with my system (a PC), I plan to use only standard color and very high resolution black and white. I don't want to pay the speed penalty for very high resolution color.

INSTALLING THE EGA

The installation instructions that accompany the EGA are clear and easy to follow. If you use them, you should have no problems. But to give you an overview of the steps involved, the following describes what you need to do: Turn your PC off, unplug all power sources, and take the cover of your machine off. If you're using the EGA with additional memory, the next step is to install the piggyback, or daughter board, to the EGA. The piggyback just plugs into the EGA (diagrams in the installation manual show you exactly where to plug this in).

Next, set the switch on the EGA to let it know what kind of monitor you're using and whether or not you have any other display cards in your system. This switch is positioned on the back end of the card, so if you change equipment, you can reset the switch without taking apart your system and removing the card. When I want to run the EGA with my monochrome monitor, I simply shine a light on that switch at the back of my system, use a ball-point pen to change the settings, plug in the monochrome monitor, and I'm ready to go.

Next, you need to change the DIP (dual inline pin) switch settings on switch block SW 1 on your system board. Switches 5 and 6 must be set to ON (a diagram in the EGA installation manual shows the location of this switch on the system board).

The last step before plugging in the card is to check the jumpers on two connectors. They must also be set for the type of display you're using. In the manual is a diagram you can use to check the jumpers' positions and, if necessary, change them.

All that's left is to plug in the card. IBM says any vacant slot will do, but recommends the far left slot (mandatory for the AT). Hold the EGA by the top, press it into the slot, and screw it in tightly.

SETTING UP WINDOWS FOR THE EGA

Once you've installed your hardware and plugged in your monitor, you still have one more task: You need to let Windows know about your new equipment by running the Setup program again. Put the first Windows disk (Setup) in drive A, type *A:*, press Enter, then type *SETUP* and follow the instructions on the screen. When you get to the section that inquires about the type of display adapter and display, indicate your equipment. The EGA choices are:

- EGA with monochrome monitor

- EGA in black and white, 640 by 350 resolution with color monitor

- EGA with no extra memory with either a standard or enhanced display (for eight colors)

- EGA with at least 64K additional memory and enhanced color display (16 colors/very high resolution)

Once you've completed the Setup program, if you've chosen to use colors, use Control Panel's Screen Colors... command from the Preferences menu to set the colors. Each time you change your type of display or resolution, you'll need to run the Setup program again to inform Windows.

12

BEYOND 640K

When the IBM PC-1 was introduced in 1981, it came equipped with 64K of memory. Those of us who upgraded our systems to 128K thought we had all the memory we'd ever need. At first, there were very few programs available that needed as much as 128K. But as more and more software became available, the complexity of the programs increased and so did their memory requirements. The next IBM PC release—the PC-2—had 256K of memory, and most serious users upgraded their systems to 320K or 512K. Just recently, companies like Intel, Tall Tree, and Persyst announced memory boards that expand the PC's RAM to 2MB (megabytes), 32 times the memory of the original PC. And you can add up to four of these memory boards, making the total RAM possible in your PC about 8MB.

WHY USE EXPANDED MEMORY?

Just as we owners of the original PCs wondered what anyone would do with more than 128K, you might wonder what anyone would do with 2MB to 8MB of RAM. The PC can only address 640K of RAM. So, it's up to the software applications to make use of the additional RAM. Right now, four programs use this additional memory directly: Lotus Symphony (Release 1.1), Lotus 1-2-3 (Release 2), Framework by Ashton-Tate, and Sorcim/IUS's SuperCalc3. These applications use this additional memory to store massive spreadsheets and databases. And before long, it's likely that many more large spreadsheet and database programs will be modified to take advantage of this additional RAM directly.

Expanded memory can also be used for a print spooler (also called a print buffer) and one or more so-called RAM "disks."

A print spooler is a part of memory reserved for documents you've sent to be printed. Instead of waiting as long as it takes your printer to print before being able to use your computer for other tasks, you only need to wait until the document is copied into this print spooler. Then the print-spooler software sends the document to the printer at a rate the printer can handle and your computer is free for other tasks. Windows has its own print spooler, but it doesn't work with standard applications. So, you may wish to assign some of your system's expanded memory to a print spooler that will work with standard applications.

A RAM disk is a program that lets you use some of your computer's memory as if it were a very fast disk. Because it has no mechanical parts, it is much faster than a mechanical disk. Windows comes with a RAM-disk program called RAMDrive (under the RAMDRIVE.SYS file name on Windows' Setup disk) that works with expanded memory boards such as the Intel Above Board/PC. RAMDrive turns as much of the expanded memory as you specify into a RAM disk. You can specify this "disk" as the swap space for Windows to use when it swaps standard applications in and out. Because it is using this very fast RAM disk, swapping is considerably faster than it would be on a mechanical disk. With the RAM-disk option, you can use more applications than will fit in conventional RAM at once and switch between applications more quickly.

It is important to understand that Windows does not yet use this expanded memory directly. If you had 640K on your PC and got messages that read "Not enough memory to run" before you installed the Above Board/PC, you will still get those same messages with the expanded memory board. Right now, Windows uses the expanded memory only as a RAM disk. Most likely, however, a future version of Windows will take advantage of this expanded memory directly. When this happens, you'll be able to have regular applications and desktop applications all running at once, and it will be a rarity to get a "Not enough memory to run" message or have a Windows application crawl along because you're running it in too little memory.

Here's how I use the expanded memory on my system now:

I have one Intel Above Board/PC fully loaded with 2MB (2048K) of RAM. I use 320K of this additional RAM for conventional memory—that is, to expand the system memory up to 640K. That leaves me with 1728K of expanded RAM. I use 64K for a print buffer, which means, when I use Microsoft Word for writing, I don't have to wait seemingly forever while my printer is printing. I use the remaining 1664K for my Windows RAM disk. I copy the Windows programs into this RAM disk (labeled D: in the MS-DOS Executive), run Windows from "drive" D, where it runs considerably faster than from my hard disk, and use the rest of the space as swap space for standard applications. But if I regularly ran a very large spreadsheet program (for example, Lotus 1-2-3), I would consider installing two Above Board/PCs. I'd dedicate one 2MB board to 1-2-3 and use the other as I do now, for a Windows RAM disk.

BENEFITS OF EXPANDED MEMORY

The benefits of using Windows and expanded memory right now are the increased speed a RAM disk gives you for running Windows and the faster swap time when switching between standard applications. And if you can also use an expanded memory board to increase your conventional memory to 640K, so much the better.

Possible future benefits are even greater. Lotus, Intel, and Microsoft have collaborated on the concept of expanded memory, and Lotus/Intel/Microsoft expanded memory specifications have recently been published. This collaboration on specifications will standardize the way programs written to use the expanded memory will work. As long as the memory board you buy conforms to these specifications, software written to take advantage of this memory will run and will use the expanded memory on your board. And when Windows is revised so that it can use the additional memory as RAM rather than as a RAM disk, the expanded memory board will be even more appealing.

ABOUT...

AT and Above Board

The IBM AT can use the Intel Above Board A/T for expanded memory in the same way as the PC. It can use some of the additional memory for a Windows RAMDisk, which can make Windows run faster, and it can use Intel's print spooler, which works with standard applications and won't take up any conventional memory. In addition, AT users can allocate some of the memory above 640K to extended memory. Extended memory can only be used in the AT's protected mode. Right now, DOS and its applications only run in real mode (8088-emulation mode). Some AT users may still prefer to allocate some of the Above Board memory as extended memory if they run the IBM Vdisk program or use the XENIX operating system and run XENIX applications that run in a protected mode and use extended memory.

LIMITATIONS OF EXPANDED MEMORY

There are two limitations of expanded memory you should be aware of. One is that if you use a RAM-disk program such as Windows RAMDrive, anything on that drive is temporary—it exists only as long as your computer is running. Each time you start your computer, you need to copy in the files you want to use. If there is a power outage or you trip over your power cord and you've stored data on the RAM disk that you haven't saved to a fixed disk, it will be lost. This is not a limitation that can't be worked around. Just remember it and, if you're storing data on the RAM disk, save it to permanent storage (floppies or hard disk) regularly. If you're using the RAM disk only for swap space, not data files, don't worry about periodically saving.

If you have a PC rather than an XT, you may need to purchase a more powerful power supply, such as the XT power supply. The PC's power supply provides 7 amps at 5 volts. If the equipment you add to your computer exceeds this amount, your PC will shut itself off to prevent damage to the computer. If, after you install the extended memory (the Intel Above Board consumes a maximum of 1.3 amps at 5 volts), your computer periodically shuts itself off (as mine did), you'll need to replace the power supply with a 15-amp XT power supply. Power supplies are not expensive and are well worth the security of knowing that your computer will continue to run while you work.

INSTALLING THE ABOVE BOARD/PC

I'll give directions for installing the Intel Above Board/PC. There are other expanded memory boards available and the methods of installing the hardware and software for these boards may be slightly different. You'll need to consult the installation manual for specifics. But setting up the board for Windows will be the same, regardless of which brand of expanded memory board you use. All expanded memory boards will work with the Windows RAMDrive program.

Installing the hardware

Before inserting the Above Board/PC in an empty slot in your PC, you first need to set two switches: one on the Intel board and one on your system board if you have a PC. (This system board switch does not have to be set on the IBM AT or XT).

The switch on the Above Board is set to indicate how much of the memory on the board will be used as conventional memory (the memory below 640K). The rest of the memory on the board will be used as expanded memory. The system board switch is set to indicate how much conventional memory you have on your system. If you're new at setting switches or need more information, consult the Installing the Above Board documentation.

Use the table shown here to set the switches on your Above Board and on your system board.

Conventional memory before Above Board	PC-1 Switch settings		PC-2 Switch settings		XT Switch settings
	System board Switch SW2	Above Board switch	System board Switch SW2	Above Board switch	Above Board switch
256K	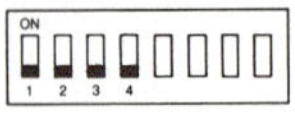	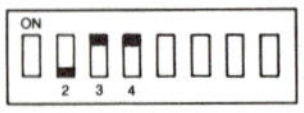	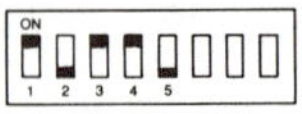	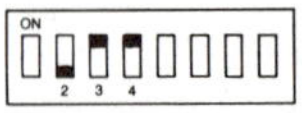	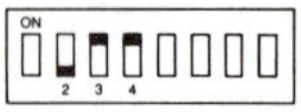
320K	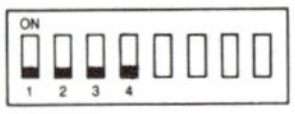	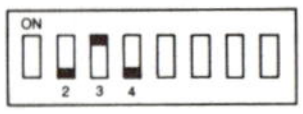		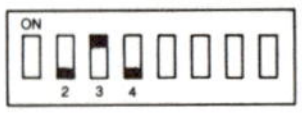	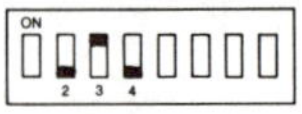
384K	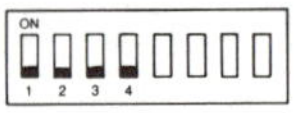	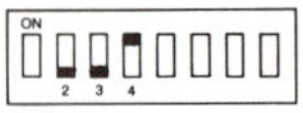		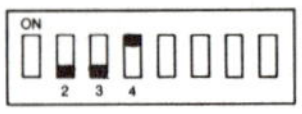	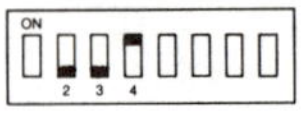
448K	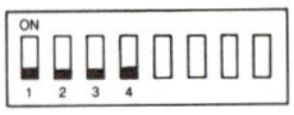			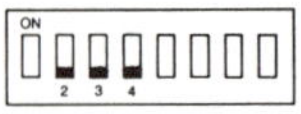	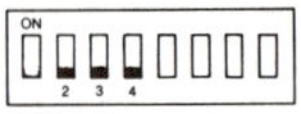
512K	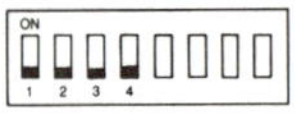	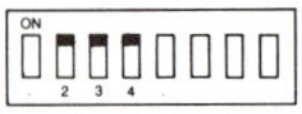	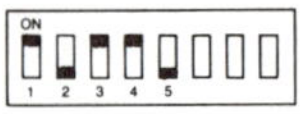	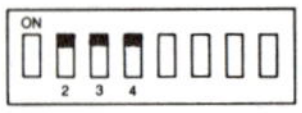	
576K	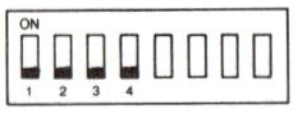		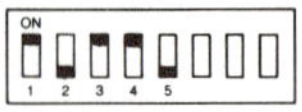	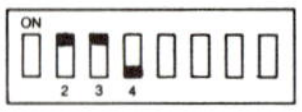	

Above Board and system board switch settings for conventional memory (table used with permission of Intel Corporation)

You must have at least 256K of conventional memory in your computer before you can install the Above Board. If you have less than 640K of conventional RAM, you'll want to dedicate some of the Above Board's memory to this to get as much conventional memory as possible. The more of Windows and the applications you're running that can fit into RAM, the fewer swaps to and from disk the memory manager will make and the faster Windows and the applications will run.

If you have 640K of conventional memory already, or if for some reason you don't want to increase the size of conventional memory, set the Intel Above Board switch 2 to ON, switch 3 to OFF, and switch 4 to ON. You also need to indicate the size of memory chips on the Above Board with switch 1. Set switch 1 to ON if you have 256K memory chips or to OFF if you have 64K memory chips. You can tell which size chip you have by looking at the labels stamped on them. For example, the label *51C256-20* contains the numbers 256, indicating it's a 256K memory chip.

Once you've set both switches, you can plug the board in, screw it down, and you're ready to install the software.

Again, if this is the first board you've installed, if you'd like to see installation diagrams, or if you already have one or more Above Boards installed, detailed instructions and diagrams are provided in the installation manual.

Installing the software

The next step is to run the Setup installation software. This is the place you specify how you want the additional memory used.

■ *Put the Intel Above Board installation and utility floppy disk in drive A and type:*

SETUPAB

You'll first see the Intel introductory screen and then a setup welcome message. Select *Y* to go ahead and set up your system disk for the Above Board. Next, you'll see a print buffer and RAM Disk setup menu.

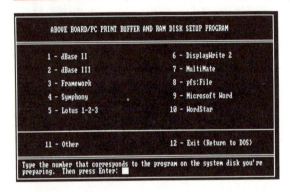

This is the place you specify whether or not you want a print spooler or RAM disk. (Intel calls the print spooler a print buffer. Spooler and buffer are interchangeable terms.) If you have a 2MB Above Board and use standard applications, I recommend you specify 64K of the expanded memory for a print buffer, particularly if you do word processing (you generally print more often when you do word processing). If you work mostly with spreadsheets, 16K to 32K may be large enough. If you use one of the standard applications listed in selections 1 through 10 on the menu, you can type one of the selections and see what size print buffer Intel recommends for that application.

A few minutes after you make your selection, the program displays the amount of conventional memory in your system, and the amount of expanded memory. Make a note of the total expanded memory. You'll need this number later when you install the Windows RAMDrive program. Then the Setup program displays its recommendations for sizes for a print buffer and RAM disk. Its choices for Word are shown here.

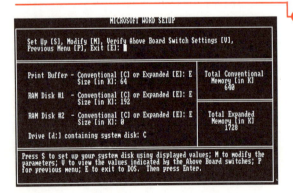

When I set up Above Board on my system, I wanted the recommended 64K print spooler and no RAM disk, because I planned to use Windows' own RAM-disk program rather than this one. So I chose the M (Modify) command shown at the bottom of the screen, changed the value of the RAM Disk #1 size to 0 (indicating no RAM disk), and then pressed S (Set Up) to have the expanded memory include a 64K print-buffer setup.

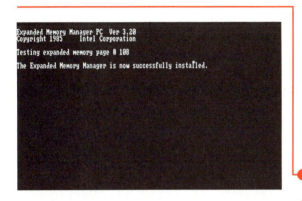

If you don't use any of these standard applications, press selection 11 (Other) in the application menu. If you want a print buffer, accept Setup's choice (16K), or type the number you want. If you don't want a print buffer, enter 0 for no print buffer. Then press S to set up the expanded memory according to your specifications.

If you are currently using a print buffer program, you may wish to abandon it and use the Above Board print buffer instead. The Above Board can locate its buffer in expanded memory and free up the conventional RAM for Windows and your applications.

Next, Setup requests information on the type of display board you're using. After you respond to this request, it writes the startup information it needs on your system disk. Finally, press E and press Enter to exit to DOS, and then reboot your computer with the Above Board installed.

A file named EMM.SYS is copied to your system disk and the line *DEVICE =EMM.SYS M0 I5* is written in your CONFIG.SYS file, a file DOS automatically reads each time your computer is started. Now when your computer is restarted, you'll first see the message shown here.

Then, if you've installed a print spooler, you see the next message shown here.

This message is comforting; it lets you know everything you thought you installed actually is installed.

Installing RAMDrive

You've installed the Above Board hardware and used the Intel software to set up your system so it knows about the expanded memory. The next step is to install Windows' RAMDrive program so that Windows can use all or part of the expanded memory to swap standard applications in and out.

First, you need to copy the RAMDrive program to your system disk or to the directory that contains your DOS startup files. The RAMDrive program is on Windows' Setup disk.

Insert the Setup disk in drive A and copy RAMDRIVE.SYS to your startup disk or directory.

Then you'll need to compute the amount of expanded memory you want to allocate to this RAM disk. Earlier, when you ran the Above Board Setup program, I had you note your total amount of expanded memory. Generally, you will want to allocate all of this amount, minus what you used for a print buffer, to the Windows RAM disk. For example, my total amount of expanded memory is 1728K. So, I'd specify 1728K − 64K, or 1664K for my Windows RAM disk.

If you have another use for part of the expanded memory and would like to use only what Windows will actually need, here's how to calculate what you'll need. Start with the amount of memory required by the largest standard application you use. Add 75K to this amount for screen exchange and program switching. Then multiply the total by the number of standard applications you plan to use. Multiply this total by 1.02, the space required by DOS, and you'll have the amount of space you'll need, as the following calculation shows:

Largest standard application		256K
Screen exchange and program switching space	+	75K
	=	331K
Number of standard applications	×	3
	=	993K
DOS space	×	1.02
Total memory required for three applications	=	1012.86
Total memory, rounded to nearest whole number	=	1013K

Now you need to put this size information into your CONFIG.SYS file. As mentioned earlier, this is a file DOS reads each time you start your computer, the same place the Above Board Setup program wrote information about expanded memory. You can use Notepad to add information to the CONFIG.SYS file.

■ *Start Notepad and choose the Open... command. Type the full file name of CONFIG.SYS (including the path name) in the typing box.*

> Your CONFIG.SYS file probably is located in the root directory or in the directory with your DOS startup files.

■ *Move the insertion point to the end of the file and add this line:*

DEVICE = RAMDRIVE.SYS 1664 /A

This installs the RAMDrive program and allocates 1664K of expanded RAM for it. Instead of *1664,* use the amount of expanded RAM you have or the amount you've calculated you'll need. You cannot enter a number greater than the total amount of expanded memory you have. The */A* tells Windows that you're using an Intel Above Board for expanded memory. If you're using another board, use */E* instead.

Your CONFIG.SYS file now has at least the two lines shown here.

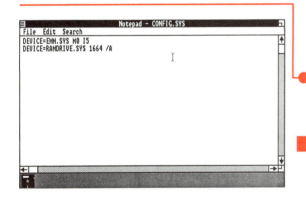

One is for the expanded memory and one is for the RAM disk.

■ *Save this file, close Notepad and Windows, and restart your system.*

> You'll see the message shown here, letting you know RAMDrive is now installed.

And when you start Windows, the MS-DOS Executive will have another disk-drive icon, one for RAMDrive (in this example, D).

USING THE EXPANDED MEMORY WITH WINDOWS

Now that you've done all the installation, there is still one more step: You need to tell Windows to use this new RAM disk as its swap area. The place to specify this is in the WIN.INI file.

■ *Double-click on the file named WIN.INI.*

    This starts Notepad and opens the file named WIN.INI.

■ *Scroll through the file until you come to the section with the heading [pif].*

    The first line in the *[pif]* section should read *swapdisk = ?.*

■ *Replace the ? with the letter of your RAM disk and a colon. On my system, RAMDrive is d:*

■ *Save WIN.INI and leave Notepad.*

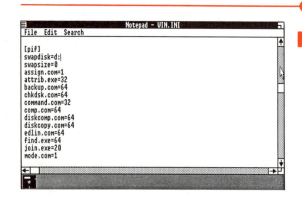

    Now you need to make a few changes to your AUTOEXEC.BAT file, a batch file that is run each time you start your computer. Because a RAM disk is not a real disk but a portion of Random-Access (temporary) Memory, as mentioned earlier, when you turn off your computer, anything in that temporary storage space disappears.

    Each time you start your computer, you need to copy the files you'll be using into the RAM disk. I suggest having the AUTOEXEC.BAT file automatically copy the Windows program files into the RAM disk. Then you won't have to copy them manually each time you start your computer, and Windows will run faster. If you use one of the desktop applications or a Windows application regularly, you may wish to copy this in, too. All you need to do is add instructions to the AUTOEXEC.BAT file to copy these files into your RAM disk each time you start. The Windows program files will take up some of the RAM disk space (about 414K), and the rest will be used as swap space for standard applications. You also can put instructions in the AUTOEXEC.BAT file, as I do, to change to the D RAM disk and start Windows from there.

Paging memory

IBM Personal Computers are limited to 640K of addressable memory. But if expanded memory is used, the PC is made to think that it has an increased amount of addressable memory, called virtual memory. It accesses virtual memory by a technique called paging. When the Intel Above Board pages, it uses a 64K piece of the PC's address space not usable by programs. This 64K space acts as a window into the Above Board's memory, which is divided into 16K pages. When a program requests some information stored in the expanded memory, the Above Board's Expanded Memory Manager (EMM) can switch any 16K page out of memory and switch another page in. The 64K window can hold four 16K pages at any time.

The following are the lines you may wish to put into an AUTOEXEC.BAT file. If you already have an AUTOEXEC.BAT file, just add these lines. If not, create one with these lines:

PATH = D:\;C:\WINDOWS

> If you already have a path command in your AUTOEXEC.BAT file, just add *D:\;C:\WINDOWS* to the end.

CD \WINDOWS

COPY WIN.* D:*

D:WIN

The first line tells Windows to look for what it needs either in D or in the Windows directory part of drive C. The second line changes to the Windows directory. The third line tells Windows to copy the Windows program files located in the \WINDOWS directory on drive C. And the fourth line starts Windows from drive D, the RAM disk.

You can use Notepad instead of Edlin to create or edit an AUTOEXEC.BAT file. Then save this file, and restart your computer. Windows will start automatically from your new RAM disk.

If you only use the RAM disk for Windows programs but not for data, you don't have to worry about periodically saving information on the RAM disk so you won't lose it in case of a power outage or accidentally turning off the machine. If you do use the RAM disk for data as well as programs, don't forget to save the data each time before you turn off your machine.

APPENDIX

The following table lists information contained in each program information file (PIF) of the PIF directory for Version 1.1 of Microsoft Windows. Rows in the table are arranged in the order in which the PIFs appear in the directory; row entries are not arranged by product or by developer. Columns in the table are arranged in the order in which the information appears in the program information file editor. For more information on PIFs, see Chapters 8 and 9.

STANDARD-APPLICATION INFORMATION FOUND IN THE PIF DIRECTORY

Program name	Name of application	Program parameters	Minimum memory (required)	Maximum memory (desired)	Runs in a window	Directly modifies	Copies to Clipboard (screen exchange)
Lotus 1-2-3 (Release 2)	123.COM	None	170K	320K	No	Screen	Graphics/ Text
Lotus 1-2-3	123.EXE	None	170K	320K	No	Screen	Graphics/ Text
BASIC Compiler	BASCOM.COM	†?	128K	128K	*Yes	None	Text
Microsoft BASIC	BASIC.COM	/C:0	80K	96K	*Yes	COM1, COM2	Text
Microsoft Advanced BASIC	BASICA.COM	/C:0	80K	96K	No	Screen, COM1, COM2	Graphics/ Text
Microsoft Chart	CHART.COM	None	128K	228K	No	Screen	Graphics/ Text
Microrim Clout	CLOUT.EXE	None	350K	512K	No	None	Text
Ashton-Tate dBASE	DBASE.COM	None	128K	256K	No	Screen	Text
Ashton-Tate dBASE II	DBASE.COM	None	128K	256K	*Yes	None	Text
Ashton-Tate dBASE III	DBASE.COM	None	128K	256K	No	Screen	Text
IBM Displaywriter 2	DW2PG.COM	None	160K	256K	No	Screen	Text

* The application may run in a window if your system has enough memory to hold both Windows and the application at once.

† When a ? appears in the Program Parameters box, you will be prompted for parameters before the standard application is run in the MS-DOS Executive.

STANDARD-APPLICATION INFORMATION FOUND IN THE PIF DIRECTORY

Program name	Name of application	Program parameters	Minimum memory (required)	Maximum memory (desired)	Runs in a window	Directly modifies	Copies to Clipboard (screen exchange)
IBM Displaywriter 3	DW3PG.COM	None	228K	310K	*Yes	None	Text
IBM Filing Assistant	FILE.EXE	None	128K	256K	No	Screen	Text
Ashton-Tate Framework	FW.EXE	None	312K	640K	No	Screen	Graphics/ Text
Ashton-Tate Framework	FWC.EXE	None	312K	640K	No	Screen	Graphics/ Text
Ashton-Tate Framework	FWT.EXE	None	312K	640K	No	Screen	Graphics/ Text
IBM Graphing Assistant	GRAPH.EXE	None	128K	256K	No	Screen	Graphics/ Text
Harvard Project Manager	HTPM.EXE	None	440K	640K	No	Screen	Graphics/ Text
IBM Filing Assistant	FILE.EXE	None	128K	256K	*Yes	Screen	Text
IBM Graphing Assistant	GRAPH.EXE	None	128K	256K	No	Screen	Graphics/ Text
IBM Reporting Assistant	REPORT.EXE	None	128K	256K	*Yes	None	Text
IBM Writing Assistant	WRITE.EXE	None	196K	256K	*Yes	None	Text
Lotus Access System	LOTUS.COM	None	170K	320K	No	Screen	Graphics/ Text
Lotus Access System (Release 2)	LOTUS.COM	None	24K	24K	No	Screen	Graphics/ Text
Microsoft Multiplan	MP.COM	None	128K	256K	‡No	Screen	Text
Microsoft Multiplan	MP40.COM	None	128K	256K	No	Screen	Text

* The application may run in a window if your system has enough memory to hold both Windows and the application at once.

‡ The application may run in a window if you deselect the Screen option under Directly Modifies.

STANDARD-APPLICATION INFORMATION FOUND IN THE PIF DIRECTORY

Program name	Name of application	Program parameters	Minimum memory (required)	Maximum memory (desired)	Runs in a window	Directly modifies	Copies to Clipboard (screen exchange)
Microsoft Multiplan	MP80.COM	None	128K	256K	No	Screen	Text
Microsoft Access	ACCESS.EXE	None	256K	320K	No	Screen, COM1, COM2	Text
Micrografx PC-Draw	PC-DRAW.EXE	†?	256K	256K	No	Screen	Graphics/ Text
IBM Personal Editor	PE.COM	None	64K	128K	No	Screen	Text
PFS Access	ACCESS.EXE	None	128K	176K	No	Screen, COM1, COM2	Text
PFS Plan	PLAN.COM	None	128K	196K	No	Screen	Text
IBM Professional Editor	PROEDIT.EXE	None	64K	128K	No	Screen	Text
Microsoft Project	PROJ.COM	None	128K	256K	‡Yes	Screen	Text
Microsoft Project	PROJM.BAT	None	128K	256K	No	Screen	Text
Microrim R:base 5000	RB5000.EXE	None	60K	60K	*Yes	Memory	Text
Microrim R:base	RBASE.EXE	None	225K	320K	*Yes	None	Text
IBM Reporting Assistant	REPORT.EXE	None	128K	256K	No	Screen	Text
IBM Initiator for Graph	RG.COM	None	52K	52K	No	Screen	Text
Sorcim/IUS SuperCalc	SC3.COM	None	128K	256K	No	Screen	Graphics/ Text
Hayes Smartcom	SCOM.COM	None	64K	64K	No	Screen, COM1, COM2	Text
Hayes Smartcom II	SCOM.EXE	None	100K	225K	No	Screen, COM1, COM2	Text

* The application may run in a window if your system has enough memory to hold both Windows and the application at once.

† When a ? appears in the Program Parameters box, you will be prompted for parameters before the standard application is run in the MS-DOS Executive.

‡ The application may run in a window if you deselect the Screen option under Directly Modifies.

STANDARD-APPLICATION INFORMATION FOUND IN THE PIF DIRECTORY

Program name	Name of application	Program parameters	Minimum memory (required)	Maximum memory (desired)	Runs in a window	Directly modifies	Copies to Clipboard (screen exchange)
Microsoft Spell	SPELL.COM	None	64K	64K	No	Screen	Text
Lotus Symphony	ACCESS.COM	None	320K	640K	No	Screen, Memory	Graphics/ Text
Lotus Symphony	SYMPHONY.EXE	None	290K	640K	No	Screen	Graphics/ Text
Turbo Pascal 8087	TURBO-87.COM	None	64K	128K	No	Screen	Graphics/ Text
Turbo Pascal	TURBO.COM	None	64K	128K	No	Screen	Graphics/ Text
Turbo Pascal BCD	TURBOBCD.COM	None	64K	128K	No	Screen	Graphics/ Text
Lifetree Software Volkswriter	VX.EXE	None	128K	256K	No	Screen	Text
Microsoft Word	WORD.COM	/X /C	192K	228K	No	Screen	Graphics/ Text
Microsoft Word (EGA)	WORD.COM	/X /C	192K	228K	No	Screen	Text
MultiMate	WP.EXE	None	256K	320K	No	Screen	Text
Satellite Software WordPerfect	WRDPERF.EXE	None	128K	256K	No	Screen	Text
IBM Writing Assistant	WRITE.EXE	None	196K	256K	No	Screen	Text
MicroPro WordStar	WS.COM	None	96K	192K	No	Screen	Text
MicroPro WordStar 2000	WS2000.COM	None	225K	320K	No	Screen	Text
Microstuff CrossTalk	XTALK.EXE	None	64K	128K	No	Screen, COM1, COM2	Graphics/ Text
XYQuest XYWrite	EDITOR.EXE	None	96K	256K	No	Screen, Keyboard	Graphics/ Text

INDEX

G

Graphic user interface, 3, 7–8, 16, 100–102, 145, 175

H

Hard disks, 19, 199
  directories
    moving around, 53–55
    trees, 25
Hayes modems, 58, 61, 67, 72
Headers, 117, 167–68

I

Icon area, 24
Icons, 5, 7
  for applications, 17, 34
  dynamic, 33
  expanding, 8 (*see also* Windows, zooming)
  starting, 37
  titles, displaying, 32
Index Technology Excelerator, 190–91
Intel Above Board/PC, 269–79
Intuition Systems WordSetter, 188–90

L

Lambert, Steve, 67
Lotus 1-2-3
  charts, changing in Paint, 254
  copying information to Write from, 251–54
  LOTUS.PIF, 251
  123.PIF, 202, 251

M

Memory
  expanded, 268–79
    benefits of, 270
    Intel Above Board/PC, 269–70
    limitations of, 271
    paging, 279
    print spooler, 269

Memory *(continued)*
    RAM disks, 268–71
    RAMDrive, 275–77
    specifications for, 270
    with Windows, 277–79
Memory management, 3, 4, 103–4
  standard applications, 103
  Windows applications, 103–4
Menu bar, 23
Menus, 6–7
  advantages of, 6
  displaying, 27
Micrografx In·a·Vision, 264
  menus, 175
  templates, 183–84
  transparencies, 174–83
  vertical text, 181
Microsoft Multiplan, 107, 175
  copying information to Write from, 226–30
  PIFs for, making, 208–9, 219
Microsoft Project
  copying information to Windows from, 235
  PIFs for, making, 219–20
Microsoft Word, 205–6
  using with Windows, 240–43
  WORD.PIF, 240
Modems, Hayes, 58, 61, 67, 72
Moving
  between applications, 9–10, 35, 40, 198
  between menus, 27
  icons, 38
  windows, 46–47
MS-DOS Executive
  commands, 27–33
  disk-drive icons, 24–25
  File menu, 28–29
  files, 26–27
    directory entries, 27
  menus, 27–33
    displaying, 27
  MSDOS.EXE, 27
  pathnames, 26
  Special menu, 31–33
  View menu, 30–31
  window, 16

W

Windows, 4–5, 7
  closing, 50
  pop-up, 10
  resizing, automatically, 4
  zooming, 48–49 (*see also* Icons,
        expanding)
Windows applications, 7–8, 100–108, 201
  converting MS-DOS applications to,
        107–8
  developers' guidelines, 186
  memory management, 103–4
  switching between, 9–10, 35, 40,
        198, 200
Windows operating environment
  benefits of, 9–11
  in color, 264–71
  desktop, 4
  EGA (Enhanced Graphics Adapter),
        setting up for, 267
  expanded memory, 277–79
  expanding the 640K limit, 8
  graphic user interface of, 100–102
  history of, 2–4
  installing, 18–19
  introduction to, 2–12
  RAMDrive, 269
  screen display, 22–24
    icon area, 24
    menu bar, 23
    size box, 23
    System menu, 22–23
    title bar, 22
    work area, 24
  Setup program, 267
  starting, 19–20
  tradeoffs, 11–12
    memory, 11–12

Windows operating environment *(continued)*
    speed, 11–12
  writing Windows applications, 107
WIN.INI, 37, 211–12, 232
Word length, 71
Word Wrap command, 42–43
Wordwrap, 111
Work area, 24
Write, 26
  boilerplate text, creating, 159
  Character menu, 114–15
  closing without saving, 244
  combining text and graphics from
        other applications in, 221–37
  copying from Paint to, 142–45,
        166–67
  Edit menu, 112–13
    keyboard shortcuts, 112
  File menu, 111–12
  fonts and sizes, changing, 121–25
  footers, creating, 168–69
  formatting, changing, 120–21
  headers, creating, 167–68
  margins, setting, 118
  paragraph alignment, changing, 119
  Paragraph menu, 116
  pictures, sizing, 144
  printing, 111–12
  repaginating, 236, 255–56
  Search menu, 113–14
  tabs, setting, 152–53
  using, 118–26, 159–71, 243–44
  Word files compatible with, 239
  WRITE.EXE, 119
WYSIWYG, 111

X

XOn/XOff, 72

Nancy Andrews

Nancy Andrews earned both Bachelor of Arts and Master of Arts degrees in English, and started her career as an English teacher. Nancy has also worked in the field of training design, as a writer of training materials. Nancy's company, Plain English, provides written documentation, as well as training and consulting services, for small businesses. Her previous book, **MICROSOFT FILE ON THE APPLE MACINTOSH**, was published in March 1986.

The manuscript for this book was prepared and submitted to
Microsoft Press in electronic form. Text files were processed
and formatted using Microsoft Word.

Cover design by Ted Mader and Associates
Interior text design by Perry Woodfin
The screen displays were created on the IBM PC XT and AT, and
were printed on the Hewlett-Packard LaserJet and by ImageSet
Corporation.

Text composition by Microsoft Press in Century Old Style with
Helvetica Bold and Helvetica Italic, using the CCI composition
system and the Mergenthaler Linotron 202 digital
phototypesetter.